"The work of José Bleger, articulating with masterly clinical grasp sources going from Pichon-Rivière to Melanie Klein, and from Margaret Mahler to French philosophy, has steadily gained recognition since his early death. The distinguished authors of this volume generously attest to its present relevance."

Jorge L. Ahumada, member of APA (Argentine Psychoanalytic Association), Training Analyst and former member of the board of *International Journal of Psychoanalysis*

"With great expertise, Bleger investigated the relationship between the subject and institutions, showing how the family, group and social belonging were organizing factors in the personality. He discovered the importance of the psychoanalytic frame, whose apparent normality may conceal primary links which never achieved representability. His ideas greatly influenced Latin American psychoanalysis."

Jorge Luis Maldonado, member of APDEBA (Psychoanalytical Association of Buenos Aires, Argentina), Training Analyst and former Vice President of APDEBA.

"Editors and authors of different generations and perspectives craft an illuminating context to meet José Bleger (1922–1972), whose thinking marked a turning point in the conception of the frame in psychoanalysis. Who could resist the temptation to read his seminal essay framed by such creative questions? A reference book."

Haydee Faimberg MD (IPA) Training and Supervising Analyst SPP (France) and APA (Argentina) and International Distinguished Fellow (British Society); author, *The Telescoping of Generations: Listening to the Narcissistic Links Between Generations* **(Routledge)**

Psychoanalysis of the Psychoanalytic Frame Revisited

Psychoanalysis of the Psychoanalytic Frame Revisited provides an in-depth discussion of José Bleger's work, broadening current knowledge and focusing on his significant contribution to psychoanalytic thinking. This work should prove especially relevant in considering the implications of changes in the treatment setting forced by the Covid pandemic.

This edited collection proposes a current debate on José Bleger's ideas on the psychoanalytic setting. The contributors here provide a broad overview of current discussions about the analytic setting, its clinical expressions and its technical management, engaging and transforming the concept of "encuadre" (frame). The book covers topics including early experiences, the psychoanalytic setting, symbiosis and applications in a pandemic. A common thread, Bleger's brilliant intuition, runs through the book, and the tense relationship between the frame and the figure maintains its dynamics throughout.

Psychoanalysis of the Psychoanalytic Frame Revisited will be of great interest to psychoanalysts in practice and in training, as well as anyone seeking to understand the work of José Bleger.

Carlos Moguillansky is MD, Master in culture, Training Analyst, Former Scientific Secretary and President of APDEBA. He is a former member of the board of the *International Journal of Psychoanalysis* and a current member of the IPA Publications Committee. He has also authored papers and books in Spanish, many of them are translated into English, Armenian, Russian, Portuguese and French.

Howard B. Levine is a member of APSA, PINE, the Contemporary Freudian Society, NYU Post-Doc's Contemporary Freudian Track, and in private practice in Brookline, Massachusetts, USA. He is the author of *Affect, Representation and Language: Between the Silence and the Cry* (Routledge 2022) and Editor-in-Chief of the Routledge W.R. Bion Studies Book Series.

The International Psychoanalytical Association Psychoanalytic Classics Revisited

Series Editor: Silvia Flechner

Titles in this series

Playing and Reality Revisited: A New Look at Winnicott's Classic Work
Edited by Gennaro Saragnano and Christian Seulin

Attacks on Linking Revisited: A New Look at Bion's Classic Work
Catalina Bronstein

André Green Revisited: Representation and the Work of the Negative
Edited by Gail S. Reed and Howard B. Levine

Psychoanalysis of the Psychoanalytic Frame Revisited: A New Look at José Bleger's Classic Work
Edited by Carlos Moguillansky and Howard B. Levine

Psychoanalysis of the Psychoanalytic Frame Revisited

A New Look at José Bleger's Classic Work

Edited by
Carlos Moguillansky and Howard B. Levine

Routledge
Taylor & Francis Group

LONDON AND NEW YORK

Cover image: Getty

First published 2023
by Routledge
4 Park Square, Milton Park, Abingdon, Oxon OX14 4RN

and by Routledge
605 Third Avenue, New York, NY 10158

Routledge is an imprint of the Taylor & Francis Group, an informa business

British Library Cataloguing-in-Publication Data
A catalogue record for this book is available from the British Library

Library of Congress Cataloging-in-Publication Data
A catalog record has been requested for this book

ISBN: 978-1-032-17205-7 (hbk)
ISBN: 978-1-032-17206-4 (pbk)
ISBN: 978-1-003-25225-2 (ebk)

DOI: 10.4324/9781003252252

Typeset in Palatino
by Taylor & Francis Books

Contents

Series Editor's Foreword   ix
GABRIELA LEGORRETA

Psycho-analysis of the psycho-analytic frame   1
JOSÉ BLEGER

Introduction   14
CARLOS MOGUILLANSKY

1 What is the setting after all?   21
   LEOPOLDO BLEGER

2 The psychoanalytic setting, embodiment and presence:
   Exploring José Bleger's concept of *encuadre*   39
   JOHN CHURCHER

3 Psychic equivalency as an aspect of symbiosis
   JUDY K. EEKHOFF   57

4 On the psychoanalytic frame and ambiguity as axes for the
   study of Bleger's works   80
   JOSÉ E. FISCHBEIN AND SUSANA VINOCUR FISCHBEIN

5 On Bleger's view of the psychoanalytic frame: A critical
   approach   96
   B. MIGUEL LEIVI

6 Of things that are not visible: José Bleger: A clinician for
   our times?   109
   HOWARD B. LEVINE

7 Thirst for infinity and the analytic frame: Reflections on Bleger
   and Matte-Blanco   119
   RICCARDO LOMBARDI

8 Understanding early experiences: Bleger's contribution to the
   undifferentiation of early states   127
   BERND NISSEN

9 Revisiting José Bleger's ideas in times of pandemia   148
   ALBERTO PIECZANSKI

   Index   158

Series Editor's Foreword

Psychoanalysis of the Psychoanalytic Frame Revisited: A New Look at Bleger's Classical Work by Carlos Moguillansky and Howard B. Levine

The Classics Revisited Series, launched by Gennaro Saragnano in 2015, was introduced after four earlier successful series published under the auspices of the International Psychoanalytic Association. The aim of this latest series is to make available to psychoanalysts and other scholars in related fields, a reinterpretation of the classics of psychoanalysis by authoritative colleagues from various countries and different theoretical approaches, in light of the most recent developments in contemporary psychoanalysis.

In a historical period characterized by the increased internationalization of psychoanalysis, and its rapid spread in Eastern Europe and Asia, we believe that there is an increased demand for psychoanalytical culture and for further investigation of the great classics of this discipline. These classics might be books, single papers or individual contributions of a specific thinker that have marked the history of the theoretical and clinical development of psychoanalysis. These works include all those contributions which, far from being comprehensible only if viewed against a specific historical and cultural backdrop, are capable of continuously stimulating psychoanalytic thought in a creative and non-dogmatic manner, and therefore remain as basic theoretical and clinical landmarks, regardless of personal opinions and the approach of each psychoanalyst.

The Publications Committee is pleased to launch the fourth volume of this series with the book *Psychoanalysis of the Psychoanalytic Frame Revisited: A New Look at Bleger's Classical Work.* This volume is an acknowledgment of José Bleger's important contributions and his seminal paper, "Psychoanalysis of the psycho-analytic frame". Bleger is one of the most renowned pioneers of Latin American psychoanalysis. He was born in Argentina in 1922 and died in 1972 at 49 years of age. He was creative thinker, an intellectual with multiple interests.

In "Psycho-analysis of the psycho-analytic setting", Bleger presents new and striking insights about the setting. While Bleger agrees with Winnicott, who considered the frame as the psychoanalytic situation composed of the "summation of all the details of management", Bleger introduces a distinction between the process and the frame. The frame consists of the constant elements within whose limits the process occurs. What is most original in Bleger's ideas about the frame is his endeavor to explore it using a psychoanalytic inquiry and lens. He designates the psychoanalytic frame as a non-process within which the analytic process takes place, the background of a figure as in Gestalt psychology. If the setting is kept constant, it remains unperceived. When for different reasons, disruption occurs, the setting suddenly changes its status: "from the background of a *Gestalt* into a figure, that is, into a process" (Bleger, 2013 [1967], p. 229).

A clinical aspect that ensues because of this new perspective of the frame, now seen as a non-process, is that its disruptions reveal that something has been projected onto it. Bleger considered the most primitive aspects of the personality, that is, the symbiotic and psychotic part of the personality, to be deposited in the frame and to remain silent until they were disturbed. The analysis of these primitive aspects of the personality, when they become part of the process, are amenable to psychoanalytic interpretation.

In this book, the contributors from the different regions of the IPA highlight and discuss the way in which Bleger's work on the notion of the frame has influenced their psychoanalytic thinking. We hope that the diverse points of view, will bring about a fruitful debate that could result in a broadening of the definition and scope of the notion of the frame. It is important to underline that these different conceptualizations have important clinical implications. The way one conceptualizes the frame, will, without a doubt, influence the direction of analytic work. Most of the chapters in this book include clinical material which enriches and clarifies the ideas discussed.

We are thankful to the editors of this book, Carlos Moguillansky and Howard B. Levine for having gathered excellent contributions. The variety, richness and originality of the contributions makes this book a valuable addition to the IPA Classics Revisited Series. It will be of great value to those who want to become more acquainted with Bleger's seminal paper which should be considered a classic in the way Italo Calvino considers it: "A classic is a work which persists as a background noise even when a present that is totally incompatible with it holds sway".

Gabriela Legorreta
Series Editor
Chair, IPA Publications Committee

Psycho-analysis of the psycho-analytic frame[1]

José Bleger

Winnicott (1956) defines "setting" as "the summation of all the details of management". I suggest, for reasons that will become clearer further on, that we should apply the term "psycho-analytic situation" to the totality of phenomena included in the therapeutic relationship between the analyst and the patient. This situation comprises phenomena which constitute a *process* that is studied, analysed, and interpreted; but it also includes a *frame*, that is to say, a "non-process", in the sense that it is made up of constants within whose bounds the process takes place.[2]

The analytic situation may be thus studied from the point of view of the methodology it stands for, its frame corresponding to the *constants* of a phenomenon, a method or technique, and the process to the set of *variables*. Methodological considerations will, however, be left out and they have only been mentioned here to make it clear that a process can only be examined when the same constants (frame) are being kept up. Thus, we include within the psycho-analytic frame the role of the analyst, the set of space (atmosphere) and time factors, and part of the technique (including problems concerning the fixing and keeping of times, fees, interruptions, etc.). The frame refers to a strategy rather than to a technique. One part of the frame includes "the psycho-analytic contract" which "is an agreement between two people into which enter two formal elements of mutual exchange: time and money" (Liberman, 1961).

I am here concerned with the psycho-analysis of the psycho-analytic frame, and there is a great deal in the literature about the need for keeping it up and about the breaks and distortions caused by the patient in the course of any psycho-analysis (varying in intensity and features from exaggerated obsessive fulfilment to repression, acting out, or psychotic disintegration). My work in the psycho-analysis of psychotic cases has clearly revealed to me the importance of maintaining and protecting the fragments or elements which might have remained and which can sometimes only be achieved by hospitalization. Yet I do not want to consider now the problem of "disruption of" or "attack on" the frame. I want to study what is involved in the maintenance of an *ideally normal frame*. The problem is similar to what physicists call an ideal experiment, that is to

DOI: 10.4324/9781003252252-1

say a problem which does not occur fully and precisely in the way it is being described or stated, but which is of great theoretical and practical use. This is perhaps what Rodrigué had in mind when he once referred to the patient whose history nobody has written and nobody will ever be able to write.

The way I have stated the problem seems to imply that such study is impossible, since ideal analysis does not exist, and I agree with this opinion. The fact is that at times permanently, and at other times sporadically, the frame changes from the mere background of a Gestalt into a figure, that is to say, a process. But even in these cases, it is not the same thing as the process of the analytic situation itself because, whenever "flaws" occur in the frame, we still tend to maintain it or restore it with our interpretation; this is quite different from our attitude in the analysis of the process itself. In this sense, I am interested in examining the psychoanalytic meaning of the frame *when it is not a problem*, in the "ideal" analysis (or at the moments or stages when it is ideal). Thus, I am interested in the psycho-analysis of the frame when it is maintained and not when it is broken, when it remains a set of constants and not when it has turned into variables. The problem I want to look into concerns those analyses in which the frame is not a problem—precisely to show that it is a problem— a problem, however, which has not been defined or hitherto recognized.

A relationship which lasts for years, in which a set of norms and attitudes is kept up, is nothing less than a true definition of *institution*. The frame is then an institution within whose bounds certain phenomena take place which we call behaviour. I was led to this study partly by a series of seminars on Institutional Psychology and as a result of my experience in this field (though at present limited). What became evident to me was that each institution is a portion of the individual's personality; and it is of such importance that identity is always, wholly or partially, institutional, in the sense that at least one part of the identity always shapes itself by belonging to a group, institution, ideology, party, etc. Fenichel (1945) wrote: "Unquestionably the individual structures created by institutions help conserve these institutions". But besides this interaction between individuals and institutions, institutions always work in varying degrees as the limits of the body image and as the basic centre of identity.

The frame is maintained and tends to be maintained (actively, by the psycho-analyst) as invariable; and while it exists as such it seems to be non-existent or it does not count, just as we become aware of institutions or relationships only when they are missing, are blocked, or have ceased to exist. (I do not know who it was who said about love and children that we only know they exist when they cry.) But, what is the meaning of the frame when it is maintained, when "it does not cry"? It is, in all instances, the problem of symbiosis, which is "dumb" and only reveals itself when it breaks or is on the verge of rupture. This is what happens, too, with the body image whose study started with pathology which first proved its existence. In the same way as we speak of the "ghost member", we must accept that institutions and the frame *always* make up a "ghost world", that of the most primitive and undifferentiated organization. What is always there is never noticed unless it is missing; we might apply to the frame the term used by Wallon for what he called "ultra-things", that is to say, all that which in experience appears as vague, undefined, without conception or knowledge of itself. What makes up the ego are not only the steady relationships with objects and institutions but the ulterior frustrations and gratifications with them. There is no awareness of what is always present. Awareness of the missing or gratifying object comes later; the first step is the perception of a certain "incompleteness". What exists in the individual's perception is that which experience has taught him might be missing. On the other hand, steady or motionless relationships (the non-absences) are those which organize and preserve the non-ego, and serve as a basis for the building up of the ego according to frustrating and gratifying experiences. The fact that the non-ego is not perceived does not mean it does not exist psychologically for the organization of personality. The knowledge of something is only apparent in the absence of that something, until it is incorporated as an internal object. But what we do not perceive is also present. And precisely because of this, that "ghost world" is also present in the frame even when this has not been broken.

I want to digress again, hoping to provide more elements for the present study. Until recently, we were comfortably working in the field of science, language, logic, etc., without realizing that all of these phenomena or behaviours (I am interested in all of them in so far as they are behaviours, that is to say, human phenomena) take place within a context of assumptions which we ignored or thought nonexistent or invariable; but we know now that communication contains a meta-communication, science a meta-science, theory a meta-theory, language a meta-language, logics a meta-logics, etc., etc. If the "meta-" varies the contents vary radically.[3] Thus, the frame is constant, and is therefore decisive in the phenomena of the process of behaviour. In other words, the frame is a *meta-behaviour*, and the phenomena we are going to distinguish as behaviour depend on it. It is what remains implicit, but on which the explicit depends.

The meta-behaviour works as a "bulwark", as M. and W. Baranger have called it, a phase in which the analysand tries not to risk avoiding the basic rule. In the meta-behaviour, I am interested in analysing the cases in which the basic rule is fulfilled, and I am concerned precisely with examining that fulfilment. I agree with these authors in regarding the analytic relationship as a symbiotic relationship; but in the cases in which the frame is being respected, the problem lies in the fact that the frame itself is the receiver of the symbiosis and that the latter is not present in the analytic process itself. Symbiosis with the mother (immobility of the non-ego) enables the child to develop his ego. The frame has a similar function: it acts as support, as mainstay, but, so far, we have been able to perceive it only when it changes

or breaks. The most powerful, endurable, and at the same time least apparent, "bulwark" is, then, the one that lies on the frame.

I want to illustrate the description I have offered of the frame with the
example of a patient Mr A., with a phobic character and an intense dependence disguised under the form of reactive independence. For a long time he
wavered between hesitation, desire and fear of buying a flat in a purchase
that was never accomplished. At a certain point, he came to know by mere
chance that I had, some time before, bought a flat that was still being built,
and this was the starting point of a period of anxiety and acting out.

One day he told me about what he had learnt and I interpreted his reaction:
the way he said it contained reproach at my not informing him of my purchase, knowing it was a fundamental problem of his. He tried to ignore or
forget the incident by presenting strong resistance every time I insistently
related this fact to his acting out, till strong feelings of hatred, envy, frustration, coupled with verbal attacks, began to appear, and were followed by a
feeling of detachment and hopelessness. As we advanced further in the analysis of these situations, the "background" of his childhood experience gradually began to emerge from the narration of different recollections. At home,
his parents had done nothing without informing or consulting him about it;
he knew all the details of the development of the family life. After the emergence of these memories and my interpretation of them against great resistance, he began accusing me of having broken our connexion, and he said that
he would not be able to trust me. Fantasies of suicide appeared as well as
derangement, frequent confusion and hypochondriacal symptoms.[4]

For the patient, something had broken, something which *was so* and *had to be*
as it had always been; and he could not conceive of its being otherwise. He was
demanding a repetition of what had been lived, of what for him had "always
been so", a demand or feature he had managed to keep through his life by
restricting or limiting his ego in social relationships and by constantly control-
ling relationships himself, demanding a strong dependence from his objects.

I want to stress in this example how the "non-repetition", because the
frame was respected, brought to light the steadiest and most permanent
element of his personality, his "ghost world". The delusional transference
(Little) or the psychotic part of his personality was a non-ego that constituted the groundwork of his ego and his identity. It was only with the
"unfulfilment" of his "ghost world" that he was able to see that my frame
was different from his, that even before the unfulfilment, his "ghost
world" already existed. I must emphasize, however, that the maintenance
of the frame was what led to the analysis of the psychotic part of his personality. The important question is not how many of these phenomena are
due to frustration or the clash with reality (the frame), but how much of
this area does not appear and is therefore never likely to be analysed. I am
able not to give an answer to this question, but only to delineate the problem. It is similar to what happens with the character feature that must be
turned into a symptom in order to be analysed, that is to say, it must stop

being ego-syntonic. Should not whatever is done in the analysis of character be done with the frame? The problem is different and more difficult since the frame is not ego-syntonic on the one hand, and on the other hand is the groundwork on which the ego and the identity of the individual are built up; and it is strongly separated off from the analytic process, from the ego that shapes the neurotic transference.

Even if we assume that, in the case mentioned above, this material would have emerged in one way or another because it was there, the problem persists in reference to the psycho-analytic meaning of the frame.

Summing up, one might say that the frame (thus defined as a problem) is the most perfect repetition compulsion[5] and that actually there are two frames, one which is suggested and kept up by the analyst, and consciously accepted by the patient, and the other, that of the "ghost world", on which the patient projects.[6] The latter is the most perfect repetition compulsion since it is the most complete, the least known, and the least noticeable one. Rodrigué (1966) talks about a "pending transference" and the "difficulty arises because we are speaking about a phenomenon which, if it existed in its pure form, would have to be dumb by definition".

It has always seemed surprising and exciting to me, in the analysis of psychotic cases, to note the coexistence of a total denial of the analyst with exaggerated sensitivity to the infringement of any detail of the "habitual", the frame, and how the patient might become confused or violent, for example, because of a few minutes' difference in starting or finishing the session. Now I understand it better in that what becomes disorganized is his "meta-ego", which to a great extent, is all he has got. I think it is jumping to conclusions to talk all the time about a patient's "attack" on the frame when he does not adhere to it. He brings what he has got and it is not always an "attack" but his own organization, even though disordered.

In psychotic transference, affection is not transferred but "a total situation, the whole of a development" (Lagache); it would be better to say, the whole of a "non-development". For Melanie Klein, transference repeats the primitive object relationships, but I think that what is still most primitive (the non-differentiation) repeats itself in the frame. The ambiguity of the "as if" of the analytic situation studied by W. and M. Baranger (1961–62) does not cover "all the aspects of the analytic field" as they express it, but only the process. The frame does not accept ambiguity, either on the part of the patient or on the part of the analyst's technique. Each frame *is*, and does not admit ambiguity. Similarly, I believe that the phenomenon of participation (Lévy-Bruhl) or of syncretism admitted by these authors for the analytic situation, only applies to the frame.

Jaques (1955) says that social institutions are unconsciously used as a defence against psychotic anxiety. I believe them to be the depository of the psychotic part of the personality, i.e. the undifferentiated and non-dissolved portion of the primitive symbiotic links. Psychotic anxieties take

place within the institution, and, in the case of the psycho-analytic situation, within what we have described as the process—what "is in motion"
against what is not: the frame. Reider (1953) describes different types of
transference to the institution instead of the therapist and psycho-analysis
as an institution seems to be a means of recovering the lost omnipotence
of sharing in the prestige of a great institution. I believe that what is
important here is to consider the psycho-analytic situation as an institution
in itself, especially the frame.

The development of the ego, in analysis, in the family, or in any institution, depends on the immobility of the non-ego. This denomination of
non-ego makes us think about it as something non-existent, but which
actually exists to the extent that it is the "meta-ego" on which the very
possibility of formation and maintenance of the ego depends. Hence we
might say that identity depends upon the manner in which the non-ego is
kept up or handled. If the metabehaviour varies, the whole ego undergoes
changes in probably equivalent degrees as regards its quantity and its
quality. García Reinoso (1956) has said that just as it is true—as Freud had
pointed out—that the ego is corporal, so is the non-ego. We might add
something else: that the non-ego is a different ego, having different features, and I suggest (Bleger, 1967) calling it a *syncretic ego*. This also
implies that there is not only *one* sense of reality and a lack of it: there are
different structures of the ego and sense of reality.

The non-ego is the background or the frame of the organized ego; the
"background" and "figure" of a unique Gestalt. Between the ego and the
non-ego, or between the neurotic and psychotic part of the personality,
there is no dissociation but a cleavage, as I have described it in a previous
paper.

Miss N was a very rigid and limited patient who always lived with her
parents in hotels in different countries; the only thing she always carried
with her was a small picture. The unsatisfactory relationship with her
parents and the constant moving had turned this picture into her "frame",
what gave her the "non-change" for her identity.

The frame is the most primitive part of the personality, it is the fusion
ego-body-world, on whose immobility depend the formation, existence,
and differentiation (of the ego, the object, the body image, the body, the
mind, etc., etc.). Patients with "acting-in" tendencies or psychotic patients
also bring "their own frame", and *the institution of their primitive symbiotic
relationship*; yet not only they, but all patients bring it too. Hence we can
better recognize the catastrophic situation which to a variable degree is
always created by the analyst's breaking the frame, e.g. holidays, changes
of time, etc., because in these breakings a "crevice" is opened into which
enters a reality that appears catastrophic to the patient; "his" frame, his
"ghost world" remains without depository and it becomes evident that his
frame is not the psycho-analytic frame, as happened with Mr A.

I now want to give an example of a "crevice" that the patient maintained till he felt the need to recover his omnipotence, "his" frame.

Mr Z, the only son of a family who in his childhood was wealthy and socially influential and united, lived in a huge, luxurious mansion with his parents and grandparents, for whom he was the centre of attention. For political reasons, a lot of their possessions were expropriated, and this brought about a great economic decline. The whole family tried hard for a while to live like rich people, concealing their disaster and poverty, but his parents finally moved into a small apartment and accepted a job. (In the meantime his grandparents had died.) When the family faced and accepted the change, he continued living up to appearances. He withdrew from his parents to live on his profession as an architect and he covered up his great insecurity and economic instability so well that everybody thought him rich. He lived and encouraged his fantasy that "nothing had happened", preserving in this way the safe and idealized world of his childhood, his "ghost world". The impression he gave me in the course of treatment was that of a "well-to-do" person, belonging to the social and economic upper class, who, without the showing-off of a "parvenu", maintained an air of security, dignity, and superiority, of being over and beyond the "miseries" and "pettiness" of life, including money.

The frame was well kept, the patient paying regularly and punctually. As the cleavage in his personality was being more deeply analysed, as well as his acting in two worlds, he began to owe me money, to be unpunctual, and to speak—with great difficulty—about his lack of money, a fact which made him feel very "humiliated". The breaking of the frame meant here a certain disruption of his omnipotent organization, the appearance of a "breach" which became the way to get in "against" his omnipotence (the steady and safe world of his childhood). The fulfilment of the frame was the depository of his omnipotent magic world, his childish dependence, his psychotic transference. His most profound fantasy was that analysis would strengthen that omnipotence and would give him back his "ghost world". "To live" in the past was the basic organization of his existence.

The following material comes from a session just after his parents were seriously injured in an accident. During the previous session he paid me part of his debt, and he began the present session by telling me that he had brought me so much money and still owed me so much. He felt the debt "as a breach, as something missing". After a pause, he went on: "Yesterday I had sexual intercourse with my wife and at the beginning I was impotent and that frightened me". (He had been impotent at the beginning of his marriage.) I interpreted that as he was now living a difficult situation because of his parents' accident, he wanted to go back to the security he enjoyed in his childhood, to his parents and grandparents within him, and the relationship with his wife, with me, and with the present reality made him impotent to accomplish that. He had a need to close the breach by paying me the whole of the debt, so that the money might disappear between us, so that I, and everything that made him suffer now, might also disappear. He answered that the day before he had thought that he in fact only needed his wife not to be alone, she was a mere addition in his life. I interpreted that he also wished me to satisfy his reality-needs so that they might disappear and he might thus go back to the security of his childhood, and to his fantasy of reunion with his grandparents, father and mother, just as had happened in his early years.

After a silence, he said that when he heard the word fantasy he found it strange that I should talk of fantasies, and was afraid of going mad. I told him that he wanted me to give him back all the security of his childhood which he tried to preserve within himself so as to cope with the difficult situation and that, on the other hand, he felt that I, and reality with its needs and sufferings, got in through the breach which his debt had created between us. He finished the session by talking about a transvestist; and I interpreted that he felt like a transvestist: at times like a rich and only son, at times like his father, at times like his mother, at times like his grandfather, and in each one of them both *poor and rich*.

Any variation in the frame brings the non-ego to a crisis, "contradicts" the fusion, "challenges" the ego, and compels reintrojection, re-elaboration of the ego, or stirs the defences to immobilize or reproject the psychotic part of the personality. Mr Z could accept the analysis of "his" frame till he had defensively to get it back; and what is important is that his "ghost world" appears and is questioned with "flaws" to the frame (his debt) and that the recovery of his "ghost world" was linked to the fulfilment of *my* frame precisely to ignore me or destroy me.

The phenomenon of reactivation of symptoms at the end of a psycho-analytic treatment, which has often been described, is due, too, to a mobilization and regression of the ego because of a mobilization of the "meta-ego". The background of the Gestalt becomes a figure.[7] The frame, in this way, may be considered as an "addiction" which, if not systematically analysed, may become a stabilized organization, the foundation of the organization of the personality, and the individual gets an ego "adjusted" and modelled upon the institutions of which he is part. It is the basis, I believe, of what Alvarez de Toledo, Grinberg, and Langer (1966) have called the "analytic character", which the existentialists call a "factic" existence, and which we might recognize as a "factic ego".[8]

This "factic ego" is an "ego of belonging"; it is made up and sustained by the admission of the subject to an institution (which may be the therapeutic relationship, the psycho-analytical society, a study group, or any other institution); there is no "internalized ego" to give internal stability to the subject.

Let us say, in other words, that his whole personality is made up of "characters", that is to say, of roles, or—to put it another way—that his whole personality is a façade. I am now describing the "extreme case" but quantitative variation must be taken into account because there is no way to abolish completely this "factic ego"; neither do I think this necessary.

The "pact" or the negative therapeutic reaction represents a perfect fixation of the patient's non-ego in the frame and even its non-recognition and acceptance by the psycho-analyst; moreover, we might say that the negative therapeutic reaction is a real perversion of the transference-countertransference relationship. The "therapeutic alliance" is, on the contrary, an alliance with the healthiest part of the patient (Greenacre, 1959); and this is true of the process but not of the frame. In the latter, the alliance is established with the psychotic (or symbiotic) part of the patient's personality (whether with the corresponding part of the psycho-analyst's personality I do not know yet).[9]

Winnicott (1947) says:

> For the neurotic, the couch and warmth and comfort can be symbolical of the mother's love; for the psychotic it would be more true to say that these things are the analyst's physical expression of love. The couch is the analyst's lap or womb, and the warmth is the live warmth of the analyst's body. And so on.

As to the frame, this is always the most regressive, psychotic part of the patient (for every type of patient). The frame is a permanent presence, like the parents for the child. Without them, there is no development of the ego, but to keep the frame beyond necessity, or to avoid any change in the relationship with the frame or with the parents, there may be even a paralysis of development. Rodrigué, in a book on transference (1966), compares the psycho-analytic process with the process of evolution.

It has been emphasized that the child's ego organizes itself according to the mobility of the medium that creates and provides his needs. The rest of the medium which does not generate needs, is not distinguished and remains as a background in the structure of personality, and as yet this has not been given proper considerations.

In every analysis, even one with an ideally kept frame, the frame must become an object of analysis. I do not mean that this is not occurring in practice, but I want to stress the meaning or significance of what is being done or remains undone, and its importance. The de-symbiotization of the analyst-patient relationship is only reached with the systematic analysis of the frame at the right moment. And here we are likely to find the strongest resistance because it is not a repressed thing but something split and never differentiated; its analysis disturbs the ego and the most mature identity reached by the patient. In these cases we don't interpret what is repressed; we give rise to the secondary process. It is not interpreted on amnesic gaps but on what never was part of the memory. It is not projective identification either; it is the expression of syncretism or the patient's "participation".

The frame is part of the patient's body image; it *is* the body image in the part that has not been structured and differentiated. It is thus something different from the body image itself; it is the body-space and body setting non-differentiation. That is why the interpretation of gestures and body attitudes frequently becomes persecutory, because we do not "move" the patient's ego, but rather his "meta-ego".

I want to present now another example which also has the peculiarity that I cannot describe the "dumbness" of the frame but only the moment when it reveals itself, when it has stopped being dumb. I have already compared it with the body image, the study of which was started precisely by the consideration of its disturbances. In this case, however, the psycho-analyst's frame itself was vitiated.

A colleague brought to a supervision session the analysis of a patient whose transference neurosis he had been interpreting for several years; but the intractability of the case induced him to bring it to supervision. The patient "respected" the frame and in this sense "there were no problems"; he associated well; there was no "acting-out"; and the analyst interpreted well in the area on which he was working. But the patient and the therapist used the familiar form of address to each other because the patient had suggested this at the beginning of his analysis, and the therapist had accepted it. The analysis of the therapist's countertransference took many months till he finally "dared" to correct this familiar form of address, interpreting to the patient what was happening and what was hidden behind it. To stop using the familiar "tu" to each other as a result of its systematic analysis revealed the narcissistic relationship and the omnipotent control, and how the person and role of the analyst had been suppressed because of this familiarity.

By using this familiar form of address, the patient imposed his own frame, overlapping the analyst's, but really destroying the latter. The analyst was compelled to cope with a task that represented too great an effort in the session with his patient (and in his countertransference), and this led to an intensive change in the analytic process and rupture in the patient's ego, which was surviving under unsafe conditions and with a very limited "spectrum" of interest, with intensive and extensive inhibitions. The change of the form of address through analysis led to the conclusion that this was not an obsessive phobic character but a simple schizophrenia with a phobic-obsessive characterological "façade".

I do not think it would have been efficient enough to modify the familiar form of address from the very beginning since the candidate did not have the technical experience to handle a patient with a strong narcissistic organization. The analyst must not agree to use the familiar form of address himself, though he may accept it on the part of his patient and analyse it at a suitable time (which I cannot place retrospectively). The analyst should accept the frame the patient brings (which is his "meta-ego") because there the non-solved primitive symbiosis is found summed up. But we must state, at the same time, that to accept the patient's "meta-ego" (the frame) does not mean to abandon one's own, by means of which one is able to analyse the process and to transform the frame itself into a process. Any interpretation of the frame (not altered) stirs the psychotic part of the personality. It makes up what I have called a split interpretation. But the analyst-patient relationship outside the strict frame (as in this example), as well as the "extra-analytic" relationships, enable the psychotic transference to be concealed and favour the "development" of the "psycho-analytic character".

Another patient, Mrs C, maintained her frame until she progressed in her pregnancy. She had never shaken hands since treatment started, but she now stopped greeting me when arriving or leaving. I strongly resisted including in the interpretation that she had stopped greeting me, but I could see in this the mobilization of her symbiotic relationship with her mother, of highly persecutory features, which became active because of her pregnancy. Not to shake hands when arriving or leaving has been maintained but there still lies an important part of "her frame", which is different from "mine". I believe that the situation is even more complex, because not to shake hands is not a mere detail which is missing to round up the frame. It is evidence that she has another frame, another Gestalt which is not mine (that of the psycho-analytic treatment) and in which her idealized relationship with her mother remained split. The more we deal with the psychotic part of the personality, the more we must take into account that a detail is not just a detail, but an expression of a Gestalt, that is to say, of a special organization or structure.

Summing up, we may say that a patient's frame is his most primitive fusion with the mother's body and that the psycho-analyst's frame must help to re-establish the original symbiosis in order to be able to change it. The disruption of the frame, as well as its ideal or normal maintenance, are technical and theoretical problems, but what basically blocks off any possibility of a profound treatment is the disruption the analyst himself introduces or admits in the frame. *The frame can only be analysed within the frame*, or, in other words, the patient's most primitive dependence and psychological organization can only be analysed within the analyst's frame, which should be neither ambiguous, nor changeable, nor altered.

Summary

I propose to call the *psycho-analytic situation* the sum total of phenomena involved in the therapeutic relationship between the analyst and the patient. This situation includes phenomena which make up a *process* and which is studied, analysed and interpreted; but it also includes a *frame*, that is to say "a non-process" in the sense that it represents the constants, within whose limits the process occurs. The relationship between them is studied and the frame is explained as the set of constants within whose limits the process takes place (variables). The basic aim is to study, not the breaking of the frame, but its psycho-analytic meaning when "ideally normal" conditions are maintained.

Thus, the frame is studied as an *institution* within whose limits phenomena occur which are called "behaviours". In this sense, the frame is "dumb" but not non-existent. It makes up the non-ego of the patient, according to which the ego shapes itself. This non-ego is the "ghost world" of the patient, that lies in the frame and represents a "meta-behaviour". The role of the frame is illustrated with some clinical examples which reveal the placement in the frame of the patient's most primitive "family institution". It is thus the perfect repetition compulsion, which brings up the primitive undifferentiation of the first stages of the organization of personality. The frame as an institution is the receiver of the psychotic part of the personality, i.e. of the undifferentiated and non-solved part of the primitive symbiotic links. The psychoanalytic meaning of the frame defined in this way is then examined, as well as the relevance of these considerations for clinical work and technique.

Notes

1 Paper read at the Second Argentine Psychoanalytic Congress, Buenos Aires, June 1966. This chapter was originally published as J. Bleger (1967) "Psycho-Analysis of the Psycho-Analytic Frame", *Int. J. Psycho-Anal.*, 48: 511–519. Copyright © Institute of Psychoanalysis, reprinted by permission of Taylor & Francis Ltd, http://www.tandfonline.com on behalf of Institute of Psychoanalysis. For many years this was the only version available in English. The Spanish original was also first published in 1967, but as Chapter 6 of J. Bleger's monograph *Simbiosis y ambigüedad: estudio psicoanalítico*. Buenos Aires: Paidós. An English edition of the entire monograph was published 46 years later as Bleger, J. (2013). *Symbiosis and Ambiguity: A Psychoanalytic Study*. Edited by J. Churcher and L. Bleger. Translated by S. Rogers, L. Bleger, and J. Churcher. New Library of Psychoanalysis. London: Routledge. This 2013 edition corrected some significant errors in the 1967 translation of Chapter 6. Together with an Introduction explaining its conceptual roots in the preceding chapters, the 2013 version of Chapter 6 has been reproduced in Tylim, I. and Harris, A. (Eds.) (2018) *Reconsidering the Moveable Frame in Psychoanalysis: Its Function and Structure in Contemporary Psychoanalytic Theory*. London & New York: Routledge. The entire text of the 2013 edition of *Symbiosis and Ambiguity* is expected to be available in the 'Other Classic Books' section of PEP-Web from 2023.
2 Here we might compare this terminology with that used by Liberman (1962) and Rodrigué (1966) respectively.
3 This variation in the "meta-" or variation of the fixed or constant assumptions is the origin of non-Euclidean geometry and Boolean algebra (Lieber, 1960). In psychotherapy, each technique has its assumptions (its frame) and therefore, its own "contents" or processes.
4 As Little (1958) describes it in patients whose transference is delusional, body associations of very early experiences began to appear in my patient. When he felt immobilized he associated to having been wrapped up as a baby in a band that kept him motionless. The non-ego of the frame includes the body and if the frame breaks, the limits of the ego made up by the non-ego have to be recovered through hypochondriacal symptoms.
5 This repetition compulsion is not only a way of remembering but a way of life on the requirement to live.
6 Wender (1966) has said that there are two patients and two analysts, to which I now add: two frames.
7 It must be this fact which has led some authors (Christoffel, 1952) to the breaking of the frame as a technique (giving up the couch and having the interview face to face) a point of view I do not share.
8 8I have dealt more intensively with the "factic ego" and the "syncretic ego", the "corporal ego" and the "internalized ego" elsewhere (Bleger, 1967).

9 I do not believe that this psychotic split transference which is placed on the frame is the consequence of repression of infantile amnesia.

References

Abraham, K. (1919) "A particular form of neurotic resistance against the psycho-analytic method". *Selected Papers*. London: Hogarth, 1927.

Alvarez de Toledo, L. C., Grinberg, L. and Langer, M. (1964). "Termination of training analysis". In: *Psychoanalysis in the Americas* (ed. Litman). New York: Int. Univ. Press, 1966.

Baranger, W. and Baranger, M. (1961–2). "La situatión analítica como campo dinámico". *Rev. Urug. Psicoanal.* 4.

Baranger, W. and Baranger, M. (1964). "El insight en la situación analítica". *Rev. Urug. Psicoanal.* 6.

Bleger, J. (1964). "Simbiosis: estudio de la parte psicótica de la personalidad". *Rev. Urug. Psicoanal.* 6

Bleger, J. (1966). *Psicohigiene y Psicología institucional*. Buenos Aires: Paidos.

Bleger, J. (1967). *Simbiosis y Ambiguedad*. Buenos Aires: Paidos.

Christoffel, H. (1952). "Le problème du transfert". *Rev. franc. psychanal.* 16.

Fenichel, O. (1945). *The Psychoanalytic Theory of Neurosis*. New York: Norton.

Freud, S. (1914). "Remembering, repeating and working-through". *S.E.* 12.

García Reinoso, D. (1956). "Cuerpo y mente". *Rev. Psicoanal.* 13.

Greenacre, P. (1959). "Certain technical problems in the transference relationship". *J. Am. Psychoanal. Assoc.* 7.

Jaques, E. (1951). *The Changing Culture of a Factory*. London: Tavistock.

Jaques, E. (1955). "Social systems as a defence against persecutory and depressive anxiety". In: *New Directions in Psycho-Analysis* (ed. Klein et al.). London: Tavistock.

Klein, M. 1955 "The psycho-analytic play technique: its history and significance". *New Directions in Psycho-Analysis* (ed. Klein et al.). London: Tavistock.

Lagache, D. (1952). "Le problème du transfert". *Rev. franc. psychanal.* 16 (Spanish: *Rev. Urug. Psicoanal.* 1, 1956).

Liberman, D. (1962). *La comunicación en terapeutica psicoanalítica*. Buenos Aires: Eudeba.

Liberman, D., Ferschtut, G. and Sor, D. (1961). "El contrato analítico". *Rev. Psicoanal.* 18

Lieber, L. R. (1960). "The great discovery of modern mathematics". *General Semantics Bull.* 26–27.

Little, M. (1958). "On delusional transference". *Int. J. Psychoanal.* 39.

Nunberg, H. (1951). "Transference and reality". *Int. J. Psychoanal.* 32.

Reider, N. (1953). "A type of transference at institutions". *Bull. Menning Clin.* 17.

Rodrigué, E. and Rodrigué, G. T. de (1966). *El Contexto del Proceso Analítico*. Buenos Aires: Paidos.

Wender, L. (1966). "*Reparación patalógica y perversión*". Paper read to the Argentine Psycho-analytic Assoc.

Winnicott, D. W. (1945). "Primitive emotional development". *Collected Papers*. London: Tavistock, 1958.

Winnicott, D. W. (1947). "Hate in the countertransference". *Collected Papers*. London: Tavistock, 1958.

Winnicott, D. W. (1956). "Clinical varieties of transference". *Collected Papers*. London: Tavistock, 1958.

Introduction

Carlos Moguillansky

Setting, frame, framework, context, scope ...

This book tries to develop the idea of *encuadre*, setting or frame, as it is translated into English. But what are we talking about with this idea?

In *Les mots et les choses*, Foucault pointed out that ideas need a certain conceptual framework to emerge and spread as a thought of the time. In another conceptual context, they do not survive the lack of interest or misunderstanding they arouse. Two thousand, five hundred years ago, the Greeks wondered how the earth was supported without falling. The myths of Atlas and Hercules spoke of Titans with the strength necessary to sustain the world. At the same time, Anaximander of Miletus thought that perhaps the earth was not falling to either side, but his ideas were not taken into account. It took more than 2000 years for Kepler and Newton to give us a more approximate view of universal gravitation. The Greek world failed to realize that the earth was orbiting at incredible speed around the sun. The framework of Anaximander's ideas had to change dramatically so that later, Newton could think that nothing fell, since everything was attracted under the rule of gravity or rotated in orbits at incredible speeds. The path of access to common reason, accepted and verified by all people, is paved with the reason of each individual. Each one of them deserves to be taken care of. Although not all of them are correct. Only healthy debate offers a reflexive framework for all men and women to access that sought common reason, preventing us from the arrogance of believing that we are the only ones who are right.

Let's see another version of encuadre, as a predefined space to frame an image. Let's imagine for a moment one of Van Gogh's paintings, with its emblematic sunflowers. Then, let's imagine that those sunflowers grow and proliferate until they literally exceed the limits of the frame and make it explode. Is this not one of the problems that we find in the development of a person's potentialities every time they go beyond the framework of their loyalty to their family and their origins? This image can alert us to the role of the original frame that made the sunflowers' exhibition possible, but that paradoxically become a prison that prevents their future

DOI: 10.4324/9781003252252-2

normal development. The frame is an object but it also refers to a multiple ensemble of functions.

Let's continue a little bit with our imagined scene: the occasional visitor asks his partner if they are in a museum or in the middle of a field of sunflowers. The partner answers: "No, we are in a museum. It is just your exalted imagination." We can see the functions of the frame as a context of meaning, which allows us to distinguish the fictional realm of fantasy from the realistic plane of practical facts. As we can see with the field of sunflowers that proliferates on the museum's walls in which both visitors are wandering.

The aim of the present volume is to broaden the current knowledge of José Bleger's work and to focus on his significant contribution to psycho-analytic thinking. In doing so, this book hopes to bring forward his ideas and clinical experience, which deserve to be known and discussed by present-day psychoanalysts. Bleger was one of the most renowned pio-neers of Latin American psychoanalytic thinking. His ideas deserve to be shared with the psychoanalytic community, to build a productive debate on his paper with readers. The urgency and depth of this debate is an urgent need to resolve the rough edges of its most extreme positions. Thus, hopefully, a reasonable balance of the overview can be achieved.

José Bleger was the prototype of the intellectual. He set out to be con-troversial and lived up to the challenge of addressing the multiple and contradictory aspects of human experience of his time. The rigor and seriousness of his scientific ideas paralleled his ideological commitment. This attitude was fruitfully rewarded and resulted in discoveries regarding the clinic of the analytic setting and the development of ideas about human drama, following the ideas of Georges Politzer and Enrique Pichon-Rivière.

The reader unfamiliar with the ideas of José Bleger will be able to find a broad overview of current discussions about the analytic setting, its clin-ical expressions and its technical management. In this book, authors from different regions present their ideas which has resulted in generating a fruitful and controversial panorama of the new perspectives on this topic that psychoanalysis has developed to date. The authors have appropriated and transformed the concept of *encuadre* following their clinical experi-ences and psychoanalytic tradition. However, the reader may also note the common red thread of Bleger's brilliant intuition in the development of their different positions. Well indeed, the tense relationship between the frame and the figure, well known since their discovery by Gestalt theory, maintains its dynamics throughout all the contributions.

One may wonder if the relationship between frame and figure recalls the link between container and contained. This perspective runs the risk of falling into a binary view of the problem, which alternatively empha-sizes one or the other of these two factors. Bleger's ideas help us move away from this risk. His pluricausal thinking prevents an exaggerated polarization. As an example of his pluricausal thinking, we can consider the current misunderstanding between different versions of his term 'encuadre', generated by the different languages in our community and the associated translation problems 'traduttore traditore'. The Spanish term encuadre has two possible versions in English: setting and frame. Interestingly, this translation problem has a productive side, because these two terms illuminate two well-defined aspects of the encuadre, as a disposition of rules and as a scope of exposure and development of the analytic process.

Let's see briefly the first aspect of the term, encuadre as a disposition of rules. In the first place, psychoanalytic practice needs to solve the difficulties regarding the controversy concerning the rules for analytic practice that arise from the analyst's side. The question of "impostors", analyst psychoanalysis and lay analysis—*Laienanalyse*—raised a huge controversy between those who defended psychoanalysis as a medical practice and those who believed that lay people could practice psychoanalysis. Among those considered to be lay analysts, there were brilliant ones, such as Melanie Klein, Joan Riviere and James Strachey. The encuadre contains a hidden aspect referred to the ability—ethical, technical and psychological— of those who exercise it. The second aspect, referring to the encuadre as a place of exposure and development of the unconscious functioning of a person, is far more interesting.

Emotional interaction creates a certain tension between the necessary freedom of expression and the limit imposed by its full understanding. The dynamic between expressive freedom and the need to understand speech is illustrated in all fields of language. In visual arts, in music, in literature, in theater and cinema, certain framing rules are imposed. And this background frame acts as an expressive context which fixes the figure of what is expressed.

In appearance, this background often has the prosaic format of a frame: a wooden rectangle, a set of pages of a book, a sonata, the dramatic order of a play, a film. However, these material forms refer to a subjective agreement between the one that expresses and the one that attempts to understand, which meets expectations and rules of exchange. In psychoanalysis, this set of expectations and rules has acquired different names: Setting, analytical situation, working alliance. These different expressions emphasize one aspect of that setting, depending on the varied clinical or theoretical loyalty of those who coined them. This book will probably be an example of this semiotic variety, since it brings together authors from different latitudes.

However, all of these terms pay their respects to the expressive format. As in Fargue's poem: "the piano lights up at the edge of the waves" (1895), the figure of the piano plays with the frame of the waves. But it also evokes more than what it says: how can one refer to the unknown light that illuminates the piano? In the same way, the analytic setting imposes an unspoken question that requires the patient to give an account to himself of why he is there, what prompted him to attend, who is that being behind himself, who has proposed the encounter with the analyst and with himself. The setting places the question within the framework of a scene and calls its different characters to speak. In the setting the patient and the analyst will talk about reality and ghosts, desires and pain, the known and the unknown background of experiences never fully understood. Because of the heterogeneous spectrum of the characters of the patient encompasses both his identity and his otherness. And probably, the silent question of the frame forces the weakness of that apparent monolithic identity to emerge.

At the beginning of psychoanalytic practice, the setting was often confused with the contract. It was only considered as an agreement regarding the frequency of the sessions and the terms of the social, clinical and economic exchange between the patient and the analyst. We can see that these ideas changed. Many authors paid attention to the clinical expressions and manifestations of the frame and to its technical handling. Edward Glover (1927), D.W. Winnicott (1947, 1954), Ida Macalpine (1950) and Maurice Bouvet (1958), among others, made important observations on the emotional experiences of the patient and the analyst. José Bleger published "Psycho-analysis of the Psycho-analytic Setting" in 1967. His text was followed by interesting papers by André Green (1979, 1982), Jean-Michel Quinodoz (1992), and Thomas Ogden (1994). These contributions showed that setting is the stage of multiple emotional and pragmatic expressions, that appear in actions and accomplished deeds. Moreover, they warned the analysts, regardless of their clinical and theoretical orientation, to be attentive to them since they have to handle them.

In his study of the maintenance and rupture of the setting, Bleger noted the silent role that it plays in the analytic situation. For Bleger, the setting supports the patient's most indiscriminate anxieties—which he called the psychotic part—and allows the analytical work of the most discriminated elements of the personality. We face two different but cooperative functions. Certain variables, kept as constant, allow the free play of other experiences that, being sustained by the former, allow the approach of psychoanalytic work.

The subsequent study of the subject allowed us to understand that this situation—the impact of the different aspects of the setting—also applies to the analyst. And it is one of the reasons for the attachment of some analysts to a strict setting. When the setting is broken, both the patient and the analyst face their own anxiety deposited on it. We may see that the outcome of that emotional collision is often unpredictable. As it can create a catastrophe or a creative or evolutionary crisis. According to Bleger, analysis implies the existence of a double relationship, including an evolutionary process and a fixed setting—which he thought of as a non-process—that is the depository of the silent symbiosis of the patient and the analyst. Thus, in his thinking, the setting reedits the primitive fusion with the maternal body. The variation of the setting causes a crisis when this fusion is broken and mobilizes symbiotic anxieties. In this crisis, processes similar to the primary process arise and the feeling of identity is altered.

Freud recommended two rules governing the analyst's ethics: the *Indif-ferenz*—translated by Strachey as neutrality—and the *Abstinentzregel*—the abstinence rule. These rules make the setting be very different to the role of a mere catalog of formal agreements. And they establish it within an ethical framework that gives emotional containment and ethical security to the intimate exposure of the patient. These rules raise a subject of debate regarding the role of the analyst's desire and his emotional contact with the patient. Freud considered that a benevolent positive transference favored the initial course of an analysis. Would we say the same about the analyst's emotional attitude? Probably, this debate needs to be sustained. On one hand, the health and neatness of the setting defends the analysis from the intrusion of the analyst's personal desire. On the other hand, certain flexibility is necessary. We imagine that few analysts would dispute the use of holding, containing and of concern, promoted by D.W. Winnicott, Wilfred Bion and Otto Kernberg respectively.

The different contributions in this book consider the setting in the light of two opposing qualities: as a ritual game and as a playing area. Its ritual function institutes a formal relationship. Its rhythmic and repetitive series of acts promote a stable working relationship. But, behind this manifest goal, its steady rhythm helps to establish contact; what is known as the relational or the phatic function of the communication channel between a sender and a receiver. The multiple purposes of this phatic function are: start, prolong, interrupt, end a conversation or simply check if there is a contact. This phatic function is closely linked to the anxieties that are fixed or mobilized in communication. When the ritual is mobilized, the associated anxieties arise as a threat of separation, of encounter or as a crisis of a stable situation. These anxieties, well studied by the Kleinian school, could be understood as the manifest expression of the threat of a rupture of a stable relationship, related to the referential worldview of the feeling of identity.

The meaning of the frame also offers a space for the expression and play of the signifiers. At this point, the discussion between setting and frame goes beyond a translation problem. Well, once again the two different functions of the frame, proposed by Bleger, are at stake. As a set of fixed dispositions and as a psychic room, or a frame of an action in progress or of a potential action. Psychic room and frame imply each other. It is a frame by delimiting and establishing a place in a specialized area of action, with its possibilities and its rules. Within this specialized area, an agreement of rules and expectations is maintained, on what and how certain exchanges will take place. The frame is also an empty space—a blank—which is available to be used as a pause, as a punctuation of the discourse or as a space to be occupied by a new idea or a new specific action. This function was studied through the clinical manifestations of the repetition compulsion, which needs a setting for its deployment, until the nonsense aspects of this repetition are linked in the "framework of action" of the transference.

Bleger was familiar with Winnicott's ideas on the setting as the function that facilitates the survival of the analytic function to the patient's destructive attack. The setting could allow the patient to move away from their intended self-analysis and would put him in a position where they can use the analytical aid. This is an active function of the setting. It allows us to see in retrospect that its muteness is relative. The setting only manifests itself when it fails, as with any vital function. In pragmatic disorders, that is, patients with disorders of concrete thinking and tendency to action, the setting loses its fixed and mute character and is an active factor in the process. In these cases, when the patient uses it as the scenario for the interaction of their transference, the verbal disorder slides toward a pragmatic level of communication, in which action—often imperative— replaces speech.

This perspective introduces Green's ideas. Green thought that the frame was a structure that, far from being a formal agreement of hours and fees, served as a framework or a stage for representation. In this role, the analytic setting participates as a contextual factor in the communication of the analysis. The speech always builds its meaning in a strong dialogue with the context. Its recursive meaning is the fruit of this mutual interaction. This same idea is presented in Ogden where he describes the isolation between patient and analyst. It arises when the frames of the patient and the analyst are not congruent and they act in different contexts. In this case, Ogden offers a similar description to that of Phyllis Greenacre, who described that the pragmatic disorder coincided with the difficulty to access verbal language. The patient's own framing, very different from that of the analyst, is a form of projective transference of his communicative failure in childhood. Christopher Bollas described the same disturbance when talking about the efficacy of parental projective identification in the patient's speech.

Following these ideas, the difficult-to-access patient is distinguished not by the intensity or quality of his transference, but by his effort to establish a different setting from that offered by the analyst. Bion added that this situation creates a misunderstanding produced by the reversal of their mutual perspectives. They overlap, but they do not meet each other. That divergence of points of view creates a misunderstanding, where the analyst's interventions are unacceptable, and the patient silently disdains the contact. Meltzer also postulated that the analyst could modulate the setting—especially at the beginning of an analysis, to establish the recollection of the transference. In his study of the psychoanalytic process, he described a first step characterized by the recollection of the transference.

At that time, the analysts' maneuvers prioritize the management of the frame and the modulation of anxiety.

In short, these varied perspectives illustrate the setting as a living and changing context of verbal and non-verbal exchanges. Among its multiple functions, it implies messages, installs a phatic link in the emotional relationship and offers containment to the anxieties of the patient and the analyst. Its function has been compared to that of an institution. Its legality is often explicit and, sometimes, it is only the result of the regularity of its use.

This book collects the contributions of analysts from different geographies and theoretical and clinical traditions. Its intention is to recreate a debate that will broaden the definition and scope of the encuadre. This debate has the potential of being transformed into a useful tool for clinical work. The reader may evaluate for himself the different, sometimes openly controversial perspectives, and make his own critical judgment. Within this debate, different positions are developed on the role of the Oedipus Complex, the transference and the linking relationship. Each position proposes to see the setting either as a linguistic context, as an emotional depository or as a formal establishment of rules and conventions. Although it can be said that encuadre participates in all these definitions, it is without doubt that each approach generates a different direction of the cure, in its methods, and in its goal. The editors of this book gave the authors the freedom to express their opinions, with the idea of building a creative polemic about the ideas of an author who did not shy away from debate. As in fact José Bleger was in his life.

The contingency of the COVID-19 pandemic brought humanity to its knees and made the question of the frame uniquely topical. Analysts from different latitudes had to modify their ways of working to mitigate the risks of contagion. And we still do not know all the derivations and clinical consequences of this modification. We sincerely and humbly hope this book can help to illuminate a little the shadows of a path still so unknown.

1   What is the setting after all?

Leopoldo Bleger

Since the late 1990s, the subject of the setting has become more and more important; the bibliography growing steadily. For instance, the entry "setting" in the *IPA Encyclopedia* includes more than a hundred references, although some of these are not entirely relevant to our subject matter. In what follows, I will mainly be considering the very first period of the history of the setting, as well as the so-called "internal setting".

I must say that I am somewhat perplexed about the ways in which the notion of setting has evolved. This paper reflects an attempt to better grasp what this development is all about. Perhaps my comments and critiques will be considered "classical", "conservative", even "reactionary" by some —the reflections of an "orthodox" analyst who does not understand his "modern" colleagues.

I will limit myself to noting the difficulties that some conceptions of the setting raise. I have no additional elaboration to propose, my aim being to underscore some of the elements that every analyst should have the opportunity to experience in his or her practice.

After having worked for fifteen years in a public psychiatric dispensary in Paris (a setting, therefore, where patients are not required to pay for their services) I had decided to stop.

Two half-days a week, I received five patients, among them, a man in his thirties. He had been referred to me after a hospitalization due to a long and painful period of delusion. I had seen him for almost three years, after which he had regained his interest in painting. He spoke about the latter in a way that aroused my interest in part because it seemed closely related to his delusions. During this period, he was living off his wife's earnings. However, around the time of my leaving, he had started to approach some galleries with the intention of selling his paintings.

When he found out that I was leaving, he reacted quite strongly. He inquired whether it would be possible to continue our sessions at my private office, even though he was aware that the question of payment would arise. The situation must have been so difficult for him that he ended up telling me with the greatest embarrassment that the fact of

DOI: 10.4324/9781003252252-3

seeing someone in a dispensary was by no means a consequence of his financial difficulties. I am at pains to describe his difficulty in telling me about this. He had a strong conviction, yet he also knew how strange it sounded: to his mind, it was society's responsibility to provide him with free psychotherapy. The announcement of my departure helped reveal an element of great significance, an element whose relation to the treatment process was difficult to evaluate.

In fact, the whole theme of gratuity and money was intimately linked to the figure of his father: as if a dam had broken, a flood of associations emerged. Among all of his associations, one stands out. It felt like a confession. He had never told me that, when he was about ten years old, he had been seeing a psychotherapist for a long time in another dispensary. At that time, he had been stealing money. These thefts continued during his teenage years when he worked in a market and later, as a young man, when he worked as a cashier in a grocery store. As I recall it, he justified these thefts consciously by referring to something his father used to say, however, adding to it his own connotation. His father's words were: "The important thing is to make money", which he heard as implying "… no matter how".

Therefore, the psychotherapy itself appeared to be an act of stealing. The sine qua non "condition" of the situation was *to not pay* a psychotherapist or an analyst: it had to be free. The important aspect was not, as it seemed for other patients, that psychotherapy should take place in a public setting, an institution. Perhaps the term "condition" can be used here as Freud used it, to refer to the conditions of sexual life. For this patient, the "condition" was non-payment.

This situation left me stunned and more than a little perplexed. Looking back now, after many years have passed, I wonder if this aspect of the clinical material could had been overshadowed by the fact of having taken place in a public dispensary where the fees were provided by the government.

Perhaps my reasoning is flawed and the question is irrelevant. Would this material have emerged through other means, perhaps a dream, when the transference conditions made it possible? This is what one hopes for, ideally. One also hopes that the (ideal) analyst will be sharp and perceptive enough to sense that there is something strange going on.

Unfortunately, this is far from guaranteed. Sooner or later, we all come across patients who have undertaken a second or third analysis and for whom crucial issues and aspects of psychic life have remained "untouched" in previous treatments. This is not because we are better analysts than the previous ones were, even though some patients make us feel that way.

My example concerns psychotherapy, not psychoanalysis, at a frequency of two sessions per week. Nevertheless, it points to aspects which can easily remain hidden to the analyst, silently embedded in the "reality" of the setting.

It is wise to assume that any psychoanalysis contains much more than meets the eye. Sometimes a very important aspect of an analysis suddenly comes to light years after termination. The rich polysemy of the analytical situation is probably one of the reasons we so often find ourselves talking about clinical experiences with a close colleague.

At the origins

Since the setting is considered as a psychoanalytic *concept* and not anymore as a *description*, no longer considered merely as a set of rules, it seems mainly in the service of changes in technique. In 1954, D.W. Winnicott postulated the existence of three types of patients according to the technical provisions they required from the analyst: Freudian patients; patients for whom the question of the depressive position was central; and finally, patients who required a profound process of regression because the personal structure was not yet securely founded (Winnicott, 1958 [1954], pp. 278–279).

Winnicott makes clear that his experience with one of these cases led him to re-examine his technique, even that used with more usual cases (ibid., p. 280). In his view, Freud's neurotic structure had led him to "take for granted" the early mothering situation, and consequently, *"it turned up in his provision of a setting for his work"* (ibid., p. 284, emphasis by Winnicott).

Still according to Winnicott, Freud considers that there are usually three people in the analytical situation, one of whom is excluded from the scene. If there are only two, there has been a regression of the patient in the analytic setting, "the setting represents the mother with her ministrations and the patient is an infant". When regression is more profound, there is only one person (ibid., p. 286). Freud's neurotic character would thus have been, according to Winnicott, a serious limitation to his grasp of the non-neurotic stakes in the treatment. In other words, you have to be psychotic to work with psychotics.

Two years earlier, in the very first version of his paper on the transitional object, Winnicott had already made maternal care the "setting" *par excellence*. The mother-child relationship was the paradigmatic model of treatment: "… an infant in a certain setting provided by the mother" (Winnicott, 1958 [1951], p. 239).

Winnicott's description of the third type of patients seems to strike a chord with many analysts who are gripped by a kind of nostalgia for a treatment where the analyst would finally be the mother they have dreamed of. Not having had the possibility of experiencing it themselves, they wish to provide it for their patients.

Winnicott writes that the couch, with its comfort and warmth, can symbolically evoke mother's love, whereas for the psychotic patient, these qualities *are* the physical expression of the analyst's love; "The couch *is* the analyst's lap or womb" (emphasis by Winnicott, 1958 [1949], p. 199). As we will soon learn, Bleger does not hesitate to quote Winnicott's statement, but with a different conception.

The setting in Argentinian psychoanalysis

Some authors prefer the term "frame" to that of "setting" or even make a conceptual distinction between them. In the first translation of José Bleger's paper, in 1967, the term was "psycho-analytic frame". In the 2013 version, it became "setting". The translator of the 1967 version is unknown and it seems Bleger could not review the translation. Furthermore, both terms (frame and setting) can be used as translations of the *same* word in Spanish, "encuadre". The editors of the 2013 version remarked that in his paper, Bleger refers to Winnicott's idea of "setting", using the word in English. In those days, Argentinian analysts used both the Spanish and the English word interchangeably. Etchegoyen does this as well in his book. In the *IPA Encyclopedia*, both terms are used as synonyms (p. 406).

According to Bleger, as it is well known by now, the analytical situation includes the process and the setting, which he designates as *non-process*. He uses several models or points of view to study the setting, among others, the body schema, the logic of "I" and "not I" (ego and non-ego), repetition compulsion and, above all, the institution.

Some papers take as an object of consideration a problem or phenomenon that has already been identified, in an attempt to deepen or criticize it. Others are attempts to point to an x and to transform this x into an object of thought. One should *not* take Bleger's paper to be a doctrinal text, rather, it is an attempt to identify an x, to define it and to study it.

A first misconception would be to think that Bleger's paper *advocates* the setting, that it is a *plea* for the setting.

No. Bleger's paper acknowledges the *existence* of a setting. The proof is that no matter how many sessions are held, a setting is created, whether in an analysis, in a psychotherapy or in a working group. It is not that we give ourselves a setting, but that, whether we like it or not, there *is* one.

It's a kind of reversal of perspective: it is not the setting that defines the analysis, but as soon as an analytic modality takes place, there is necessarily something we can call "setting".

This is why Bleger is interested in the moments of the treatment when the setting *does not* pose a problem. As we will see later on, André Green bases his distinction precisely on this point, that is, on whether the setting represents a problem or not. In general, the setting only comes into view when it is disrupted or broken, as was the case with my patient at the dispensary. Should we consider that at other times the setting does not exist?

José Bleger thinks that some very important aspects of the treatment are deposited, or even immobilized in the setting, especially those craziest or most problematic aspects of the situation and of its *two* participants. These are aspects that are highly invested by the patient and also, in his or her own way, by the analyst—so much so that touching them could throw them off balance.

One of the obstacles to a better grasp of the issues concerning the setting is to think of the analytic situation as an "as if" situation, one that is not altogether "real".

For my part, I cannot imagine how unconscious issues could really take place if the analytic situation were merely "as if". Some authors who think in terms of indications and contraindications for psychoanalysis seem to base themselves precisely on the patient's ability to go along with this "as if" quality of the analytic situation. Treatment would be possible for these patients but not for the rest, because the latter would not be able to "play the game".

Between the 1950s and early 1970s, Bleger and other analysts of the *Río de la Plata* (the river between Buenos Aires and Montevideo) trained in a rather Kleinian spirit, and were not very concerned with the question of indications and contraindications. According to them, we are all—neurotic, psychotic, perverse or borderline—confronted from the very beginning of life with psychotic anxieties. This is not to say that psychic life is psychotic: it is the *intensity* and the *type* of anxiety we are confronted with that can be described as psychotic. It is then up to each one of us to contend with it as best we can!

Contradicting Winnicott's position, Bleger, as any good Kleinian (or Freudian, for that matter), presupposes a continuum between neurosis and psychosis: differences having to do with symbolization and non-symbolization of reality do not, in his mind, distinguish different types of patients, but rather different levels of analytical work with *all* patients. There are significant zones of non-symbolized psychic life in each one of us. This is a point I wish to highlight.

At the core of psychic life, there is a kind of "raw reality" that psychotic patients allow us to glimpse. Work with these patients is therefore invaluable for psychoanalysts, it makes us perceive the common background where the wildest and craziest of psychic experiences are always present. At times, while listening to a patient, we are reminded of the difficulty of containing all of our human savagery, including love, in such an intimate situation as that of an analytic treatment.

The question of the setting thus ceases to be a "technical" issue. This is what Bleger remarks in a note in his paper which may, at first glance, seem a little enigmatic: "the setting corresponds much more to a strategy than to a technique" (Bleger, 2013 [1967], p. 229, n.173). In other words, what we do with the setting and, above all, *what the setting does to us without our knowing it,* is intricately related to the orientation and the meaning we give to the psychoanalytic cure, the conception we have of it, the psychoanalyst's point of view.

While Bleger shares with most of his colleagues from the Río de la Plata a certain conception of analysis, his proposals on the setting collide with at least two prevailing perspectives at the time: on the nature of anxieties involved in the analytical session, and the distinction between process and setting.

Joël Zac: Setting and acting out

A year after Bleger's presentation of his paper on the setting in Buenos Aires (1966), another Argentinean analyst, Joël Zac, presented a paper whose title hints at his position: "Setting and acting out: Relationship between week and weekend". Zac defines the setting as "a set of stipulations, explicit or implicit, which ensure, on the one hand, a minimum of interference in the activities that develop between patient and analyst, and on the other hand, a maximum of usefulness to the analyst in making diagnostic and/or prognostic estimates" (Zac, 1967, p. 32). I leave aside the second part of his definition, which would steer us away from the subject.

"Minimizing interference" seems tantamount to reducing the setting to a purely static element with no particular meaning for the analytical situation. Yet, when Zac studies the analytical situation in terms of constants and variables, he includes the analyst's theory and even the "real person" of the analyst among the constants, and interestingly, he also includes the setting! On closer examination, he may be right: *the idea* one has of a setting which allows work to take place is indeed a fundamental element.

However, the first part of the paper serves as an introduction to a second part, which gives the real foundations of his position, that is, his theory. Zac believes that the most important anxieties are separation anxieties: from the very first losses of the object and the pain they cause to early traumatic experiences, it is in relation to experiences of bonding and separation, with the specific anxieties that these situations involve, that essential aspects of the analytical treatment take place. In a similar line of thinking, Etchegoyen does not hesitate in dedicating an entire chapter of his book to separation anxieties and the psychoanalytical process.

Zac describes the development of the theoretical understanding of separation anxieties, starting with Freud and Melanie Klein, then moving to Otto Fenichel, John Bowlby and Margaret Mahler. But it is above all his reading of Melanie Klein's conception of the integration of the self that guides his thinking. Four pages of his paper (Zac, 1967, pp. 37–40) deserve particular attention because they shed light on the theoretical conceptions underpinning the importance of the rhythm and frequency of weekly sessions, also as this relates to interpretative technique. Among the constants that Zac invokes is the stipulation that sessions be consecutive during the week, from Monday to Thursday or from Tuesday to Friday, in order to significantly mark the weekend break.

Clearly situated within a certain, let us say, classical current of thought of the time, Zac's paper is, in its own way, a response to and a critique of Bleger's thesis.

Weekend separations during treatment confront patients with object losses where the primitive situations of separation and abandonment are actualized as are difficulties in their elaboration (ibid., p. 46). To properly mark the moment of separation and be able to interpret the anxieties it creates, a sustained rhythm is needed. At the time, in Argentina, the norm was to have four sessions per week and *not* to "spread" these sessions over the week (for example, Monday–Tuesday and then Thursday–Friday), a rhythm which would not have potentiated the emergence of such anxieties. This illustrates how the choice of setting follows from a particular theoretical conception of analysis.

His conception of acting out contributes yet another twist. Taking as a starting point the Freudian definition of acting as a way of remembering, Zac soon deviates from this. At the time, the Freudian notion of *agieren* was often understood as acting out (following Strachey's translation of *agieren* as "acting out"), and the tendency to act out was seen as typical of the "psychopathic" trends in the personalities of some patients. In other words, a tendency to act, even through language, instead of a more symbolized modality. Under Zac's pen, this becomes "the patient with acting out".

In his paper, which is one of the best examples of a certain conception of the setting, Zac tends to strongly "rigidify" the analytical situation, to the point that it becomes difficult to question or think about.

Etchegoyen's conception

Despite profound differences, Zac and Bleger's conceptions are very well presented in *The Fundamentals of Psychoanalytic Technique* (Etchegoyen, 1986), in which he gives rightful place to the thinking of the Río de la Plata group between the 1950s and 1970s. The choice of the word "fundamentals" in the title clearly indicates that Etchegoyen considers it possible to cogently articulate technique. For him, technical rules are not arbitrary choices.

For Etchegoyen, Bleger's definition of the analytical *situation* in terms of *process* and *setting* (or non-process) comes into conflict with his own position, whereby the terms analytical *situation* and *process*, albeit difficult to define and distinguish precisely, remain useful in orienting our thinking as analysts.

To his mind, Bleger's distinction between process and setting is a "speculative definition that takes away from the concept of analytic situation" (Etchegoyen, 1986, p 480). While he shares Bleger's understanding of the muteness of the setting, he does not agree with making this muteness a depository for the symbiotic aspects of the psyche: this is truly the crux of their disagreement.

However, like Bleger, he also points out that a disruption of the setting often brings about new configurations, which is not to say that this gives the analyst license to provoke disruptions, since this would then introduce an extraneous variable. "The process inspires the setting but should not determine it" (ibid., p. 482).

If the analyst comes down with a cold, this may bring to light the existence of a heretofore inaccessible fantasy of the patient, for instance, that his analyst is invulnerable to illness, or to hypochondriacal fantasies that remained embedded in the setting as long as the analyst did not fall ill (ibid., p. 484). Bleger had described it as the *muteness* of the setting. Etchegoyen believes that the function of the setting is to be *silent*, so that, against this silent background, the process can speak. However, defining the setting as mute by nature does not imply that it cannot have meaning. One can discern meaning without this having any bearing on this backdrop function, in other words, although the setting remains silent, it nevertheless speaks in its own way. For Etchegoyen, the setting is not mute by definition, it always has a meaning, and the meaning can be grasped through the material that the patient brings concerning the setting.

Here is one of the clinical examples proposed by Etchegoyen: A patient interpreted the fact that his analyst always greeted him in the same manner in the context of an aristocratic fantasy in which the analyst opened him the door and walked behind him, eventually to "wipe his ass". No way for the analyst to change his way of receiving him! The analyst's interpretations had very little impact on the patient until one day, Etchegoyen was obliged to greet him differently (he does not say precisely how or why). Suddenly, the fantasy emerged "with a force and degree of conviction that were quasi-delusional" (ibid., p. 487).

In fact, he had, in the past, perceived a superior attitude from the patient, which was based in part on the patient's higher social status, but, Etchegoyen adds that he had never interpreted "that he [the patient] really believed that this circumstance unquestionably defined the roles of master and valet in the transference".

It's all about "really believing"! This example underscores the power of conviction of the patient's psychic reality in the context of the analytical situation, that is, the hallucinatory realization that takes place in any treatment. The analytical situation allows this hallucinatory realization to unfold. We are no longer in the realm of the "as if".

For Etchegoyen, the setting is something objective proposed by the analyst, something the patient will use to express his fantasies. From an instrumental point of view, the setting is instituted because it offers the best conditions for the analytical task; and curiously enough, a good part of this task consists in seeing what the patient thinks of the situation we are establishing and what his theories are. The setting, Etchegoyen adds, is the Rorschach ink-blot on which the patient projects aspects of him or herself (ibid., p. 486).

On one occasion, I had to cancel the sessions of a whole day at the last minute. At the next session, a patient told me that she had imagined, no, that she *thought*, I had needed to give this time slot to someone else and that given that, her analysis would soon be finished, I had considered that it did not matter. It is "logical" that this alteration of the setting would have felt like an inherent part of her fantasy world, which involved rivalry and comparison.

Etchegoyen's position, in many ways typical of a traditionally Kleinian position (the analyst must interpret the patient's fantasies), leaves me doubtful to say the least. As we have seen with Zac, the fact of not distinguishing between acting out and *agieren*, particularly *agieren* as transference, leaves aside everything the patient *does* with the analytical situation without knowing it, and which is not thought of in terms of fantasy. It is the iron-clad conviction of the "aristocratic" patient in his clinical example. The bedrock level of fantasy is an indisputable subjective position, obtuse to the point of relentless repetition.

Taking a historical perspective on the question of the analytical process, Etchegoyen discusses the position of a majority of Ego Psychologists for whom it is the setting that allows for regression. Etchegoyen argues rightly (in my view) that regression is a characteristic of the pathology and of what the patient brings to the situation. The setting is the current locus of the expression of conflict, and according to Freud, the central conflict is infantile (ibid., p. 511). Etchegoyen adds that the setting was not designed to promote regression but, rather, to reveal and contain it. The transference neurosis is not a product of the setting; on the contrary, the setting is our most valid response to the phenomena of transference.

In comparison, regression, as it is postulated by Winnicott, is clearly temporal, and is primarily process-related (ibid., p. 517). It is the positive aspect of analytical holding which set the conditions for regression to take place—a position that is almost completely opposed to that of other authors (Ida Macalpine in this case), for whom it is the frustrating aspects of the setting that promote regression (ibid., p. 519).

Etchegoyen proposes a useful means of classifying regression. On the one hand, there are analysts who believe the setting allows for, or creates, regression, which in turn helps promote an analytic process (therapeutic regression). Then there are those who think that regression is primarily determined by the pathology of the patient and not the setting (psycho-pathological regression). Finally, there are those, like Winnicott and Balint, who believe that regression is curative in itself, because it allows the individual to find his or her true self and to grow (ibid., p. 543). In a certain way, analysts who think along the lines of Winnicott and Balint put aside the question of the setting to focus primarily on "holding".

The containing function of the mother's breast is used as a model for the function of the setting, taking as a starting point Freud's study of separation anxiety and absence of the object (mother) in *Inhibitions, Symptoms and Anxiety*. For Etchegoyen, the analyst's task consists, to a large extent, in detecting, analyzing and resolving the various anxieties related to separation (ibid., p. 528). It is difficult, he contends, to interpret these properly without it coming across as hollow or rote.

Etchegoyen notes that, often, the analyst does not understand this type of anxiety in all its magnitude and that the patient is quite determined not to understand it since to take it into account, to assume it, would lead him to a situation of dangerous dependence on the object, in this case, the analyst. A correct interpretation of separation anxiety can potentially bring to light one of the most painful of human problems, that of the need for bonding, dependence and the "orphan condition". We confront the patient with his solitude and we attack his omnipotence (ibid., p. 542).

André Green's Winnicott

It seems that the issue of the setting emerged in Argentina in the 1960s, and in the following decade in France. I write "it seems" because this would require a more thorough historical investigation. However, we can live with a certain imprecision (Roussillon, 1995).

Jean-Luc Donnet was the first French analyst to write a paper focused explicitly on the setting, although this was partly to argue against its extension. "Le divan bien tempéré" [The well-tempered couch] was published in 1973 in the *Nouvelle Revue de Psychanalyse*.[1]

It is probably another paper, dizzying in its amplitude, which marked a sort of starting point for the elaboration of the setting in France, I am referring to "L'analyste, la symbolisation et l'absence dans le cadre analytique", by André Green, published in 1974 and presented as a report to the IPA Conference the following year.

Green's paper begins with the diagnosis of a crisis in psychoanalysis, at a societal level, within analytical institutions and with respect to the contradictions of theory and practice. This concerned not only France, but the entire psychoanalytical community.

On the basis of this diagnosis, Green identified three main points: the role of the analyst, in particular his imaginative elaboration, the function of the setting, and the place of narcissism (Green, 1990, pp. 64–65).[2]

Although he refers to José Bleger's definition of the psychoanalytic situation in his 1967 paper, he quickly diverts the notion of the setting to Winnicott's sense of a facilitating environment. Moreover, his paper is dedicated to Winnicott. Green makes clear that his experience was enriched by the analysis of patients who *could not* use the setting as a facilitating environment.

Green makes a rather debatable distinction between two situations: one in which the setting fades into the background, mainly due to the holding or containment capacity of the analyst as a person, and one in which the analyst feels that something is happening against the setting: "the analysis is not taking place between people but between objects, as if the persons involved had lost their reality to give way to a poorly known object field" (ibid., p. 84). Although Green writes that his description of the analytical situation with difficult cases also applies to certain critical moments in so-called classical analyses (ibid., p. 86), he is nevertheless making a clear distinction. All the more so when he refers to a person versus object distinction.

Further in his paper, he insists that the setting does not reproduce an object relationship, rather, it allows the birth and development of an object relationship. It is safe to assume that this concerns the maternal figure and, thus, it makes sense that, in the next section, he approaches the analyst's work as a *construction* of symbolization and not as a *process* of symbolization (ibid., p. 87). In other words, for some patients, it is the capacity to symbolize itself that needs to be constructed.

In the preface to his 1990 book, in which the 1974 text appears as a chapter, he returns to this question with an emphasis on borderline cases. The alternative, according to Green, is either to exclude these borderline cases from the analytical experience and to entrust them to a form of psychotherapy, or to resort to technical variations which rely much less on interpretation as a tool for transference analysis and more on counter-transference attitudes. He goes on to say: "With the emergence of border-line pathology over the last 30 years, issues surrounding the setting have come to the forefront" (ibid., p. 33).

"All" Green is here, one might say: holding firmly onto the psycho-analytic tools with one hand while simultaneously testing their limits with the other, at the risk of leading to substantial variations. The history of the psychoanalytic movement has proven that what appears at first as an extension or a variation often produces a paradigm shift.

Green's proposals raise some questions. A first difficulty has to do with the "break" of the continuum between normal and pathological, and the continuity between different forms of pathology: more or less classical cases belonging to one category, difficult cases to another. Green had succeeded in avoiding a major pitfall by speaking of the analytical situation and of the psychoanalytic treatment itself, rather than speaking of "cases". In his 1974 paper, the emphasis was on the difficulties of the *analyst* rather than those related to the patient's pathology. However, when the same paper was republished in 1990, the *cases* took precedence over the analyst's difficulties.

The second difficulty, the most important one, is that considering the setting only as a facilitating environment means making the analyst a facilitator of the process. Yet, the setting imposes itself on the analyst as well as on the patient. This is one of the essential points I wish to make in this paper. If the analyst fails to recognize that he may be duped and is as much under the sway of the analytic situation as the patient, the risk exists of being too confident in his own perceptive abilities, leading him to technical changes.

The third difficulty relates to one's conception of psychoanalysis and the treatment. Two of Green's remarks seem relevant in this regard. The first relates to the question of indications, and the second, to the replacement of the notion of transference neurosis by the notion of process. Thus, Green is referring to a rather classical framework of thought, which he both criticizes and takes as his starting point.

As I mentioned before, I was once forced to cancel a day's work somewhat at the last minute, announcing this to my patients at the preceding session. At the first session following this break, a patient whose speech is often halting and enigmatic expressed that her anxiety and agitation had caused her to have trouble sleeping on the night following my announcement. She then added that she masturbated to calm herself down. Pouncing on the idea that her anxiety must have resulted from her having imagined that I had had a problem, I tell her that she must have been frightened, perhaps in connection to the canceled session. She tells me that she dreamt that she had cramps and I imagine that she must have dreamt this in order to tell me about her fear. I am wrong, at least in part. She expresses instead that she had experienced the *missing* session (her expression) as a sudden irruption of intimacy.

I remained silent, stunned by the accuracy of her interpretation, which had not occurred to me: by canceling a session, I, in fact, had thrown something very personal into our regular, established rhythm, I had presented myself too directly as a person. Thus, along with fear, this irruption of intimacy had also caused a strong excitement.

After she left, I realized that the payment she left me included two sessions. The *missed* session existed despite the cancellation. Or rather, she was trying to bring it into existence to help dissipate the turmoil caused by the disruption.

The conception of the treatment implicit in this clinical vignette and that of my patient at the dispensary is quite different from Green's in his 1974 paper.

Some elements of technique may appear to be arbitrary, established for the sake of convenience, convention, or due to a lack of imagination. In other words, one setting or another could be considered a matter of personal choice.

But whenever we change an element of the setting, canceling sessions to go to a conference, for instance, we feel a certain discomfort. We have the feeling that we are "doing" something to the situation and sometimes to the patient themself. Especially when the treatment goes through a somewhat complicated period, we think that this is not the time to "touch" the setting, as though we are touching the patient themself.

In short, we are reluctant to make this kind of alteration and we tend to respect the conditions of treatment as much as possible. This means that the setting also applies to the analyst, that the analyst is not simply its "guarantor", as some colleagues would say, but that the "guarantor" has a responsibility to be as reliable as possible.

"Internal" setting

In recent years, the notion of setting has been enriched by the reference to an "internal" setting, a very fashionable term that seems to have a bright future. I am rather skeptical about the idea of an internal setting, which seems to be somewhat redundant with the classical idea of "analytical attitude" (Schafer, 1983).

Let's consider the arguments of Mariam Alizade, an Argentinean analyst, as early as 2002. The reasons for introducing the notion of internal setting are, in essence, the usual justifications: current transformations in clinical practice, new pathologies and socio-cultural changes mean that today's demands no longer fit into the traditional setting. It is therefore necessary to find new ways of conducting psychoanalysis without losing its specificity (Alizade, 2002a, p. 2).

For Alizade, the internal setting is already implicit in the fundamental rules of free association, evenly hovering attention and abstinence. It is especially present in the role and attitude of the analyst, that is, the internal organizations or configurations that are gradually created in the analyst's psyche when he internalizes the psychoanalytic discipline. I underscore two terms: discipline and internalization. These are *gestalts*, involving elements of a protective superego, which ensure the proper conduct of the psychoanalytic act.

On his part, the patient will also internalize the setting throughout the process of analysis. It is an endo-psychic and intersubjective geography. It is the enveloping freedom of the setting that allows for successive reorganizations. Thus, the internal setting allows the "elimination" [Mrs Alizade's term] of certain elements of the external invariants (couch, number of sessions and meeting place). This is not necessarily accompanied by the collapse of the internal setting and do not compromise the effectiveness of the treatment.

According to Alizade, there is a number of elements belonging to the internal world of the analyst, the patient and the field of action of the analysis which compose an invariant set, a system, incorporated into the mind of the analyst and working its way into the atmosphere of the session. It influences the external variables and constitutes an organizing schema for exploration.

The rules laid down as guiding principles have, according to Alizade, lent a certain objectivity and scientific solidity to psychoanalysis but they "have slowed down a certain audacity in the investigation of potential variants of the analytical treatment" (ibid., p. 1).

The internal setting, according to Alizade, includes the capacity for empathy, the analyst's permeability to his or her own unconscious and that of the patient, unconscious transmission and interaction, and the use of creativity. It is Reik's famous "third ear" made of "inner voices", of what is not said with words and is in the range of the inaudible. We are dealing with a phenomenology of the invisible, where perception translates into action.

So, the patient can challenge all the traditional elements of the setting (schedules, regularity, rhythm, fees, couch) but he cannot, according to Alizade, escape the impact and the implication of the internal setting: of "what must be".

Of course, Alizade is not totally unaware of the risks of her proposal: the idea that all forms of treatment are equally valid; the use of suggestion rather than elaboration; oversimplification; the loss of a conception of the external frame as depository for the patient's psychotic anxieties; as well as the loss of an indispensable dose of analytical rigor (Alizade, 2002b).

To her mind, the dismantling of the conventional notion of external setting is an inevitable reality in contemporary psychoanalysis. Group sessions, use of the couch twice a week, with one weekly session of psychodrama, psychoanalysis conducted at low frequency, with or without the couch—all such combined or mixed forms are possible.

One may wonder whether the notion of an internal setting is not invoked as a way to justify dispensing with the difficulty of creating a more or less traditional analytical setting. To set aside the traditional conception of setting, Alizade must emphasize all the elements that are essential to the analytical situation ("the fundamental rules"), adding as well the more or less ineffable elements with which every analyst is familiar from his experience.

Some years later, John Churcher, a colleague from Manchester and member of the British Society, wrote an interesting and articulate paper, elaborating on the definition of setting. In it, he identifies implicit references to the notion of setting in Freud's technical recommendations, and makes his way to the subtleties and difficulties of Bleger's 1967 proposals (Churcher, 2005).

Churcher came across the formulation "internal setting" in an unpublished paper by another English analyst, Marie Bridge, who used the term in describing the increased intensity and duration of treatments in her psychotherapeutic practice. She attributes these increases to the effects of her own analysis and to the possibility of finding a very particular space in her own mind that allowed her patients to venture into a more disturbed transferential relationship. To her mind, a sustained rhythm of five sessions a week and the timelessness of the unconscious are the essential factors in the equation.

Churcher's interest is to delineate the internal conditions necessary for the work of analysis to take place. He also refers to Alizade and to the relation between external and internal setting for the analyst and for the patient. For Churcher, it is the setting created in the analyst's mind that becomes a constant, this is what safeguards the conditions that allow the mobilization of psychotic anxieties.

Churcher is sensitive to the current work conditions shared by many psychotherapists in public health systems (in England, the National Health Service), who are confronted with managerial evaluation techniques with goals and indicators that create a climate of institutional pessimism. He does not hesitate to describe these conditions as "crazy" (Churcher, 2005, p. 11). He also notes that psychologists working with organizations and institutions need to adhere to a strict setting, accompanied by equally strict technique.

Churcher therefore proceeds in a very different way from Alizade, almost the opposite. For Alizade, it is the contemporary context of clinical practice that forces change in the "external" setting (this term, as well as that of "internal", remain very problematic for me) and it is therefore the internal setting that must contain and deepen the process. Churcher sees the internal setting as a kind of bulwark that helps us preserve the essential conditions of practice. All the more so since Churcher, following in the footsteps of several authors, including Bleger, believes institutions are not external to individuals.

Churcher later returned to the notion of internal setting in two more papers (Churcher, 2016, 2017), taking, as a starting point, moments when the analyst maintains his setting and a clinical attitude which aims to restore the setting to the background after it has been disrupted.

Shortly after Churcher's first paper, in 2006, Michael Parsons presented a paper to the British Society discussing the notion of "internal setting" (Parsons, 2014 [2007]).

From the outset, Parsons does not hesitate to distinguish the external structure of the treatment (the office, chair, couch, payment, vacations) from an internal structure linked to the identity of the analyst (ibid., p. 155). The internal setting defines and protects an area of the analyst's mind where anything that happens, including in the external setting, can be seen from a psychoanalytic perspective. The setting may not be respected on the outside (e.g., very loud noises or someone entering the room) as well as on the inside (an acting-out of the patient or an error by the analyst). Note that here the interior is the space of the consulting room. However, relying on his inner setting, the analyst can still consider the meaning of these situations or breaches, and bring it into the analysis.

Parsons believes that Winnicott's experiments with modifying the setting (and those of Ferenczi long before him) were an attempt to develop a sense of the internal setting. The internal setting would thus be a space where analysts become "listeners" of themselves (ibid., p. 166), a function of counter-transference, so to speak.

In other words, Parsons, like Alizade, tries to identify elements of the analytical situation that do not refer only to "formal" parameters.

Questions regarding the flexibility of the external setting arises once more. But it seems to me that if Alizade advocates a complete de-regulation of these so-called "formal" parameters (the term "de-regulation" is the emblem of a whole current of contemporary psychoanalysis, especially in Latin America), Parsons seeks greater freedom of action for the analyst in a very Winnicottian spirit. As long as the analyst remains attentive to himself and his or her counter-transference, the risks of the analyst's acting out are minimized. The clinical examples that Alizade and Parsons present clearly show the differences in their orientation.

Concluding remarks

This paper is an attempt to better orientate myself with regard to a very puzzling question which cannot be reduced to a simple clinical or technical "detail".

As conditions for the practice of psychoanalysis are becoming more and more difficult in Latin America and in the United States, many colleagues have to turn, for instance, to remote analysis to be able to earn a living. The situation in France and in some other European countries is, at least for the moment, an exception. However, although inter-related, there is a difference between the economic, political and social situation on one side, and the theoretical elaborations of psychoanalysis, on the other.

Let me try to recapitulate the causes of my perplexity. First, why has the setting become a more and more important "notion"? I don't know. I don't think it is simply a reflection of advances in psychoanalytical thinking. So many brilliant ideas and theories have perished over a century! Some of these were clearly attempts to thwart other propositions, beginning with Freud's. Some are reactions against the mainstream like Kohut's Self-Psychology in relation to Ego Psychology. There are lots of other examples.

I understand (at least I think so) why the concept of "internal" setting has gained favor: it allows for the introduction of modifications of the setting in the name of clinical necessities. However, to put it briefly: the clinical problems are not simply facts, they are also a creation of the analyst who necessarily organizes his perspective and his understanding of the clinical situation through the lens of his own version of psychoanalysis and psychoanalytical treatment (Widlöcher, 1994).

The idea that the analyst can remain attentive to himself and his counter-transference raises the question of the unconscious aspects of counter-transference—unless one wants to believe that counter-transference is above all conscious or preconscious.

This is, after all, my main concern: the analyst's unconscious functioning in the session. Every analyst has probably had occasion to measure the degree of omnipotence we all put in our clinical work. The setting is thus a good recommendation for the analyst. Even more than for the patient.

Notes

1 Donnet came back several times to the subject, especially in the introduction to the 1995 book, which takes up the title of the article, *Le divan bien tempéré*.
2 The quotations below follow the pagination of the French edition.

References

Alizade, M. (2002a). *Colloque APA-SPP*. Available at https://web.archive.org/web/20050409073643/http://www.spp.asso.fr/Main/DebatSansFrontiere/ApaSpp/2002/Discussions/texte2.htm.

Alizade, M. (2002b). El rigor y el encuadre interno. *Revista Uruguaya de Psicoanálisis, 96*: 13–16.

Bleger, J. (2013 [1967]). Psycho-analysis of the psycho-analytic setting. In: *Symbiosis and Ambiguity*. London: Routledge.

Bridge, M. (2013 [1997]). Why five times a week? A candidate's perspective. *Bulletin of the British Psychoanalytical Society, 49*(7): 3–9.

Churcher, J. (2005). *Keeping the psychoanalytic setting in mind*. Unpublished paper, presented to the Annual Conference of Lancaster Psychotherapy Clinic.

Churcher, J. (2016). Der psychoanalytische Rahmen, das Körperschema, Telekommunikation und Telepräsenz: Implikationen von José Blegers Konzept des "encuadre". *Psyche – Zeitschrift für Psychoanalyse und ihre Anwendungen, 70*(1): 60–81.

Churcher, J. (2017). Privacy, Telecommunications and the Psychoanalytic Setting. In: Scharff, J.S. (ed.) *Psychoanalysis Online 3*. London: Karnac. Paper given at the 28th Annual Conference of the EPF, Stockholm, 26–29 March 2015. Also available in *European Psychoanalytical Federation Bulletin, 69*: 221–223.

Donnet, J-L. (1995). *Le divan bien tempéré*. Paris: Presses Universitaires de France.

Donnet, J-L. (2005). *La situation analysante*. Paris: Presses Universitaires de France.

Etchegoyen, H. (1986). *Los fundamentos de la técnica psicoanalítica*. Buenos Aires: Amorrortu.

Green, A. (1990). *La folie privée: Psychanalyse des cas-limites*. Paris: Gallimard.

IPA. *Inter-Regional Encyclopedic Dictionary of Psychoanalysis*. Entry, 'Setting' (The Psychoanalytic). Available at: www.ipa.world/en/encyclopedic_dictionary/English/home.aspx

Parsons, M. (2014 [2007]). Raiding the Inarticulate: Internal Setting, Beyond Countertransference. In: *Living Psychoanalysis. From Theory to Experience*. London: Routledge. Originally published in *International Journal of Psychoanalysis, 88*(6): 1441–1456.

Roussillon, R. (1995). *Logiques et archéologiques du cadre psychanalytique*. Paris: Presses Universitaires de France.

Schafer, R. (1983). *The Analytic Attitude*. London: Routledge.

Widlöcher, D. (1994). A case is not a fact. *International Journal of Psychoanalysis, 75* (5–6): 1233–1244.

Winnicott, D.W. (1958 [1949]). Hate in the Countertransference. In: *Collected Papers: Through Paediatrics to Psycho-Analysis* (pp. 194–203). London: Tavistock Publications.

Winnicott, D.W. (1958 [1951]). Transitional Object and Transitional Phenomena. In: *Collected Papers: Through Paediatrics to Psycho-Analysis* (pp. 229–242). London: Tavistock Publications.

Winnicott, D.W. (1958 [1954]). Metapsychological and Clinical Aspects of Regression within the Psycho-Analytical Set-Up. In: *Collected Papers: Through Paediatrics to Psycho-Analysis* (pp. 275–294). London: Tavistock Publications.

Zac, J. (1967). Encuadre y acting out: Relación semana-fin de semana. *Revista de Psicoanálisis, 25*: 1.

Zac, J. (1971). Un enfoque metodológico del establecimiento del encuadre. *Revista de Psicoanálisis, 28*: 593–610.

2 The psychoanalytic setting, embodiment and presence

Exploring José Bleger's concept of *encuadre*[1]

John Churcher

Introduction

José Bleger's book *Symbiosis and Ambiguity: A Psychoanalytic Study* was first published in Spanish in 1967 (Bleger, 1967a). In the same year a single chapter from it was published in English in the *International Journal of Psychoanalysis* under the title 'Psycho-analysis of the psycho-analytic frame' (Bleger, 1967b). This chapter has become a classic among writings on the psychoanalytic setting, but in isolation from its original context of the book as a whole, and with some serious deficiencies in the translation. Translations of the entire book into French, Italian and Portuguese have been available for some time but it was more than forty years before an English edition was eventually published, in the New Library of Psychoanalysis series (Bleger, 2013 [1967]).

Symbiosis and Ambiguity is an ambitious and complex work, both clinically and theoretically. In this paper I summarise only some of the concepts that José Bleger uses to understand the psychoanalytic setting, and explore some of their implications. Then, in a thought experiment, I consider how these concepts might be applied in an imagined, impossible, radically modified setting involving telecommunications.

Process and non-process

Within the psychoanalytic situation José Bleger distinguishes the analytic process from something that he calls a 'non-process'. The process can be regarded as a set of variables which change over time, and the non-process as a set of constants, whose values do not change, or which in any case are held as constant as possible. As with the so-called 'parameters' of psychoanalytic technique (Eissler, 1953), we should not take this quasi-mathematical terminology too literally.

In terms borrowed from Gestalt psychology, Bleger describes the process and the non-process as related in the same way as figure and ground. In the Gestalt psychology of perception this is an asymmetrical relation: a figure has a boundary, whereas the ground is unbounded and extends

DOI: 10.4324/9781003252252-4

behind the figure as well as behind and beyond any frame in which the figure may be set (Rubin, 1958 [1915]). The Spanish word that Bleger uses to refer to this non-process is *encuadre*. In the version published in the IJP this was translated as 'frame', but in the English edition of *Symbiosis and Ambiguity* we have retranslated it as 'setting'. 'Frame' and 'setting' can each have various senses in English, and as psychoanalytic terms they are often used more or less interchangeably, although the context sometimes favours one more than the other. In this paper I shall use 'setting', except when reporting the work of those who have preferred 'frame'.[2]

The central idea was already well-expressed in Marion Milner's original analogy between the psychoanalytic setting and the frame around a painting, when she wrote:

> The frame marks off the different kind of reality that is within it from that which is outside it; but a temporal spatial frame also marks off the special kind of reality of a psychoanalytic session. And in psychoanalysis it is the existence of this frame that makes possible the full development of that creative illusion that analysts call the transference.
>
> (Milner, 1952, p. 183)[3]

Leopoldo Bleger (2022) emphasises that the setting exists independently of our wishes:

> Bleger's paper acknowledges the *existence* of a setting. The proof is that, no matter how many sessions are held, a setting is created, whether in an analysis, in a psychotherapy or in a working group. It is not that we give ourselves a setting, but that, whether we like it or not, there *is* one. (Chapter 1, this volume).

I would only add that the setting is created *by us*; we did not find it already existing in nature, like water or sunshine.

The 'ideally normal' setting

As long as the setting is kept constant, Bleger points out, it remains unnoticed, unperceived. When for some reason a disruption occurs, the setting suddenly changes its status: 'from the background of a *Gestalt* into a figure, that is, into a process' (Bleger, 2013 [1967], p. 229). Conversely, the process suddenly moves to the background in a figure-ground reversal. The reversal is only temporary, however, because as psychoanalysts we preserve a distinct attitude towards the setting: we do our best to maintain or restore it, to return it to the background, in order to be able to continue to observe and analyse the process. We strive to maintain the setting as an ideal norm, even though we inevitably and repeatedly fail.

Instead of focussing on the disruptions, Bleger wants to study the maintenance of the norm as an ideal. He likens this endeavour to a 'thought experiment' in physics, or *Gedankenexperiment*, which cannot actually be performed, but which is nevertheless a useful fiction.[4] He is interested in the setting as it exists while it is being successfully kept in the background. He wants to consider it when it is being seen as *non*-problematic, in order to show that in fact it *is* a problem which hasn't been recognised as such.

What, then, is the nature of the problem that Bleger believes has gone unrecognised? In short, it is that *something has been deposited in the setting*, and silently inhabits it, the psychoanalysis of which will be essential. To understand what this something is, we need to unpick a cluster of connected ideas in Bleger's account. He presents these as interdependent but I am here separating them out for the sake of clarity.

Setting, institution, personality, ego, body schema

First, *the setting is an institution*. Bleger is here simply pointing out that because it involves lasting relationships, with the maintenance of certain norms and attitudes, the setting is a particular kind of social institution. Other examples include the family, schools, hospitals, psychoanalytical societies.

Second, *every institution forms part of the individual's personality*, so that personal identity always has a group or institutional aspect. The psychoanalytic setting thus becomes a part of the personality of anyone who participates in an analysis, and by implication this is true for the analyst as well as for the patient. Other institutions also form parts of the personality, and Bleger refers to institutions as forming multiple 'nuclei of personal identity'. On this model, an individual's personality is not something fixed that pre-exists their involvement in an institution and remains unchanged by it; rather, the history of an individual's participation in various institutions is an integral part of the continuing history of their personality.[5]

Third, *the setting forms part of the body schema*. Bleger introduces this idea initially by way of an analogy, between the way in which the setting comes to our attention only when it is disrupted in some way, and the way in which a 'phantom limb', the experience of a living, functioning arm or leg where one no longer exists anatomically, demonstrates the existence of a body schema. Just as I might discover, if I were to lose a limb in an accident, that I also have an invisible 'phantom' limb, a live internal version of that part of my body, as part of my body schema – so, Bleger suggests, there is a live internal version of the entire psychoanalytic setting, which I only become aware of when it is broken in some way, but which always existed. It becomes clear, however, that this is more than just an analogy. He writes:

The setting forms part of the patient's body schema. It *is*[6] the body schema in the part where this has not yet been structured and discriminated. This means that it is something different from the body schema in the narrow sense of the term: it is the undifferentiation of body and space, and of body and environment.

(Bleger, 2013 [1967], pp. 238–239)[7]

Undifferentiation, symbiosis and the psychotic part of the personality

What Bleger means by this dense statement becomes clearer if we restore the chapter on the setting to its context in the book as a whole. He regards the normal, silent, continuous presence of the setting as affording the patient an opportunity for a symbiotic relationship that reproduces an early symbiosis of the infant with the mother. He hypothesises that the infant is in an initial psychological state of undifferentiation in which there is not yet a real object relation, but neither is there a purely objectless primary narcissism.

Bleger's concept of undifferentiation implies a specific structure and organisation. Prior to the paranoid-schizoid position as described by Melanie Klein, he argues, there is a more primitive position, whose characteristic defences are abnormal splitting, immobilisation and fragmentation (what Bleuler had called *Zerspaltung*), which gives rise to confusional rather than persecutory anxiety, and in which instead of a real object relation there are various 'ego nuclei' together with the objects to which they correspond. These nuclei exist psychologically, but in an undifferentiated state because the splitting (Bleuler's *Spaltung*) that later will characterise the paranoid-schizoid position has not yet occurred.

This more primitive position Bleger terms the 'glischro-caric position',[8] and the residue of its relational structure persists throughout normal and pathological development as an 'agglutinated nucleus', which he equates with what Bion (1957) called 'the psychotic part of the personality'. Throughout life, the agglutinated nucleus remains ready to form symbiotic relationships characterised by massive projective identifications. It is this nucleus that is deposited in the setting, and remains hidden there, unanalysed, until a disruption to the setting causes it to become manifest.

Boundaries and social origins of the body schema

Insofar as the world is constant, present and dependable, Bleger argues, it provides no occasion for differentiating between self and not-self. Within the undifferentiated part of the body schema the patient's body is not discriminated from the couch, the walls, or the space that they enclose. This undifferentiated world exists psychologically only as a 'non-ego', a necessary foundation upon which a more or less integrated ego, with its capacity for thinking and differentiation, is built up through experiences of frustration and gratification. Just as the setting is a 'non-process' which forms the background to the psychoanalytic process, so in the individual there is a 'non-ego', a background to and basis for the formation of the ego. The 'non-ego' is maintained by the stable, unchanging aspects of experience, including the experience in an analysis of the setting as unchanging.

Although the setting as an institution is the part of the body schema in which the body is not differentiated from its environment, Bleger also states that institutions function as limits, or boundaries, of the body schema. This idea becomes more intelligible in the context of his discussion of symbiosis in the earlier chapters of *Symbiosis and Ambiguity*. In Chapter 2, for example, he discusses a novel (Rochefort, 1958) in which the narrator recalls an intensely symbiotic relationship with a man she meets. She says: 'I was a white whale and completely mad, ready to burst out of my skin.' Bleger comments that she is describing not only the establishment of a new bodily ego but an invasion that tends to break through the boundaries of the ego and the body schema that are operating up to that moment. In the face of this danger of 'bursting' or suddenly losing boundaries, bodily contact is indispensable, a new kinaesthesia that re-configures the boundaries of the body scheme. (Bleger, 2013 [1967], p. 52).

In Rochefort's novel, the 'institution' that stabilises this re-configuration is a compulsive sexual relationship, but the stabilisation is only temporary. In a clinical situation, by contrast, the psychoanalytic setting with its systematic avoidance of physical contact may, if all goes well, be effective in gradually establishing a more enduring result. Either way, Bleger is implying a view of the body schema as essentially social: its boundaries are continually being determined and redefined through interaction with others in a space that is simultaneously physical and cultural.

Bleger probably derived his concept of the body schema from Paul Schilder, influenced by discussion with Enrique Pichon-Rivière and their reading of Merleau-Ponty (see Tubert-Oklander and Hernández de Tubert, 2004, p. 71). Schilder was building on the pioneering neurological work of Head and Holmes (1911–12) and had expanded the concept to include both libidinal and 'sociological' dimensions. Recently Schilder's work has been criticised for not distinguishing clearly between the body *schema* as the postural model of the body that is involved in the organisation of bodily movements, and body *image* as the mental image of the body (e.g. by Gallagher, 2005).

The developmental origins of both the body schema and the body image are controversial questions in neurology and developmental psychology. There has been much discussion of *aplasic* phantoms: the phantom limbs experienced by individuals who are born with missing limbs. Gallagher and Meltzoff (1996) argue that early undifferentiation is only ever partial, and that the newborn infant already has a rudimentary differentiation of self and non-self based in an innate, supramodal aware-ness of its own body. 'In effect', they write, 'this supramodal *intra*-corporeal communication is the basis for an *inter*-corporeal communication and has profound implications for the child's relations with others.' The conclusion they draw is that: 'The experiential connection between self and other is operative from birth, and is not, as Merleau-Ponty suggests, a syncretic confusion' (Gallagher and Meltzoff, 1996, pp. 224, 229).

Although this view represents a strong current of opinion in the world of infancy research, it relies on a philosophical prejudice in favour of the individual as primarily a subject of knowledge rather than a participant in shared action, and on an *a priori* assumption that communication occurs between individuals whose separate identities as embodied beings are pre-given. An alternative interpretation of the same findings is offered by Wood and Stuart (2009), who place greater emphasis on the role of embodied action and interaction, both pre- and post-natally, in the onto-geny of the body schema. Instead of requiring explanation in terms of an innate body schema, they argue,

> the aplasic phantom can be understood ontogenetically, as a funda-mentally social acquisition. Thus, just as nonaplasic phantom limb experience might be understood as "called forth" by the world of graspable, manipulable objects (Merleau-Ponty 1962), so the aplasic phantom could be enacted through the medium of intersubjectivity and the visual and somatosensory experience of others' actions in a world of graspable, manipulable objects. The experience of interacting with conspecifics, of joint action often featuring the coupling of hands and other effectors in the service of shared goals, could provide the stimulus for the aplasic individual's incorporation of absent limbs into her own body schema.
>
> (Wood and Stuart, 2009, pp. 501–502)

Susan Stuart has coined the term 'enkinaesthesia' for this kind of experi-ence (Stuart, 2011), which fits well with Bleger's phrase 'a new kinaesthe-sia that re-configures the boundaries of the body scheme' (Bleger, 2013 [1967], p. 52).

The two settings and the idea of an 'internal' setting

Up to now we have referred to *the* psychoanalytic setting, but Bleger introduced the idea that there are *two* settings: the analyst's and the patient's, and that the analyst must 'accept' the latter without abandoning the former. Therefore, as he states in a final paragraph:

> *The setting can only be analysed within the setting*; in other words, the patient's dependence and most primitive psychological organisation

can only be analysed within the analyst's setting, which should be neither ambiguous, nor changing, nor altered.

(Bleger, 2013 [1967], p. 241)

Haydee Faimberg discusses this in terms of Hegel's concepts of *Aufhebung* and 'determinate negation',[9] and she explains that she has changed her preferred translation of *encuadre* from 'setting' to 'frame' to better develop this idea (Faimberg, 2018, p. 51n.). Bleger's 'most original central thesis', she writes, is that 'there are *two frames* (not only one) to be *differentiated each from the other*. One frame, proposed and maintained by the psycho-analyst, is consciously accepted by the patient; the other *is brought by the patient* and long remains mute' (Faimberg, 2018, p. 46).

In Faimberg's view, Bleger is saying that the frame, an institution established for the purpose of psychoanalytic understanding, tends like all institutions to negate itself by substituting for this purpose over time its own survival as a raison d'être, thereby turning itself into mere ritual. This can be reversed, but only by the analyst keeping his or her own frame constant, while at the same time listening, waiting for the patient's frame to 'speak', to make its existence known. Thus, paradoxically, only the analyst's preserving the ritual makes possible an end to the ritualisation (Faimberg, 2012).

Ritualisation clearly involves a compulsion to repeat, and in a separate paper Faimberg addresses the question of what is being repeated. Her answer has two parts: firstly, that '… *what is insistent is an attempt to con-firm a timeless "solution"* to unconscious conflicts' (Faimberg, 2013, p. 870). To which I would add that the timelessness is intrinsic to the repetitive temporal structure of the setting, with its daily, weekly, and annual rhythms. Sabbadini (1989) has referred to a 'contrast of temporalities', between the timelessness of the content of a session and the actual passage of time between its fixed boundaries, whereas I am making the different and complementary point that by equating two dates as anniversaries in the calendar, or by giving two days of the week the same name ('it's Friday again'), we have already symbolically denied the passage of time.[10] The second part of Faimberg's answer is that '*what is being insisted upon changes as well*', when (or if) as a function of analytic listening the patient is heard in a new way (Faimberg, 2013, p. 871). Only then can the patient's frame be differentiated from the analyst's. In this potential for change can be seen what Faimberg calls the 'transformational quality of the psycho-analytic method itself', and the paradox that insistence on keeping things constant is a precondition for psychic change.

The analyst's insistence on maintaining the setting, on waiting, and the 'analytic attitude' of seeking to restore the setting to the background fol-lowing a disruption, all suggest the possibility of a concept which may have been latent in our clinical practice for some time. I mean the concept of an '*internal* setting', which has been articulated now by numerous authors, including: Temperley (1984), Guillaumin (1987), Ribas (1989), Alizade (2010 [2002]), Donnet (2007), Bridge (2013 [1997], 2013), Parsons (2007), Civitarese (2013 [2011]), Labarthe (2012), Churcher (2005, 2019), Schachter, Tabakin and Blucher (2019).[11] Not all of them think of the internal setting in precisely the same way but they generally agree that it is when the external setting is disrupted or under threat that the internal setting is most essential for maintaining or restoring the analytic process.

Leopoldo Bleger (2022), however, has questioned the need for such a concept and I share his concern that the distinction between 'internal' and 'external', so prevalent in psychology, is problematic in this context. José Bleger used the Barangers' conception of the 'bastion' (*baluarte*, translated in the 1967 version as 'bulwark') to make the point that: 'The most persistent, tenacious and unnoticeable "bastion" is the one deposited in the setting.' From within this conception, when a disruption causes the analyst to prioritise restoration of the setting, the restoration occurs as a process in what the Barangers called 'the bipersonal field', and not simply 'inside the analyst's head'. The concept of a 'field' in this sense, though less formalisable than its physical original, has the merit of including in a single totality the bodies and minds of both analyst and patient, the physical space they share in common, and the social 'space' and 'time' in which the analytic session is demarcated as a framed region of Milner's 'special kind of reality' (Baranger and Baranger, 2008 [1961–62]), Churcher, 2008). It thus displaces, to some extent, what Hyppolite (1954) called the 'primary myth' of inside and outside (see also Bachelard, 1994 [1964]).

Telecommunications, presence, and embodiment: a thought experiment

From the beginnings of psychoanalysis there have been experiments with modifications of the classical setting, some more successful than others, most of them controversial. In the final part of this paper I want to consider some implications of Bleger's concept for one category of modified settings: those in which telecommunications are used to substitute for the physical co-presence of analyst and patient at the same location. These include: the telephone, which historically was available from the earliest days of psychoanalysis, although the dominant view within the profession was against its use until quite recently; Skype, which became widely available in the last decade or so; and, accelerated by the COVID-19 pandemic beginning in 2020, Zoom, WhatsApp, and various similar systems.

To explore this topic, I will follow Bleger's example by making a further thought experiment, one in which the setting is modified by technology in a more radical way than is actually possible. The purpose of this exercise is not to consider what technological parameters may be feasible or desirable, but to understand better the settings in which psychoanalysis is actually conducted. Let us imagine that psychoanalyst and patient are meeting not in a real consulting room, nor by telephone, nor even in the kind of hybrid space created in a video conversation,[12] but solely through the medium of artificial proxies of themselves, or *avatars*. In such a world you control the movements, actions, utterances, etc. of your personal avatar in real time, like a virtual puppet or mask. Instead of seeing someone in front of you or their image on a video screen, you encounter his or her avatar as an animated figure interacting with your own in a virtual space.

One example of such a world is *Second Life*,[13] created in 2003, and which by 2013 had a million regular users. In *Second Life*, avatars and the interactions between them exist entirely in a virtual space, but we can imagine a world in which avatars would exist as robots interacting physically somewhere in real space. Moreover, we can imagine their being controlled via immersive virtual reality (VR), rather than using keyboards and mice.[14] It was work on remotely controlled robots that led Marvin Minsky, forty years ago, to coin the term 'telepresence' to emphasise the importance of high-quality sensory feedback for tools that would 'feel and work so much like our own hands that we won't notice any significant difference.' He added: 'The biggest challenge to developing telepresence is achieving that sense of 'being there.' Can telepresence be a true substitute for the real thing? Will we be able to couple our artificial devices naturally and comfortably to work together with the sensory mechanisms of human organisms?' (Minsky, 1980, p. 48).

Since then the technology of teleoperation has made steady progress and its field of application widened. The first transatlantic surgical operation was successfully performed twenty years ago by a surgeon in New York upon a patient in Strasbourg (Marescaux, et al., 2002). Remote surgery uses high-quality video and sophisticated robotics, but progress is constrained by the difficulty of providing adequate sensory mechanical (haptic) feedback to the surgeon's hands, and by unavoidable transmission delays which, across large distances, interfere with the exercise of visuo-manual coordination and may require special compensatory training. Clearly, our sense of presence depends on the situation and the task as well as on the technology, and the requirements for psychoanalysis are likely to be rather different from those for surgery. The term 'telepresence' was soon replaced by the more general term 'presence', but Minsky's criterion of 'not noticing any significant difference' remained central to attempts to theorise the phenomenon. For example, an influential review defined presence as 'a psychological state in which the virtuality of experience is unnoticed' (Lee, 2004, p. 32; see also Russell, 2015, Chapter 8; Slater, 2018).

It is a general feature of systems which support an experience of presence that their virtuality remains unnoticed only until something goes wrong, whereupon the technology which up to then had been cognitively transparent suddenly becomes opaque. The parallel with the analytic setting is clear, and *Bleger's concept of the setting implies that if used as a medium for psychoanalytic consultation the telecommunication system itself will inevitably become a depository for the psychotic part of the personality.* This has far-reaching implications for the ongoing debate about 'remote analysis'.

The concept of presence enables us to specify the thought experiment more precisely: if we imagine a communications system using avatars, but unconstrained by the limitations of current technology, do we suppose that we could ever, even in principle, use it as a medium in which to conduct a psychoanalysis? Some years ago I suggested that the answer would depend on two conditions: whether the participants are able to feel that they really are in each other's presence, and whether it is capable of supporting the establishment and maintenance of an analytic setting (Churcher, 2000). Andrea Sabbadini made a similar point about the use of video-links such as Skype: 'The important issue ... is whether the simultaneous presence of the analytic dyad in a physical space is a condition *sine qua non* for the psychoanalytic process to occur.' (Sabbadini, 2013, p. 31). The questions that both Sabbadini and I were asking are in principle independent of any particular technology or method of representing the participants to each other. Part of the purpose of my thought experiment is to make clear that we are obliged to use artificial representations of *some* kind whenever we telecommunicate. Is it then simply an empirical question whether psychoanalysis by means of avatars will one day be possible?

Sabbadini makes an important observation about the classical psychoanalytic setting. Although physical contact is avoided and visual contact is limited, he writes,

> ... the mere *possibility* of, say, bodily contact between them, be it of an erotic, affectionate or aggressive nature, is central to the experience (both actual and transferential) that therapist and patient have of each other. The absence of such a possibility in skypanalysis, therefore, is not a matter of indifference.
>
> (Sabbadini, 2013, p. 27)

Similar observations have been made by others, including Gillian Isaacs Russell, who quotes a patient as saying that in screen relations there is no 'kiss or kick' (Russell, 2015, pp. xvii and 39). An example of what this means occurred in a case that I am familiar with: a patient who, at a certain moment during a session, was afraid that his analyst might be about to kill or seriously injure him with a blow to the head from behind, using a hammer or other blunt instrument. Fortunately, it was possible to do some work on this experience, which did not recur, but if the session had been conducted remotely by audio or video telephony such an experience would have been impossible, as would the subsequent psychoanalytical work. What if the session had been conducted via the mediation of avatars, and if moreover these avatars existed not just virtually, but were also physically embodied as robots? Clearly, the possibilities depend on the nature of the interface. We can imagine one such avatar being 'assaulted' by another, but there will always be limits due to irreducible differences between the human organism and a machine. In the virtual consulting room, 'murder' of an avatar might be possible, and even physical injury to its human operator, but cannibalism would not.

If at this point my thought experiment stretches the imagination, it also serves its purpose by forcing us to consider the status of the body in relation to the setting, both in the classical setting and in one mediated by telecommunication. To Bleger's thesis that the setting forms part of the body schema, we need to add something which has gone largely unnoticed theoretically even if it has always been implicit: *the body itself is part of the setting*. Alessandra Lemma (2014) arrived at the same conclusion. She refers to the 'embodied setting', and stresses that it includes the analyst's body as well as the patient's. Both are no less part of the physical setting than are the couch or the chair, and like everything else that is there, the body is taken for granted only until it goes wrong. In an explicit comparison with Bleger's concept, André Green referred to the body as 'silent in health' (Green, 1975, p. 10).[15]

A perspective from developmental psychology that I find helpful in thinking about this was taken by André Bullinger (2012), for whom the body *qua* organism is an object of perception whose interactions with the environment give rise to regularities which allow the extraction and interiorisation of invariants which are then used to guide further interactions. Although the organism is innately preadapted to function in various ways, the biomechanical invariants of this functioning have to be discovered through the same interactions as do the invariant properties of things in the world. For example, even the invariant spatial relations between the fovea and the peripheral retina, although innately determined by the morphology of the eye, must be interiorised through visual experience before they can be used perceptually.[16]

This interiorisation of invariants extends beyond the biological body. When we use a tool, as various authors have observed (Merleau-Ponty, 1962, p. 143; Polanyi, 1966), we tend to incorporate it into our body-schema as a prosthesis. Interiorising the invariant properties of a stick, for example, enables a blind person to use it as an extension of the body. The avatar in the thought experiment described above can be considered a complex prosthesis. If it then imposes on its user a body schema different from the one that he or she would otherwise have, this only illustrates what has been called 'the cyborg's dilemma'. In 1997, Frank Biocca wrote:

> As we approach the year 2000, another version of our grappling with embodiment is coming to the fore. It is evident in our fascination with the idea of the cyborg, the interface of the physical body with

technology (e.g., Gray, Figueroa-Sarriera, and Mentor, 1995). The embodiment advanced in the form of virtual environment technology can be characterised as a form of cyborg coupling. This coupling underscores what I call the cyborg's dilemma, a kind of Faustian trade off: Choose technological embodiment to amplify the body, but beware that your body schema and identity may adapt to this cyborg form.

(Biocca, 1997, p. 24)

Biocca concluded his paper by warning against the self-deception of believing that there is a 'natural' option of *not* being wedded to technology, because the dilemma is already present

in a piece of clothing, in a wrist watch, in a baseball bat, in short, in all technologies that attach themselves and augment the body.

(Biocca, 1997, p. 24)

Alessandra Lemma has argued, following Deleuze, that we need to move beyond the binary logic of virtual and real, and to see the virtual as part of reality (Lemma, 2017). Similarly, Anda Zahiu follows the 'extended mind' thesis of Clark and Chalmers (1998) to argue that avatars controlled by immersive virtual reality are 'negotiable bodies that constitute a genuine part of who we are' (Zahiu, 2020). It does *not* follow, however, that our natural bodies lose their unique status as original and ultimate sources of the psyche. My avatar may be as much a part of me as my voice or my handwriting, but the reverse could not be the case. Even as a cyborg I would never be merely a component of my own avatar.

Conclusion

I have not attempted to discuss or summarise all of the ideas which underlie Bleger's view of the psychoanalytic setting, nor any of the considerable quantity of clinical material that he adduces in support of it. Nor have I considered his wider view that our inner life is to be understood, as Georges Politzer (1928, 1965–66) proposed, in terms of the category of drama. Instead, I have concentrated mainly on those aspects which relate directly to the body and the body schema in the psychoanalytic setting.

I want to conclude by returning from the exotic to the familiar, from the *unheimlich* scenario of avatar robots in the consulting room to the everyday familiarity of the telephone and, increasingly nowadays, of videotelephony and videoconferencing. Although there are evident differences between the possibilities afforded by these various technologies, many of the conditions presupposed in the thought experiment described above apply to all of them. A telephone, for example, can give a reasonably good experience of auditory presence, so that when involved in a conversation one ceases to be aware of the instrument itself, which disappears into the background. There is a distinctive phenomenology of space in ordinary telephone conversation, in which each participant simultaneously occupies their own primary zone and, secondarily, the zone of the other (see, e.g. Backhaus, 1997). It is only necessary to observe someone speaking on the telephone to see, in the language of posture and gesture, that their whole body is experienced as being at least partially somewhere else. An unexpected break in communication will divert attention to the instrument itself and away from the conversation, which is more or less disrupted, and this will be manifest also in a shift in posture and gesture. In everyday life the dependence of our sense of presence on the situation and the task, as well as on the technology, is evident. An emotionally-laden telephone conversation with someone whom you know well is affected differently by disruptions than a conversation with an insurance salesman in a call centre.

It is an implication of Bleger's view, I think, that we tend to establish a symbiotic relation with *any* invariants that we discover, adapt to, and interiorise, whether in our own bodies or in the rest of the world, and that we do so not only in the psychoanalytic setting but also in everyday life.[17] Wherever we find something stable, secure, constant, we sooner or later come to 'take it for granted'; a primitive part of the mind establishes a silent and hidden symbiotic relation with the invariant, using it as a depository for the undifferentiated parts of ourselves that are forever seeking a home. This happens always through processes that are social as well as physical, as we participate in various institutions in parallel, each of which forms part of the body schema and contributes to determining its boundary. The psychoanalytic setting is framed within the wider setting of our everyday life. Whenever everyday life is seriously disturbed, as for example, by war or natural disaster, or the exigencies of a global pandemic, we long for 'normality' to be restored as soon as possible, so that we may once again unconsciously deposit part of ourselves in it for safe keeping.

Psychoanalysis is unique among human situations and tasks by virtue of its cultivation of curiosity about what has been deposited unconsciously in the setting. For the reasons I have outlined, in psychoanalytic clinical work that is undertaken remotely, we need to be curious about the phantoms, invisible parts of ourselves, that silently take up residence in the body schema of the patient, in that of the analyst, and in the telecommunication system itself. Not to be curious is a form of denial.

Notes

1 An earlier version of this paper was published in German (Churcher, 2016). It originated in a shorter paper, titled 'Some implications of José Bleger's concept of *encuadre* ('setting' or 'frame'), presented at the 5th British German Colloquium, 11–13 October 2013, Møller Centre, Cambridge, UK.

2 We are familiar with the fact that what appear to be merely questions of translation may hide deeper conceptual problems. Even among those writers who explicitly rely on Bleger's concept, or who discuss it extensively, there is little consistency in the ways in which *encuadre* has been translated. In the English translation of Etchegoyen's *The Fundamentals of Psychoanalytic Technique* (Etchegoyen, 1991) it is translated as 'setting'. In the Italian text of his book *l'Intima Stanza*, as well as in its English translation ('The Intimate Room') Civitarese uses the English word 'setting' (Civitarese, 2008, 2010 [2008]). René Kaës, on the other hand, translates it into the French *cadre* in his book *Un singulier pluriel*, which is rendered as 'frame' in the English translation published by the IPA (Kaës, 1990, 2007). The 1993 German translation of Bleger's book has *Rahmen* (Bleger, 1993 [1967]).

René Kaës distinguishes between 'setting' (*dispositif*), 'situation' (*situation*), and 'frame' (*cadre*). For Kaës, the *dispositif* consists in certain physical and practical arrangements that the analyst makes use of, '… both that which the analyst has at his disposal and that which he puts in place for practising psychoanalysis' (Kaës, 2007, p. 57). On this basis a situation develops, within which the frame can exist as a place where the archaic elements (Bleger's agglutinated nucleus) are deposited. Kaës treats *dispositif* and *cadre* as distinct concepts that should not be confused, but in a note to the English translation of his book he acknowledges that Bleger's concept of *encuadre* includes both of them (Kaës, 2007, p. 67, n.1).

Similarly, Kamran Alipanahi (cited in Jarast, 2013, p. 159) argues that *encuadre* and 'setting' are essentially different concepts, and that the concept of *encuadre* derives from the cinema of *montage* as developed by Eisenstein. He contrasts the 'setting' as a physical space and chronological time in which events occur, with '*encuadre*' as the space that is captured in the frame of a camera. He suggests that framing, because it implies a subjective choice, is always a political act, whereas 'setting' lacks this subjective dimension. I am not convinced by the implied proposition that realistic cinema lacks a subjective dimension; its main exponent, Bazin, held that 'deep focus', the hallmark technique of realistic cinema, allows the viewer a freedom of choice that *montage* does not.

3 Civitarese has made a similar argument, in which he refers to 'la cornice del setting' (Civitarese, 2011, p. 159), which in the English translation is rendered as 'the frame of the setting' (Civitarese, 2013, p. 166).

4 The Spanish translation of this originally German term is *experiencia ideal*.

5 In this respect, Bleger follows a similar path to that taken by Freud, Fenichel, Bion and others.

6 The italicisation echoes Winnicott's 'The couch *is* the analyst's lap or womb …', which Bleger quotes in the previous paragraph but one.

7 In the Spanish original this last phrase is: '*la indiferenciación cuerpo-espacio y cuerpo-ambiente.*' (Bleger, 1967a, p. 247). The English version in IJP has: 'the body-space and body setting non-differentiation' (Bleger, 1967b, p. 517), whereas the English translation of *Symbiosis and Ambiguity* has: 'the undifferentiation of body and space, and of body and environment' (Bleger, 2013 [1967], p. 239).

8 From the Greek: *glischros* = sticky, adhesive; *karion* = kernel, nucleus.

9 *Bestimmte Negation*, usually translated in English as 'determinate negation' but in Faimberg's text rendered as 'determined negation'.

10 When we speak of the 'constants' of the setting we necessarily employ a kind of shorthand which obscures an abstraction. The sessions may occur at regular times each day but each session is unique; the notion of 'the same time each day' implies a background which includes both a natural diurnal cycle and

humanly imposed clock time. Weekends, monthly accounting dates and annual holidays imply a background which includes a calendrical system that is an achievement of centuries of science and culture. Within this system, the 'same' time of day, or day of the week, refers to an invariant that only exists as a function of the system. The symbolic denial of the passage of time is concretely parodied by Lewis Carroll in *Alice in Wonderland*, where at the Mad Tea-Party it is 'always six o'clock now'.

11 Ferruta (2014) refers instead to the 'mental' setting (*setting mentale*). Kaës (2007) writes that the frame is 'first constituted by the analyst's psyche'.

12 Lin Tao (2012) discusses the structure of this space.

13 http://www.secondlife.com

14 *Sansar* (https://www.sansar.com/) is an example of a purely virtual world in which avatars can be controlled by immersive VR headsets, whereas immersive VR teleoperation of robots is currently an active area of research. See, e.g. Toet et al. (2020).

15 Bleger himself discusses the way the body serves as a 'buffer' which moderates the reintrojection of previously projected fragments of experience, but he doesn't make clear that the body as part of the setting is also the recipient of projections in the first place (Bleger, 2013 [1967], p. 24).

16 Bullinger's perspective is rooted in the pioneering work of Piaget on sensorimotor coordination in human infants (Piaget, 1948). There are some parallels with recent discussion of embodiment and development in human and artificial systems under the banner of 'Embodied Cognitive Science', e.g. Leuzinger-Bohleber (2014), Leuzinger-Bohleber, Emde and Pfeifer (2013). Piaget's work is often unacknowledged in contemporary discussion in this area, although there are exceptions, such as Di Paolo et al. (2014, 2017); see also Churcher (1984).

17 This is hinted at by Bleger's reference to Wallon's *ultrachoses* (Bleger, 2013 [1967], p. 230).

References

Alizade, A.M. (2010 [2002]). *Psychoanalysis and Positivity*. [*Lo positivo en psicoanálisis: Implicancias teórico-técnicas*]. London: Karnac.

Bachelard, G. (1994 [1964]). The Dialectics of Outside and Inside. In: *The Poetics of Space*. Boston: Beacon Press.

Backhaus, G. (1997). The phenomenology of telephone space. *Human Studies, 20*(2): 203–220.

Baranger, M. and Baranger, W. (2008 [1961–1962]). The analytic situation as a dynamic field. *International Journal of Psycho-Analysis, 89*(4): 795–826.

Biocca, F. (1997). *The Cyborg's Dilemma: Embodiment in Virtual Environments*. CT '97: Proceedings of the 2nd International Conference on Cognitive Technology (pp. 12–24). Washington, DC: IEEE Computer Society.

Bion, W.R. (1957). Differentiation of the psychotic from the non-psychotic personalities. *International Journal of Psycho-Analysis, 38*: 266–275.

Bleger, J. (1967a). *Simbiosis y ambigüedad: estudio psicoanalítico*. Buenos Aires: Paidós.

Bleger, J. (1967b). Psycho-analysis of the psycho-analytic frame. *International Journal of Psycho-Analysis, 48*: 511–519.

Bleger, J. (1993 [1967]). Die Psychoanalyse des psychoanalytischen Rahmens. *Forum der Psychoanalyse, 9*: 268–280.

Bleger, J. (2013 [1967]). *Symbiosis and Ambiguity: A Psychoanalytic Study*. [*Simbiosis y ambigüedad: estudio psicoanalítico*]. Edited by J. Churcher and L. Bleger. Translated by S. Rogers, L. Bleger, and J. Churcher. New Library of Psychoanalysis. London: Routledge.

Bleger, L. (2022) What is the setting after all? (Chapter 1, this volume).

Bridge, M. (2013 [1997]). Why five times a week? A candidate's perspective. *Bulletin of the British Psychoanalytical Society, 49*(7): 3–9.

Bridge, M. (2013). Moving out – disruption and repair to the internal setting. *British Journal of Psychotherapy, 29*(4): 481–493.

Bullinger, A. (2012). *Le développement sensori-moteur de l'enfant et ses avatars: Un parcours de recherche.* Toulouse: ERES.

Churcher, J. (1984). Implications and Applications of Piaget's Sensorimotor Concepts. In: O. Selfridge, E. Rissland and M. Arbib (eds.), *Adaptive Control and Ill-defined Systems.* New York and London: Plenum Press.

Churcher, J. (2000). Clinical meetings, communication technology and presence. *Bulletin of the British Psychoanalytical Society, 36*(1): 26–31.

Churcher, J. (2005). *Keeping the Psychoanalytic Setting in Mind.* Paper given at the Annual Conference of Lancaster Psychotherapy Clinic in collaboration with the Tavistock Clinic, at St Martin's College, Lancaster, 9 September 2005. Available at: https://www.academia.edu/4527520/.

Churcher, J. (2008). Some notes on the English translation of The Analytic Situation as a Dynamic Field by Willy and Madeleine Baranger. *International Journal of Psycho-Analysis, 89*(4): 785–793.

Churcher, J. (2016). Der psychoanalytische Rahmen, das Körperschema, Telekommunikation und Telepräsenz: Implikationen von José Blegers Konzept des 'encuadre'. *Psyche: Zeitschrift für Psychoanalyse und ihre Anwendungen, 70* (1): 60–81.

Churcher, J. (2019). *Going to sea in a sieve: 'remote analysis', the internal setting, and disavowal.* Contribution to a Panel on 'Confidentiality as a Container – Clinical and Theoretical Issues, 51st IPA Congress, London, 23–25 July 2019.

Civitarese, G. (2008). *l'Intima Stanza: Teoria e tecnica del campo analitico.* Rome: Borla.

Civitarese, G. (2010 [2008]). *The Intimate Room: Theory and Technique of the Analytic Field.* London: Routledge.

Civitarese, G. (2011). *La violenze delle emozioni: Bion e la psicoanalisi postbioniana.* Milan: Rafaello Cortina Editore.

Civitarese, G. (2013 [2011]). *The Violence of Emotions: Bion and Post-Bionian Psychoanalysis* [*La violenze delle emozioni: Bion e la psicoanalisi postbioniana*]. Translated by I. Harvey. New Library of Psychoanalysis. London: Routledge.

Di Paolo, E.A., X.E. Barandiaran, M. Beaton, and T. Buhmann (2014). Learning to perceive in the sensorimotor approach: Piaget's theory of equilibration interpreted dynamically. *Frontiers in Human Neuroscience, 8*: 1–16.

Di Paolo, E.A., T. Buhrmann, and X.E. Barandiaran (2017). *Sensorimotor Life: An Enactive Proposal.* Oxford: Oxford University Press.

Donnet, J-L. (2007). La neutralité et l'écart sujet-fonction. *Revue française de psychanalyse, 71*(3): 747–762.

Eissler, K.R. (1953). The effect of the structure of the ego on psychoanalytic technique. *Journal of the American Psychoanalytic Association, 1*: 104–143.

Etchegoyen, R.H. (1991). *The Fundamentals of Psychoanalytic Technique.* Trans. P. Pitchon. London: Karnac.

Faimberg, H. (2012). José Bleger's dialectical thinking. *International Journal of Psycho-Analysis, 93*, 981–992.

Faimberg, H. (2013). The 'as-yet situation' in Winnicott's 'Fragment of an Analysis': Your father 'never did you the honor of' ... Yet. *The Psychoanalytic Quarterly, 82*(4): 849–875.

Faimberg, H. (2018). José Bleger and the Relevance Today of his Dialectical Frame. In: I. Tylim and A. Harris (eds.), *Reconsidering the Moveable Frame in Psychoanalysis*. London and New York: Routledge.

Ferruta, A. (2014). The analytic setting and space for the other. *The Italian Psychoanalytic Annual, 8*: 97–110.

Gallagher, S. (2005). *How the Body Shapes the Mind*. Oxford: Clarendon Press.

Gallagher, S. and A.N. Meltzoff (1996). The earliest sense of self and others: Merleau-Ponty and recent developmental studies. *Philosophical Psychology, 9*(2): 211–233.

Green, A. (1975). The analyst, symbolization and absence in the analytic setting (On changes in analytic practice and analytic experience)—In memory of D.W. Winnicott. *International Journal of Psycho-Analysis, 56*: 1–22.

Guillaumin, J. (1987). Le préconscient et le travail du négatif dans l'interprétation. *Revue française de psychanalyse, 51*(2): 701–711.

Head, H. and H.G. Holmes (1911–12). Sensory disturbances from cerebral lesions. *Brain, 34*: 102–254.

Hyppolite, J. (1956). Commentaire parlé sur la *Verneinung* de Freud. *La Psychanalyse, 1*: 29–40.

Jarast, G. (ed.) (2013). Debate online sobre el artículo de José Bleger: Teoría y práctica en psicoanálisis: la praxis psicoanalítica. *Libro Anual de Psicoanálisis, 28*: 129–162.

Kaës, R. (1990). *Un singulier pluriel: La psychanalyse à l'épreuve du groupe*. Paris: Dunod.

Kaës, R. (2007). *Linking, Alliances, and Shared Space: Groups and the Psychoanalyst*. London: The International Psychoanalytical Association.

Labarthe, C. (2012). El encuadre interno del analista. Available at http://www.revistapsicoanalisis.com/el-encuadre-interno-del-analista/.

Lee, K.M. (2004). Presence, explicated. *Communication Theory, 14*(1): 27–50.

Lemma, A. (2014). The body of the analyst and the analytic setting: Reflections on the embodied setting and the symbiotic transference. *International Journal of Psycho-Analysis, 95*(2): 225–244.

Leuzinger-Bohleber, M. (2014). Den Körper in der Seele entdecken Embodiment und die Annäherung an das Nicht-Repräsentierte. *Psyche – Zeitschrift für Psychoanalyse ihre Anwendungen, 68*: 922–950.

Leuzinger-Bohleber, M., R.N. Emde, and R. Pfeifer (eds.) (2013). *Embodiment: Ein innovatives Konzept für Entwicklungsforschung und Psychoanalyse*. Göttingen: Vandenhoeck & Ruprecht.

Lin, T. (2012). Skype analysis: problems and limitations. *Bulletin of the British Psychoanalytical Society, 48*(4): 1–10.

Marescaux, J., J. Leroy, F. Rubino, M. Smith, M. Vix, M. Simone, and D. Mutter (2002). Transcontinental robot-assisted remote telesurgery: Feasibility and potential applications. *Annals of Surgery, 235*(4): 487–492.

Merleau-Ponty, M. (1962). *Phenomenology of Perception*. London: Routledge & Kegan Paul.

Milner, M. (1952). Aspects of symbolism in comprehension of the not-self. *International Journal of Psycho-Analysis, 33*: 181–194.

Minsky, M. (1980). Telepresence. *OMNI Magazine, 2(9)*: 44–52.

Parsons, M. (2007). Raiding the inarticulate: The internal analytic setting and listening beyond countertransference. *International Journal of Psycho-Analysis, 88*: 1441–1456.

Piaget, J. (1948). *La naissance de l'intelligence chez l'enfant.* Paris: Delachaux et Niestlé.

Polanyi, M. (1966). *The Tacit Dimension.* Chicago: University of Chicago Press.

Politzer, G. (1928). *Critique des Fondements de la Psychologie.* Paris: Les Éditions Rieder.

Politzer, G. (1965–66). *Escritos psicológicos de Georges Politzer.* 3 vols. Translated by E. Ramos. Edited by J. Bleger. Buenos Aires: Jorge Alvarez.

Ribas, D. (1989). De la peur de l'objet au désir d'aliénation et à la mort (l'identification adhésive et le démantèlement vus comme désintrication pulsionnelle). *Revue française de Psychanalyse, 53(4)*: 1111–1129.

Rochefort, C. (1958). *Le repos du guerrier.* Paris: Éditions Bernard Grasset. Translated by L. Bair (1962 [1960]) *Warrior's Rest.* London: The New English Library.

Rubin, E. (1958 [1915]). Figure and Ground. In: D.C. Beardslee and M. Wertheimer (eds.), *Readings in Perception* (pp. 194–203). Princeton, NJ: Van Nostrand Company, Inc.

Russell, G.I. (2015). *Screen Relations: The Limits of Computer-mediated Psychoanalysis and Psychotherapy.* London: Karnac.

Sabbadini, A. (1989). Boundaries of timelessness. Some thoughts about the temporal dimension of the psychoanalytic space. *International Journal of Psycho-Analysis, 70*: 305–313.

Sabbadini, A. (2013). New Technologies and the Psychoanalytic Setting. In: A. Lemma and L. Caparrotta (eds.), *Psychoanalysis in the Technoculture Era.* London: Routledge.

Schachter, J., J. Tabakin, and T. Blucher (2019). Setting (The Psychoanalytic). In: *The IPA Inter-Regional Encyclopedic Dictionary of Psychoanalysis* (pp. 394–414). Available at: https://www.ipa.world/IPA/en/en/Encyclopedic_Dictionary/English/Home.aspx.

Slater, M. (2018). Immersion and the illusion of presence in virtual reality. *British Journal of Psychology, 109*: 431–433.

Stuart, S.A.J. (2011). Enkinaesthesia: The fundamental challenge for machine consciousness. *International Journal of Machine Consciousness, 3(1)*: 145–162.

Temperley, J. (1984). Settings for psychotherapy. *British Journal of Psychotherapy, 1*: 101–111.

Toet, A., I.A. Kuling, B.N. Krom, and J.B.F. van Erp (2020). Toward enhanced teleoperation through embodiment. *Frontiers in Robotics and AI, 7* (11 February 2020). https://doi.org/10.3389/frobt.2020.00014.

Tubert-Oklander, J. and R. Hernández de Tubert (2004). *Operative Groups: The Latin American Approach to Group Analysis.* London and New York: Jessica Kingsley Publishers.

Wood, R. and S.A.J. Stuart (2009). Aplasic phantoms and the mirror neuron system: An enactive, developmental perspective. *Phenomenology & the Cognitive Sciences, 8*: 487–504.

Zahiu, A. (2020) I, avatar: Towards an extended theory of selfhood in immersive VR. *Információs társadalom, 19(4)*: 147–158.

3 Psychic equivalency as an aspect of symbiosis

Judy K. Eekhoff

Just as there is something gained when anything is translated from one language to another, there is hopefully also something gained in the transformation of ideas from one person to the next. Of course, in each instance there is always something lost. My gratitude to José Bleger contains appreciation for what he gives us and for the inspiration he fosters. My hope is to convey respect for his wisdom and to expand on his ideas that remain relevant to us today.

Bleger's understanding of a psychic organization prior to the paranoid schizoid position enables analysts today to work more deeply and effectively with unrepresented states as they appear in the consulting room. He describes symbiosis and ambiguity as being a function of undifferentiation. Bleger wrote at a time when prominent analysts, himself included, believed there was an infantile stage of primary autism. He knew and studied Mahler's work. Years after Bleger's untimely death, Mahler and Tustin (1991, 1994) reversed their professional opinions on primary autism. Infant research taught them that infants at birth were able to differentiate themselves from their parents. Prenatal research finds that the infant also has a primal sense of the other and intentionality. Fetal observation via ultrasound (Maiello, 1995, 2012; Piontelli, 1985, 1987,) indicates the fetus is capable of agency, of dreaming, and of responding to sensory stimuli such as sensation, sound, and sight. Already in utero, the infant's personality is discernable. The fetus also feels pain. In other words, the fetus experiences multiple states of being, other than states of undifferentiation. It follows that so does the infant. However, undifferentiated states are present from before birth and remain forever in the psyche.

Like adults, infants experience many states of mind and body. These states mark different degrees of psychic organization. Undifferentiation as one of multiple infantile states remains a psychic phenomenon that organizes experience from infancy onward. Under normal circumstances, the molten, undifferentiated core in all of us remains as a background. When it emerges in adulthood, it becomes a symptom of overwhelming affect. Bleger (2013 [1967], p. 106) calls the undifferentiation "magma". Magma is an undifferentiated material mass. Magma is an aspect of the molten core

DOI: 10.4324/9781003252252-5

of the self where differentiation and discrimination are lacking. Whereas magma might pulsate and bubble, magma is not alive although it does adhere to surfaces.

Understanding symbiosis and undifferentiation enables us to deeply understand our patients who have survived childhood trauma. Undifferentiation informs and can comfort, even though we are unaware of it. It can be a pleasant sensory respite from a busy world and influences creative discoveries in every field. As a bodily experience, it may be an aspect of the background of safety we all need and share in order to function. States of undifferentiation also unconsciously contribute to communication with an actual other via the senses. Body relations communicate to others, and the undifferentiated state is intimately connected to the body.

Bleger understands the primitive nature of the defensive use of undifferentiated states and autistic protections evoked when necessary for psychic survival. Using different language, he explores what Bick (1968, 1986), Tustin (1986, 1990), and Meltzer (1994 [1974]), 1975a, 1975b) call adhesive identification and adhesive equivalency. He explores the psychotic aspects of our personalities, as does Bion (1957, 1958, 1959). His knowledge and understanding enables us to work deeply with patients whose poor psychic filters keep them in constant turmoil and whose primitive autistic defenses keep them psychologically isolated and alone.

I am particularly interested in applying his ideas about body relations to patients who have been traumatized as children and who use mimicry as a means of functioning. These individuals often lack a subjective sense of self and suffer from weakened projective and introjective identification processes. Their weakened processes of projective and introjective identification alternate with massive fragmentation, atomization, and leakage. These are not projective identifications.

I, like Klein and Bion, believe the infant is born object related, with a primal capacity for differentiating self from other. Moments of undifferentiation that occur during breast feeding or falling asleep come from a primal trust in the care of the other. These moments are not perceived as persecutory but as blissful, sensual oneness with the mother. These are not defensive but restorative. On the other hand, moments of undifferentiation that occur following a shock are defensive and include immobilization and dismantling the senses. They include a withdrawal from awareness of the other. The senses themselves are then used defensively (Bion, 1957) and separated one from the other, resulting in a psychic collapse (Meltzer (1994 [1974]). It is as if the person's attention itself were suspended. Infants in a state of psychic collapse are inconsolable and unreachable. They physically shake. Adults suffering from a history of trauma can also seem inconsolable and unreachable when their autistic defenses block the analytic process. Frequently they describe their collapses as *black holes* (Tustin, 1981, 1986, 1990; Eekhoff, 2022).

Using Bleger's understanding of these primal experiences enables us to analyze psychotic and autistic processes of protection from overwhelming states of body and mind. These organizational processes persist long after trauma has ceased. Further, his descriptions of these processes enable analysts today to understand and work productively with patients who have psychic delusions that they do not exist. Patients who believe they do not exist suffer from a lack of differentiation from their objects even as they appear isolated and alone. When they come for analysis, the analytic situation becomes a container or depository for the exploration of their suspensions of the self.

Bleger's brilliance lies in his ability to understand the multiple and simultaneous presence of psychic processes in all body relations and object relations. In this, he is speaking of actual two-body relationships and the concretization inherent in all relations. Reality and relationship with an external other are essential for development. His glischro-caric position occurs beneath the paranoid schizoid position and resembles what Bion (1957, 1958) calls the psychotic part of the personality. Ogden (1989a, 1989b) names it the autistic-contiguous position. I have called this earliest position the *primary position* (Eekhoff, 2022). All of these authors recognize these states as normal. Normalizing autistic psychotic experience and accepting the chaotic, unmediated sensory involvement within our perceptual identities enables us as analysts to work effectively with our severely disturbed adult patients. It also enables us to work deeper with our neurotic patients. Primary process and *perceptual identity* (Freud, 1999 [1900]) underlie all creative endeavors; but without the containment of the symbolic and the continual processes of representation, these organizational states persecute.

Many aspects of Bleger's work deserve further consideration, but in this chapter, I am exploring primal adhesive defenses against primitive agonies and the symbiotic connection to the analyst that keeps those patterns in place. These defenses are concrete in nature and rely on the body of the analyst as external scaffolding of the weak ego and *meta-ego*. The body of the analyst becomes an aspect of the analytic situation as part of the setting (Bleger, 2013 [1967], pp. 228–241). I believe it can also be part of the process (Eekhoff, 2017). This blurring of setting and process contributes to the difficulties we analysts face in the analysis of symbiosis. The healthy concretization of the analytic relation involves the bodily relation of interdependence. Patients who have ongoing access to their undifferentiated aspects vehemently deny dependence upon anyone. The analyst needs to be patient and secure and have faith in the analytic process (Bion, 1970). Further, I hope to expand on Bleger's understanding of ways in which the projective and introjective identification processes, which fuel representation, can be inhibited.

The ego functions on three (or more) levels of organization and always includes an observer. The psyche also includes areas that are non-ego and areas that cannot be represented. The primal position, Bleger's glischro-caric position, is one organizational aspect of our inner world. The para-noid schizoid and depressive positions exist simultaneously with it:

> Symbiosis is established and operates first and foremost in the area of the body and the external world. *The mental area is severely dissociated or split off* from the other two and is present as a spectator at the events and vicissitudes of symbiosis, unable to intervene in them or channel them.
>
> (Bleger, 2013 [1967] p. 35)

Bleger suggests that the mental is present even in undifferentiation, how-ever it is split-off and projected into the universe. I believe that this point of being a spectator, a witness of oneself, is a position out of which the self evolves when reality is bearable. The analyst must find ways to gather the bits and pieces of the spectator. Seeing and being seen enables differ-entiation. Primal experiences of sensation, sound and smell inform the observing participant and enable learning from experience (Bion, 1962b).

When reality is too much to bear being a spectator to one's life involves "standing beside oneself" (Ferenczi, 1988) and already implies some degree of differentiation and development. Although Bleger believes in an original state of psychic undifferentiation, he acknowledges the witness as present. When the analyst can engage the witness (Eekhoff, 2017), analytic progress is possible. The use of undifferentiation as a defense results in *psychic equivalency* that is maintained by the psychic processes of *adhesive identification* and *adhesive equivalency*. Psychic equivalency requires a lack of differentiation and is an infantile defense against premature awareness of separation between an infant and his or her mother (Tustin, 1980, 1986). Psychic equivalency is a normal part of development (Fonagy and Target, 1996). In other words, instead of being a primary state of undifferentiation that is only one of many states the infant has, undifferentiation can become a defense against awareness of premature separation from the caregiver. As a defense, psychic equivalency blocks other infantile states that are creative and helpful. It interferes with ongoing development.

Disturbance of infantile undifferentiated states shocks the undefended infant and can be traumatic. When infancy and childhood include con-tinual intrusions that violate the child's physical and psychic boundaries, symbiosis in the form of objectless sensation (Ferenczi, 1920–1932, p. 261) foregrounds to provide safety. Klein (1975) asserts that narcissism is not primary but secondary and arises out of trauma. Childhood abuse of any kind includes psychic annihilation of the child's need. When a child loses a primary object, he or she automatically also loses a subjective sense of self. Parental intrusion via projective identification into the child, and psychic threat via lack of receptivity, damages a child's capacity to make meaning out of experience. Such intrusion also evokes attacks on linking

(Bion, 1959). The same reaction occurs when the analyst prematurely highlights a patient's psychic separateness, focusing on differences and hence implying psychic distinctiveness. When such interpretations occur too early in the analytic process of patients who have a history of abuse, it can re-traumatize.

Psychic equivalency

Equivalency is present not only as a deficit in development but also as a protection against threat. Prolonged use of equivalency as a defense results in encapsulated emotional areas of the self that do not develop along with other developmental physical and cognitive abilities. Tustin (1981, 1986, 1990) would call these *autistic encapsulations*. Some patients describe these pockets as voids; others call them black holes. I believe the void and the black hole are differing manifestations of the loss of a sub-jective sense of self. Deficit and defense interact, maintaining each other. Psychic equivalency is not a regression to infancy but a position and vertex of organization of reality that persists to a greater or lesser degree in everyone. Usually, in analysis, symbiosis and psychic equivalency are mute as an aspect of the setting (Bleger, 2013 [1967]). Its defensive use originates from a primitive attempt to survive in the face of massive threat to psychic life. Psychic equivalency is both the body memory of undiffer-entiated states and a defense against manifestation in the here and now of a threat of otherness. Psychic equivalency protects against awareness of dependency upon an unreliable other by a delusion of being the other.

Psychic equivalency is an aspect of Bleger's symbiosis. It is accom-plished via the psychic phantasies of adhesive identification (Bick, 1968, 1986; Meltzer, 1974, 1975a) and adhesive equivalence (Tustin, 1986, 1990). Bick observed that disintegration occurred when the psychic skin failed. Adhesive identification is a defensive state of mind that protects the psyche from disintegration. It provides a delusional shape and form. "In adhesive identification, the experience of space between two individuals is denied and replaced with a delusion of oneness" (Eekhoff, 2019, p. 42). A delusion of oneness holds the self together by forming a sensual boundary to prevent leaking, spilling, dissolving, and evaporating. A severely abused child clings to the senses as a second skin. For example, an adult diagnosed by previous therapists as having dissociative identity disorder says he chooses which "skin suit" to wear depending upon his circum-stances. His skin suits enable him to symbiotically become the other and feel safe. They include mimicry.

Adhesive identification involves the introjection and projection of sen-sation and originates from the glischro-caric position. "Adhesive identifi-cation is the unconscious sensory use of hearing, seeing, smelling and touching to take in and fuse with the other" (Eekhoff, 2019, p. 43). It is also communication from the agglutinated nucleus of the patient and identification with a warm, live body. Adhesive identification creates a seamless symbiotic link with the analyst although there may seem to be no relationship at all. In doing so, it denies the reality of inner psychic space. Meltzer (1975b, p. 199), like Bleger, uses the word 'agglutinate' in writing about work with autistic children. In describing the slow analytic process, he says: "In this sea of meaninglessness there were little items of meaningful experience that gradually began to agglutinate, gradually filled up the Wednesdays, filled up the middle of the week or the middle of the term, as it were. These children turned out to have incredible intolerance to separation.". Adhesive identification and adhesive equivalency protect against the unbearable reality of psychic separateness.

Tustin (1986, 1990) preferred the term adhesive equation to adhesive identification. I believe these are two distinct forms of body and object relations that are revealed in an analytic process via somatic countertransference. Adhesive equation may appear to be a one-body experience; and yet I believe that even at this primal level of contact with the other as thing, there is communication, hence, separateness. Separateness is necessary for the uninterrupted flow of projective identifications. As Bion (1957) says, the non-psychotic part of the personality is always present. Primitive mentalization is found as bodily sensation and is not yet namable. Some of it may never become nameable or ever be experienced as a differentiated emotional communication of body to self or body to other.

During adhesive equivalency, both members of the dyad will not be able to differentiate who is who. As the patient appears calm and unimpacted by the analytic encounter, the analyst becomes a sensor, like a tuning fork or seismograph. The unperceivable action is knowable outside the patient in the body of the analyst. Some analysts may find this extremely uncomfortable and resist the reception of such primitive and intrusive communication, yet I believe it is inevitable, whether recognized or not. Working with traumatized patients includes the analyst's body as well as his or her mind. These *somatic communications* can be recognized and translated into language.

At the level of symbiotic body relations, where potentially, the projective and introjective identifications are weak or failing, the link can even be one of shared rhythm, of reverberation, resonance, and at-one-ment (Bion, 1970). This is a relational intersubjective state of adhesive equivalence, even more primal than adhesive identification. It is a symbiotic link. This shared state requires that the analyst be sensitive without superimposing his or her experience onto the patient. Doing so is to reenact the original trauma. The same is true of prematurely naming somatic experience as an emotional experience. At the symbiotic level, emotions have not yet emerged or differentiated themselves from affects. Naming emotions prematurely focuses attention on a higher order of development linking body and mind. Premature naming evokes mimicry.

Adhesive identification and adhesive equation involve a lack of aware-ness of a subjective self. The primal ego becomes another. The aggluti-nated nucleus can only pulse with energy and life, with seemingly no internal space. Inside and outside appear to be the same. Perhaps the inside also is, in phantasy, denied and projected via the senses, hence the term adhesive, which is to surfaces. In his paper, "On Hallucination," Bion (1958) writes about a psychotic patient who demonstrates adhesion via movement that is attuned to the analyst's movement:

> So closely do his movements seem to be geared with mine that the inception of my movement to sit appears to release a spring in him. As I lower myself into my seat he turns left about, slowly, evenly, as if something would be spilled, or perhaps fractured, were he to be betrayed into a precipitate movement. As I sit the turning movement stops as if we were both parts of the same clockwork toy.
>
> (Bion, 1958, p. 341)

Patients who use primal symbiotic process as a defense have a fascination with the sensual, which turns them into an inanimate machine with interlocking gears. It is a defense against life, against existence. Their identifications are with the surface of things and with movement. The subsequent use of sensorial experience seems to blot out the awareness of the other, but this is the result of blotting out awareness of the self—the self that has collapsed and imploded into a black hole or exploded into a universe without a depository to contain it, leaving a void where the self would be (Eekhoff, 2022). In addition, the senses are not linked in the usual way but are often separated from one another. In my attempts to understand a somatic and sensate experience in the hour, I have recog-nized that there is information about my patient within my own somatic counter-transference. Paying attention to these body relations while also noticing higher levels of organization is an aspect of the deposited and depository process described by Bleger. Since all these levels of organiza-tion are simultaneously present in every analytic encounter, the analyst pays attention to the level that seems most urgent to the patient.

The body is not separable from the mind. The psychic skin (Bick, 1968, 1986) holds the body together, enabling containment of affect and emotion and the mobilization of agency. The psychic skin-to-skin of analysand and analyst may never be interpreted, but it is present and impactful as a mute aspect of the setting. Body-to-body proximity functions as a primal con-tainer in the growth of the mind, enabling us to find our centers of gravity even when the senses are being used in reverse and hallucinations are present:

> Hallucinations and the fantasy of the senses as ejecting as well as receiving, point to the severity of the disorder from which the patient

is suffering, but I must indicate a benign quality in the symptom which was certainly not present earlier. Splitting, evacuatory use of the senses, and hallucinations were all being employed in the service of an ambition to be cured, and may therefore be supposed to be creative activities"

(Bion, 1958, p. 342).

Here Bion's understanding provides hope for the difficult analytic work.

Using Bleger and Bion's theoretical and clinical formulation's, I am exploring deficits in cognitive functioning of extremely bright and functional people as defenses against separation. These cognitive impairments show up in our offices as deficits in the capacity to classify and subordinate information. Form and content are not discriminated (Bleger, 2013 [1967], p. 35). In the absence of differentiation and discrimination, ambiguity dominates. As Bleger so brilliantly demonstrates, patients can function by using their abilities to observe and mimic. Underneath the mimicry is a lack of discrimination that means all facts are of equal weight and value. One fact cannot be subordinate to another. This failure to discriminate form and content contributes to immobilization and what looks like passivity and poor decision-making. If everything is of equal weight, discriminations necessary for decision-making are lacking. The failure to classify and subordinate information further contributes to deficits in emotional development.

Deficits require defenses. Defenses become deficits. These protections do not arise from an internal experience of conflict. They arise from an inability to perceive the other as different from oneself and arise out of being psychically overwhelmed early in their lives. Object relations suffer. Anger and aggression, conflict and doubt arise from differentiation. Psychic equivalency is found in patients who seem to be passive and calm. Such patients can look normal (Meltzer, 1974; Bick, 1968, 1986; McDougall, 1989). However, what looks like calm is in fact an inability to discriminate and differentiate. Psychic immobilization, one aspect of which is the inability to make decisions, looks like withdrawal and cannot result in learning from experience (Bion, 1962b). Whole "undrawn" (Alvarez, 1992, 2010, 2012) areas of psyche are left undifferentiated, unformed, unclassified, and unsubordinated, while other areas develop, sometimes precociously.

Arnie

My patient, whom I will call Arnie, tells me that when I speak, even when I use his own words, I "… change the subject. If I follow you, all my gears grind and the machine that is me, freezes up and cannot move." Arnie's relationship with me is primarily bodily relations. We are, in his phantasy, fused and undifferentiated. I am he and he is I. We are one person. When

I speak, I threaten the undifferentiated symbiotic phantasy he needs in order to function. When I use his words, it is more difficult for him to lose himself in the sound of my voice and the rhythms of my speech. My tone intrudes. I have drawn attention to our separateness. This is partially because in the moments between his speaking and my repetition of his words, he has moved on. I have not. He responds with anger. When I do not speak, however, he dissociates and describes himself as "gone".

This dissociation is not the dissociative repression of the depressive position, nor the dissociative divisions of the paranoid schizoid position where splitting and projecting maintain psychic equilibrium. Primal dissociation is the dissociation of psychic equivalency—an autistic defense that includes dismantling his senses (Meltzer, 1975a) and becoming one with his object. Becoming one with the object involves a collapse of his self, that I have inadvertently supported by remaining silent. He has imploded into the black hole of himself. When I do speak, his delusion of oneness with me, which is paradoxically also a defense against his collapse, is lost for him. His delusion of autonomy and safety is disrupted by my presence. He protects his sense of reality with anger.

For example, after thirty minutes of listening patiently and carefully to Arnie's concrete and detailed description of an event that has troubled him, he lapses into silence. I recognize this silence as different from a productive creative search for associations. It feels dense and impenetrable. I wait only briefly, fearing the silence marks a psychic collapse, a black hole. When I speak, I am too late. Arnie is in despair, telling me, "there is no there, there. You act like there is something there inside of me. There is nothing." I try to reach him, speaking just for the sake of my tone and sound and rhythm. But he is gone. I fail to reach him.

The next day he returns as if the previous day had not happened. Again, he begins with a monologue and presents a story of what has happened to him since we met. After some time, I finally come to an interpretation. I attempt to tie my words to his words so as to make a link with him. In fact, I even use his words to show that I have been listening and how I reached my thinking. I am then surprised by the immediate anger and the intense push back I receive. This time, he tells me I am blaming him, telling him it is his fault. I am not helping him. I am making it worse. In re-examining myself, I do not find my own tone judgmental, not that it never is. I try again to reach him. I cannot, as somehow the damage has been done. We cannot have an exchange. He cannot take in my attempt to understand him.

In fact, perhaps in that moment my unrecognized assumption that we could work together, which would imply our differentiation, missed his symbiotic relationship to me. I erroneously thought he might be able to use what I have noticed. Instead, my interpretation left him feeling like a "bug under a microscope, pinned and examined". I have heard this before from him when I use his words and add to them in order to explain my thinking. Yet, at other times, he is able to work with me. Not today. Once again, I have forgotten in this state, he is in the moment. It is not that he is in the here and now, because to be here would involve having a subjective sense of himself in the moment. He is in "the now". He experiences "now" in a bodily way. In that primal state, he lacks a sense of "going-on-being" (Winnicott, 1960, 1965). He is not aware of past or future in that his memory is impaired. In being in time, I also am different than he. I become "The Authority" and my observations become moral judgements. It will take much effort on both our parts to re-connect, and often re-connection is not possible in the session.

In this particular example, I feel I have been patient and neutral—non-judgmental and not all-knowing. I have merely described an observation of something happening in the moment between us. He tells me I am talking about something that is over. This, too, has happened before. Sometimes he denies having said what I remember. At other times, he remembers but says he said those words five minutes ago. They are no longer accurate. From his perspective, this is true. I am speaking from within a framework of time and space. I am speaking from within the symbolic order. When I do that, I am not speaking from his immediate framework of the senses and the body. I have disrupted the adhesive equivalency between us, by having a separate mind and making an observation. This separateness is ultimately necessary for growth to occur, but I have brought the reality of his dependency upon me into the session too soon. Dependency is counter to a phantasy of oneness.

Making myself different from him just be speaking an observation of our process is disturbing. I must slow down since such differentiation is disruptive. I must have patience and accept it will take time. As Bleger (2013 [1967], p. 24) says, "… the symbiotic relationship is a highly condensed relation with very complex and contradictory aspects that need to be 'broken up' in order to be introjected and worked through by degrees". Arnie was in analysis long enough to recognize the risk he faced in analysis. Breaking up feels like breaking down. Of course, he is upset because the breaking up of his symbiosis confuses him and feels dangerous.

Theoretical discussion of psychic equivalence

In the above vignettes, I have shown two ways of being with Arnie; one in being silent and the other in speaking. In each, the symbiotic fusion is present and challenged by my physical existence. Silence leaves Arnie with no center of gravity, which normally he has placed in me. He cannot sense my proximity and collapses into the black hole of himself, which sucks life and hope away. It is a collapse of space, a sucking place of undifferentiation. Anything said can only be "as if" he existed. Furthermore, everything is destroyed as it enters the psychic event horizon, including his relationship with me. No wonder he becomes claustrophobic, then experiencing me as the black hole.

In the second instance, my attempt to show Arnie the origin of my thinking implied the passing of time. Time passing is dangerous and must be defended against as it moves Arnie into a different internal psychic organization. Bleger says, "Time stops when the paralyzing of projection-introjection becomes necessary to control the confusion" (ibid., p. 54) When I challenge this by speaking, I am changing the vertex from which to witness our interaction. This has the potential of re-instating the projective and introjective cycle so necessary for learning. However, the cycle is not re-instated in this instance. Instead from Arnie's point of view, I have been violent and attacking. Quickly, I have become bad and then as suddenly, good and all knowing.

From the new vertex, I am good and he is bad. I am superior and he is inferior. Arnie feels I have pronounced judgement upon him, told him that he is evil and condemned to Hell. To him, my comment was not a neutral observation. Rather, it highlighted the truth about how hopeless the situation is and how bad he is. My words concretely make it so. He is what I said and cannot be otherwise. This concretization is another result of psychic adhesion. It too often ends with a psychic collapse and retreat into a black hole of despair.

In this case, his anger suggests projective identification processes that leave him drained and empty, with a void. And yet, if this can be tolerated, and we can speak of the process, it can mark a potential movement from the glischro-caric position where the black hole wipes out all distinctions, to the paranoid schizoid position where the Void leaves him depleted and empty.

No wonder he rages at me. No wonder he is angry. My speaking my opinion of a truth about him, even though he told me about it, is humiliating and condemning, even when I carefully include how what he has just said informed me. He has forgotten that I am an ally attempting to help him. He cannot experience my voicing an observation as simply my opinion. In a symbiotic link, relationship is a concrete experience. My interpretation is understood as a concrete unchangeable fact and he seems to "… feel betrayed *(by my interpretation)*, since if she *(he)* had already said it once why would I repeat it to her *(him)*? What is the point" (Bleger, 1967, p. 97)? (my italics).

In a world of signification and meaning, there is a point. Time and space work together to provide a context for personal meaning within a relational context. Experience accumulates. Time moves on as evidence of change. In the concrete world of psychic equivalency, nothing accumulates. There is no time. Stopping time prevents change. It also prevents confusion. Words that were spoken are the final say, are not to be added to or altered in any way. They do not need to be repeated. What is, is. This concretization, where living things do not evolve and people become things and words become law, is a means of blurring distinctions. Without distinctions there is a *delusion of safety*. This is very different from the background of safety a good enough mother provides for every infant.

Lack of distinctions and differentiations provide a feeling of being invisible. One means of being invisible is to blend concretely with whoever one is in contact. Blending concretely is the symbiotic link of adhesive equivalency. Visibility is only possible with distinctions. To see and be seen signifies difference. Difference means there is a space between us. Any hint of discrimination and differentiation becomes dangerous so it follows that a gap is dangerous in that it leaves a space to be filled by the other. Otherness raises an awareness of separateness and is dangerous, hence bad. A pounding concrete experience of difference hints at badness. Being different equals being bad.

Briefly, concretization as a defense focuses attention on the material world of the senses. In the consulting room, the body of the analyst as an aspect of the setting becomes used as a vehicle for psychic equivalence and symbiosis. Bleger confirms this: "Symbiosis functions and is stabilized on the concrete level" (ibid., p. 50).

Back to Arnie

Arnie despairs of being understood. He says he always longs for understanding from me and is disappointed not to get it. I have come to understand in such moments, I am not demonstrating understanding to him. My definition of understanding is different from his. Instead of demonstrating that I am with him in his pain, I am demonstrating that I am not he. This is a failure on my part to maintain the symbiosis long enough to be able to speak to it. My empathy comes as a shock, an intrusion into him. My understanding becomes an attack. My reflection of "his words back to him" plus a few of my own intrudes because it breaks an unconscious delusion of oneness. I am asserting my difference and my separateness. In doing so, I am responding to him from a different level of organization. I am not supporting his phantasy that I am the same as he and that we exist in a *forever now*. Instead I have become a threat to breaking up his concrete world. I have given him a glimpse of his dependency upon me, which he cannot tolerate knowing. In a world of time, there is separation and loss. Life and death become possible.

Arnie began to feel immeasurable dread each day before a session. One day he was able to name it. In this excerpt, I am primarily silent, letting him name his discoveries and even demonstrate them by losing his ability to put words together to form meaningful sentences. He says: "I am jittery. It has to be about being here, because it started on the drive over. I don't know what it is about."

He is silent for several minutes. "Hmm. The words 'breaking down' just came to me. Like my basement re-model. The contractor is jackhammering the concrete, breaking it up. You have to break things down before you can build again. It's violent."

He begins to speak very haltingly with much space between his words. His sentences are incomplete, and I am very tempted to fill in the blank spaces. I know this would be fusing with him. I feel so much pressure. Yet this may be evidence of a breakage of old patterns. "I am not functioning very well ... but ... uh ... sunk in ... stationary ... hmmm. It is violent again. Ugh ... (He sighs, rolls to face wall) ... not it ...Hmmm. (He is silent for several minutes). There is some ... ah ... I don't know if this is real or imaginary. Violence ... of the process ... of... breaking down. My ...rigid ... beliefs are together. Hmm."

He is silent for several minutes, but physically agitated. He tosses and turns on the couch, moves his toes up and down and wiggles his fingers. He is in constant motion. He starts to speak and stops. I feel tense in my body and a constriction in my throat. I feel like coughing. I want to speak. In this instance, I sense that he is working something out in the silence. His silence is not dead. After five minutes, he continues.

Maybe that is due to the part of me that doesn't give up easily. Hmmm. Why don't you just change your mind? He is silent. *To what?* He is silent for another two or three minutes. *It is not like there is a new belief system to just slip into place.* He trails off, making little sounds, but without words.

Many months after the above example, he was able to articulate something very important. He said, "When I complain you do not understand, I think I am complaining that we are not merged. You are not me. I hate you for that." His hatred is a good sign in that his indifference is breaking up and his delusion of not existing is being threatened. I exist as separate from him, who therefore may also exist. Perhaps we have moved temporarily from the adhesive equivalency of a fixed symbiotic place where existence is questionable to a black and white world of existing, but where survival is threatened. His sucking black hole, which marks an implosion, is becoming more explosive—hence projective. When he says, *"It is not like there is a new belief system to just slip into place"*, he is recognizing the absence of something inside of him, a void that has been created not just by his massive projections, but also from the deficit that exists from his previous collapses.

Psychic equivalency: Theory

Patients who have been traumatized early in their natural growth—perhaps the first three years of life before becoming verbal—bring us phantasies from all stages of their organizational development. They have access to primitive mental states that ordinarily would be repressed. These individuals perceive their worlds from differing vertexes (Bion, 1962a, 1965) or positions (Klein, 1946), depending upon their state of mind. These organizations of experience shift continuously and often are present simultaneously. Bleger brings our attention to an early position of undifferentiation, of symbiosis, which is normal, in all of us, and only becomes a difficulty when it is accessed persistently and excessively. He says:

> Furthermore, this state of primitive undifferentiation is a *particular organization of the ego and of the world,* so that we are obliged to make an effort and face a new injury to our narcissism, as Freud put it, which occurs with each scientific advance: that *our* identity and *our* sense of reality are not *the* identity and sense of reality but only one of many possible organizations.
>
> (Bleger, 2013 [1967]), p. 4.)

He goes on to describe this organization as being one of *bodily relations* (ibid., p. 5). Bodily relations of this primitive undifferentiated position are only vaguely related to object relations.

Psychic equivalency uses the senses of the body to create a delusion of oneness, where self and other are undifferentiated. Adhesive equivalency in phantasy agglutinates the two physical bodies into one body. Two bodies are psychically necessary for one person to exist (McDougall, 1989). Present in the room is a symbiotic attachment to the surface of things that uses sensation, smell, sound and sight to achieve the symbiosis. The adhesion is as much to the actual office as it is to the actual body of the analyst. The same is true even when working remotely. Discrimination and differentiation require space, as does identification. Psychic equivalency is *symbiotic oneness* where space and time are absent. In this place the projective and introjective processes are minimal. Identification itself is of sensation.

When I break the delusion of psychic equivalency with an interpretation, or even with a descriptive comment, patients similar to Arnie, maintain the symbiosis by switching the phantasy. They do not exist, but I do. There is room in such a psychic world for only one person at a time. It is not the fight or flight of the paranoid schizoid position. It is rather the symbiotic world of the glischro-caric position and the agglutinated nucleus where one person is subsumed by the other, and each is necessary for existence itself. The two cannot be separated, but one or the other may foreground. One woman told me: "We are Siamese twins, joined at the head." Later she told me she had changed her mind—we had one body and two heads. If we were to separate, both of us would die.

The action in the hour is passive in its subtlety since the subjective sense of self is subsumed by the sounds and rhythms, smells, and colors and textures of the context of the work. These include my body: my sounds, my smell, my appearance, and the tone and rhythms of my voice. It matters little whether Arnie or I am foregrounded, since in his phantasy, we are the same. When I forget that we are one and behave as if he is functioning at a neurotic symbolic level, I am doing to him what he does to me. He does not exist as himself to me but as someone more like me. This is not projective identification because I am not finding myself via identification in him. Rather I am resonating and vibrating with the bodily relations he conveys.

As much as I attempt to meet my patient without memory, desire, or understanding, I find it difficult to comprehend that from my patient's point of view, there are times we are the same. My error from his perspective is in behaving as if there were a psychic space between us that would enable a productive to and fro. Existence involves being and becoming. Not existing psychically, except as me in the moment, keeps everything the same. Equivalency concretizes and immobilizes the psyche by using bodily sensations to fuse.

In this sense, my interpretations, from his point of view, do not respect his need for me to be him or him to be me. Whereas he may be responding to the sound of my words and the tone and rhythm of my speech, I am behaving as if he is responding to my meaning. When I deviate from his words by adding to them, I am asserting a gap between us. Worse still, I am behaving as if the past moment is not the same as the current moment, while my patient remains in the *forever now.* There is no space for true collaboration and connection, and no time for discovery since I am always out of his time. Our synchronicity and rhythm are broken. I believe with Bleger, that to work effectively with patients who have ongoing access to the glischro-caric or primal position, we must allow ourselves to be used as an extension of the patient. When we fail by prematurely naming that which should not yet be named; we become dangerous. At the same time, such "failure" may be an essential element in the breaking up of the symbiosis.

I have come to realize that when I become too big by asserting myself too soon with an interpretation, my patient perceives me as the God of the Old Testament, speaking Truth. There is no room for a dialogue to come together for a back and forth of conversation and elaboration where a personal truth can be found. Such discrimination is not possible in symbiotic union. Instead, God—the God of Judgment—has spoken. Like the command to not look back at the burning Sodom and Gomorrah, if we turn to look behind to bid goodbye to all that we have loved, God will turn us both into pillars of salt, solid and inanimate. For what we have loved is other than God, other than Truth. What we have loved is absolute oneness—in other words, psychic equivalency and symbiosis. We have loved the concrete material world of the senses. In the realm of body turned to salt, pleasure is sacrificed and pain is evidence of existence.

Another biblical story comes to mind: the people of Israel decided to build a tower to reach God, to become one with God. God interrupted their efforts by changing each one's language so they no longer could be one in search of union, but became many: distinct and unable to communicate. God facilitated separateness and the symbolic order rather than the concrete material oneness of being God. Sometimes Arnie reacted by becoming God, or in the hour, becoming big like me. He would assert that he already knew whatever I said and how could I insult him by telling him what he already knew. When he did so, his hatred of the reality of separateness and the reality of his need of me became equivalent to a hatred of life itself.

Lizzy

Here is another example of a patient who is moving out of symbiosis into a two-body relationship that involves an increasing awareness of space: Lizzy tells me a story of panicking in the night as she awakens. Her whole body is buzzing with affect. It is impossible to return to sleep. She remembers a comment I made last night in her session about how chatty we were and not so analytic.

I reply that my comment about being chatty seemed to indicate a change in our relationship, one where the two of us had more space between us. It seemed to pick up on the feeling I had had that she was getting ready to leave. Perhaps in the night she could feel our differences and our separateness. She agreed. I feel close to her, recognizing and empathizing with her panic. When she describes it, I listen, feeling moved. I then repeat what she said to me. When I do, I feel her withdrawal and speak to it.

She says, "It is like we are together in an emotional place. I tell you and then you tell me what I have said. My mind knows you are doing that to show me you are with me and that you were listening. But when you do that, it is as if you become the "other" and are coming from a different location than the one I am in."

I say, "A location different than the location we were both in previously." She agrees. When I become the "other", Lizzy feels agitated and irritated. My reflection which has included the words "both of us" refers to a symbiosis. Saying it changes it. She becomes aware of separateness and difference. We are not equal. We are not the same. I am her analyst whom she needs and we come together from separate locations.

This vignette involving psychic space demonstrates the rapid shifting between simultaneous states of body and mind. Because my patient has spent many years learning to identify and discriminate, when she brings me her panic, we are able to find words for it. Such is not the case in the beginning years of working with symbiosis and ambiguity when dependency and need are denied and hidden in the symbiosis.

Discussion

In bringing to Bleger's brilliant work on symbiosis and ambiguity a contemporary understanding of autistic defenses, I am asserting that somatic responses are used defensively and inadvertently create deficits in cognitive and emotional processing. To interpret conflict or interpret aggression prematurely is to be on a different psychic organizational level than the patient. Bleger (2013 [1967], p. 85) asserts that working to shore up the ego is necessary before being able to address these more primal areas of functioning. I believe this is true because what is presented is always the deepest anxiety of the moment. When psychic equivalency is evoked via adhesive identification and adhesive equivalency, the anxiety is hard to find. Once found, the anxiety that is present is about existence itself. It is not about survival. Bion (1970, p. 103), says "Non-existence, immediately becomes an object that is immensely hostile, and filled with murderous envy towards the quality of function of 'existence,' wherever it is to be found." No wonder undifferentiated states of symbiosis are needed.

In symbiosis, anxiety is seemingly lacking, hence, too, is aggression, because the somatic fusion with the analyst keeps it at bay. Immobilization keeps the patient passive and agreeable. As mobilization begins, irritability, agitation, and anger emerge. These serve to maintain bodily relations. They also mark the hatred of existence. Bleger (2013 [1967], p. 28), says "... aggression is an attempt to control and restore the boundaries of her body, configuring them anew through abrupt contact with external objects."

As the analysis of the setting begins to impact the patient's ability to discriminate and differentiate one thing from another, insight develops. Some of this is mimicry of the analyst, but some of it is mobilization of the life instinct and the innate predisposition to grow. The epistemophilic instinct and love of knowledge is re-discovered. Both Arnie and Lizzy began slowly over time to realize those around them were confused by their actions and their words. Although they themselves did not feel confused by holding seemingly contradictory points of view simultaneously, they eventually could notice others' bafflement, including mine. They found this frustrating and at times infuriating. They felt their ability to hold contradictory views made them superior to others and me. They did not understand that ambiguity was not ambivalence.

Lizzy eventually could name this. She said she felt that everything she perceived existed on an equal level with everything else. Things were "side by side, not really touching each other." She felt this meant that her experience of things was chaotic since they didn't seem to impact each other. She noticed for example that people were pretty much interchangeable to her, not having distinguishing features. Mostly this did not bother her, but she began to see that it bothered other people, myself included. She said, "I know with my mind that these things must have some kind of relationship to each other. Other people act like they do. I am trying to figure it all out, but my mind fails me." This is stated as a fact, not to be questioned or pondered. It was not upsetting. She merely changed the focus of her attention to what was concretely happening at the moment. She felt her ability to change her focus was a strength she had. She did not perceive that changing her focus inhibited her learning and sometimes confused her objects.

A growing awareness of distinctions begins in the setting of the analysis and via my attempts to name, not interpret, somatic responses to the setting, which included my own body's response to both Arnie and Lizzy. My somatic counter-transference was often all I had to go on. I listened to the vibrations and resonances within my own body and paid attention to the rhythm of our speech more than the content of what we said. I focused on process, not content. Sometimes I would notice this aloud, knowing that when I did, I broke the rhythm. Lizzy noticed my attempts to clarify what she was saying. When she could eventually tolerate the frustration of difference—that of not being wordlessly and seamlessly understood—she was better able to think. She could also tolerate a bit of psychic space between and within us. Her experience of being understood changed from requiring merger to wanting empathy. With this change came an increased capacity to tolerate frustration. I no longer had to "get it right" every time. I could be human and so could she. This happened slowly over many years.

Our patients often teach us about psychic equivalency by describing it. Their descriptions are accurate. Simultaneously, they do not listen to or understand and remember their own descriptions. We become the depository where the words accumulate and have meaning. They only understand what they were telling us months and sometimes years later. Then we can bring their words back to them. Better still, they will tell us that they did not understand what we were saying when we used their words to reflect themselves back to them, but now they feel the significance of them in their bodies.

How are we as analysts who are used to operating from a symbolic order able to recognize psychic equivalency? If our patients' use of language is as if the words were concrete things instead of symbols, how are we to know? I suggest the concrete use of "words as things" is felt in our bodies. Words are a bodily relation that uses speech as sound and rhythm. Patients use the unconscious phantasies of adhesive identification and adhesive equivalency in order to maintain body relations with the analyst. These unconscious phantasies are the bridge between the body and mind. Body relations give them a sense of existing as a live human being, not as an inanimate thing.

The body relationship, which is dependent upon proximity, uses the senses to inform, not about safety as in the paranoid schizoid position or about concern for the other as in the depressive position, but about existence itself. Existence is a function of the glischro-caric position. Adhesive defenses provide the person with a shape. Molded by the analyst's form, the person is able to function "as if" being contained by the mind. The containment is the most primal possible, going back to early prenatal experiences of the amniotic fluid on the skin and the pulsing of blood through the placenta and umbilical cord. Whereas the fetus may not have an experience of time, it does have an experience of being contained in the amniotic sac and in the womb. This provides an experience of space and a very primal awareness of otherness—the maternal object. Maiello (1995) has called this first awareness of the object *the sound object*. This is the first experience of the other but also of the self.

Enactments with traumatized patients are frequent but do not provide the same benefit in moving the analytic work forward because the patient has difficulty with the projective and introjective processes. If the analyst and the patient are in two separate locations in space, two differing organizational levels, meeting in order to collaborate is not possible. An enactment may reveal this to the analyst; but to the patient it will only elicit a defense against the breach. Bion (1962b) says some patients have difficulty learning from experience. Without internalization via introjection, learning from experience is not possible. Without projection into an object, the healthy to and fro of projective identification cannot occur. The depository remains without a deposit.

Instead, the enactment becomes an impasse that cannot be used for learning. It becomes a means of adhering to each other. No amount of explanation will break up the symbiosis of enactment. What breaks it up is slowly over time the understanding of the analyst is communicated, not only in words, but also in the emotions and actions of the hour. These are the actions of being a depository or container that makes use of what it receives and allows accumulation to occur. These actions within the analyst are eventually introjected, breaking up the concrete autistic and psychotic protections. The process can then be internalized as a structure for processing experience.

Some patients only relate symbiotically to those to whom they are closest. With most people, they are able to maintain a healthier boundary and differentiation. However, some patients persist in using symbiosis as a defense with whomever they know. In becoming another, they develop what Bleger (2013 [1967]) calls factic personality traits (pp. xxxv, 223, 227). These are similar to what Deutsch (1964) named "as if" personalities. They use mimicry (Eekhoff, 2019) as a means of molding themselves to the surface of the other by adapting movements, dress patterns, speech patterns and other physical traits. My patient Kay (Eekhoff, 2019) was a masterful mimic. Near the end of her analysis, she said, "I have a life. I do not know if I have ever before had my own life. Maybe. Sometimes. If ever I had one, it should be now."

Bleger says, "The function of psychoanalytic treatment is to provide a symbiosis that was lacking or distorted. This function is fulfilled fundamentally by the setting, which undoubtedly includes the role of the analyst (p. 209)." He advocates a tight analytic frame while at the same time a *flexibility of technique* in order that the psychotic aspects of the personality may be analyzed. He says, "… the analyst needs to accept the setting brought by the patient (which is the patient's 'meta-ego'), because within it will be found in summary form the primitive unresolved symbiosis (p. 240)." In accepting the patient's setting, the psychic equivalency is gradually revealed. The symbiosis is invisible until minute psychic separation creates confusion and reveals entanglement.

Sometimes the entanglement and the fusion in the patient create confusion in the analyst. This confusion is a message—a message that tells us that we are being drawn to adopt the roles assigned by the patient. However, confusion may also signal movement out of symbiosis. Usually confusion comes when there are massive projections; and in fact, may indicate that the patient's projections have begun to gather into the object of the analyst, instead of into the infinite universe of outer space or compacted via implosion into a psychic black hole.

With the primarily neurotic patient, projection and introjection into and onto the analyst is more easily gathered into the transference. Transference interpretations work. Patients who have difficulty representing their experience project massively into the universe around them, even into outer space, and gathering the transference is difficult. They become their analysts in phantasy and any action on the part of the analyst that denies this symbiotic unity is a threat to their whole being. This occurs on the level of the body, not the mind and in an arena of sensuous experience. Yet the mind is always functioning, even when it is split off and projected into the analyst. Sensation and sound vibrate and move around the analytic dyad. I say dyad but the word itself is misleading in that it is a dyad in the analyst's mind, but only concretely a dyad in these moments of psychic fusion and symbiosis in the patient's mind. The patient accepts and knows there are two people in the room physically. For the patient, in these moments of deep work, it takes two physical bodies to make one person. Psychically there is only one person present.

Conclusion

In this paper, I have described Bleger's understanding of bodily relations in the earliest organizational levels of the mind. I have focused on a particular process of symbiosis—psychic equivalency—as a means of maintaining a fused relationship with the analyst. Further, I have maintained that in adulthood, ongoing access to psychic equivalency is both a deficit and a defense arising from early trauma. I suggest that trauma derails the normal course of development and impacts the creative and necessary flow of projective and introjective identifications. In a deep analysis, the concrete bodily relation with the analyst enables that which has been concretized and immobile to become free, fluid, and differentiated. This requires us to accept the setting the patient brings while interpreting the separation between the process and the setting as well as the separation between the analyst and the analysand.

I have described a process of fusion and symbiosis that occurs when patients have too much access to their own deep levels of personality. Such access is overwhelming. In order to organize their experience, these individuals become so fused with their analysts as to make transference and counter-transference experience indistinguishable. In certain moments, who is who is lost. In those times, hopefully, it is the analyst who gathers him or herself and holds what can be represented until the patient is able to bear the re-introjected aspects of the self. The analyst must maintain the separateness of a depository even when the patient cannot. This process takes many months of empathy and careful interpretation, during which intellectual description of the process can frequently result in negative therapeutic reactions or enactments of the most devastating kind. These too are helpful however, in that often they mark impasses that can only then be understood and worked through—made sensible via action.

I have described how in finding words for experience that has not been represented verbally, bodily relations are internalized and accumulate into a richly dimensional inner world of time and space. The analyst's recognition of the situation from the patient's point of view enables the symbiosis to be broken up. We know that these states of symbiosis are not only primal, but also can be defensive and persist as foreground throughout life. As Bleger teaches us, psychoanalytic treatment can successfully occur if the pathological symbiosis is broken up. The patient and the analyst begin to be able to repair the broken links. Object relations can then be re-instated and the patient gains a subjective sense of self.

References

Alvarez, A. (1992). *Live Company*. London: Routledge.

Alvarez, A. (2010). Levels of analytic work and levels of pathology: The work of calibration. *International Journal of Psycho-Analysis, 91*: 859–878.

Alvarez, A. (2012). *The Thinking Heart*. London: Routledge.

Bick, E. (1968). The experience of skin in early object relations. *International Journal of Psycho-Analysis, 49*: 484–486.

Bick, E. (1986). Further considerations on the function of the skin in early object relations. *British Journal of Psychotherapy, 2*(4): 292–299.

Bion, W.R. (1957). The differentiation of the psychotic from the non-psychotic personalities. *International Journal of Psychoanalysis, 38*: 266–275. (Reprinted London: Heinemann, 1967; London: Karnac, 1984, pp. 43–64).

Bion, W.R. (1958). On hallucination. *International Journal of Psycho-Analysis, 39*: 341–349.

Bion, W.R. (1959). Attacks on linking. *International Journal of Psycho-Analysis, 40*: 308–315.

Bion, W.R. (1962a). A psycho-analytic theory of thinking. *International Journal of Psycho-Analysis, 43*: 306–310. (Reprinted as A Theory of Thinking, in W.R. Bion, *Second Thoughts* (pp. 110–119). London: Karnac, 1984).

Bion, W.R. (1962b). *Learning from Experience*. London: Heinemann. (Reprinted London: Karnac, 1984).

Bion, W.R. (1965). *Transformations*. London: Heinemann. (Reprinted London: Karnac, 1984).

Bion, W.R. (1970). *Attention and Interpretation*. London: Tavistock. (Reprinted London: Karnac, 1984).

Bleger, J. (1967). *Symbiosis and Ambiguity: A Psychoanalytic Study*. Edited by J. Churcher and L. Bleger. Translated by S. Rogers, L. Bleger and J. Churcher. London and New York: Routledge, 2013.

Deutsch, H. (1964). Some clinical considerations of the ego ideal. *Journal of the American Psychoanalytic Association, 12*: 512–516.

Eekhoff, J.K. (2017). Finding a Center of Gravity via Proximity to the Analyst. In: H. Levine and D. Powers (eds.), *Engaging Primitive Anxieties of the Emerging Self: The Legacy of Francis Tustin*. London: Karnac.

Eekhoff, J.K. (2019). *Trauma and Primitive Mental States: An Object Relations Perspective*. London and New York: Routledge.

Eekhoff, J.K. (2022). *Bion and Primitive Mental States: Trauma and the Symbiotic Link*. London and New York: Routledge.

Ferenczi, S. (1920–1932). Notes and Fragments. In: *Final Contributions to the Problems and Methods of Psycho-Analysis* (pp. 216–279). London: Karnac, 1955. [Reprinted London: Karnac, 1994].

Ferenczi, S. (1988). *The Clinical Diary of Sándor Ferenczi*, edited by J. Dupont. Translated by M. Balint and N. Zarday Jackson. Cambridge, MA: Harvard University Press.

Fonagy, P. and M. Target (1996). Playing with reality, 1: Theory of mind and a normal development of psychic reality. *International Journal of Psychoanalysis, 77*: 217–233.

Freud, S. (1999 [1900]). *The Interpretation of Dreams*. Translated by J. Crick. Oxford: Oxford University Press. [S.E. *Vol. 4* (pp. ix–625). London: The Hogarth Press].

Freud, S. (1911). Formulations on Two Principles of Mental Functioning, S.E. *Vol. 12* (pp. 213–226). London: The Hogarth Press.

Maiello, S. (1995). The sound-object: A hypothesis about prenatal auditory experience and memory. *Journal of Child Psychotherapy, 21(1)*: 23–41.

Maiello, S. (2012). Prenatal experiences of containment in the light of Bion's model of container/contained. *Journal of Child Psychotherapy, 38(3)*: 250–267.

McDougall, J. (1989). *Theaters of the Body: A Psychoanalytic Approach to Psychosomatic Illness*. New York: Norton & Co.

Meltzer, D. (1967). *The Psychoanalytical Process*. London: Heinemann. (Reprinted London: Karnac, 2008).

Meltzer, D. (1994 [1974]). Adhesive Identification. In: A. Hahn (ed.), *Sincerity and Other Works: The Collected Papers of Donald Meltzer* (pp. 335–350). London: Karnac.

Meltzer, D., with J. Bremner, S. Hoxter, D. Weddell, and I. Wittenberg (1975a). *Explorations in Autism: A Psychoanalytic Study*. Strath Tay: Clunie Press. (Reprinted for the Harris Meltzer Trust, London: Karnac, 2008).

Meltzer, D. (1975b). The Psychology of Autistic States and of Post-autistic Mentality. In: D. Meltzer with J. Bremner, S. Hoxter, D. Weddell, and I. Wittenberg. *Explorations in Autism*. Strath Tay: Clunie Press (pp. 6–29). (Reprinted for the Harris Meltzer Trust, London: Karnac, 2008).

Ogden, T.H. (1989a). *The Primitive Edge of Experience*. Northvale, NJ: Jason Aronson.

Ogden, T.H. (1989b). On the concept of an autistic-contiguous position. *International Journal of Psychoanalysis*, 70:127–140.

Piontelli, A. (1985). *Backwards in Time: A Study in Infant Observation by the Method of Esther Bick*. London: Karnac.

Piontelli, A. (1987). Infant observation from before birth. *International Journal of Psychoanalysis*, 68: 453–463.

Tustin, F. (1980). Autistic objects. *International Review of Psycho-Analysis*, 7: 27–40.

Tustin, F. (1981). *Autistic States in Children*. Boston: Routledge & Kegan Paul.

Tustin, F. (1986). *Autistic Barriers in Neurotic Patients*. New Haven, CT: Yale University Press.

Tustin, F. (1990). *The Protective Shell in Children and Adults*. London: Karnac.

Tustin, F. (1991) Revised understandings of psychogenic autism. *International Review of Psychoanalysis*, 72(4): 585–592.

Tustin, F. (1994). The perpetuation of an error. *Journal of Child Psychotherapy*, 20(1): 3–23.

Winnicott, D.W. (1960). The theory of the parent-infant relationship. *International Journal of Psycho-Analysis*, 41: 585–595.

Winnicott, D.W. (1965). The maturational processes and the facilitating environment. *International Psycho-Analytical Library*, 64: 1–276. London: The Hogarth Press and the Institute of Psycho-Analysis.

4 On the psychoanalytic frame and ambiguity as axes for the study of Bleger's works

José E. Fischbein[1] and Susana Vinocur Fischbein[2]

Introduction

The concepts set forth by José Bleger, a Río de la Plata second generation analyst, introduces us to a thinker characterized by his creativity and investigative thoroughness. Despite his untimely death, his work significantly influenced the ideas of subsequent generations of Latin American analysts.

Our aim is to consider his developments on the psychoanalytic frame[3] and the concept of ambiguity, as these subjects were defined in the predominant 1950s and 1960s theories in the Río de la Plata, which were mainly based on the ideas of Freud and Klein. Our purpose also involves the challenge of substantiating Bleger's ideas by applying them to the analysis of current clinical material.

Bleger (1966), claims that in inquiring about *ambiguity* both of and within the psychoanalytic session, the pre-eminence of the *setting* gradually acquired precision. He considers the setting from different perspectives, that of psychoanalysis, that of the institution—as the session should be considered as an institution, together with the psychoanalytic institution itself—in addition to being seen as a Gestalt.

The *ambiguity* that characterizes *symbiosis* is revealed when examining the latter. Bleger argues that ambiguity is characteristic of the most primitive organization of the personality. At first he called this organization "primitive undifferentiation", and later "syncretism".

Though acknowledging the writings of other psychoanalysts, Klein, Fairbairn, and Fenichel among them, he felt compelled to formulate hypotheses of his own, considering primitive undifferentiation "as the starting point of human development." Little by little, this "organization of the self and the world" would become the centre of his perspective and would lead him to change his approach to clinical practice (Bleger, 1967, pp. 9–10).

The influence of Susan Isaacs was outstanding in the methodological aspects of his writings. In particular, her ideas referring to the psychoanalytic methodology of case studies, as raised in "The Nature and Function of Phantasy" (Isaacs, 1948), vis-à-vis Bleger's conceptions of the setting.

DOI: 10.4324/9781003252252-6

Thus, to identify the author's conceptual contributions in their epoch and environment, the first section refers to the context in which Bleger developed his theories. Second, the role of the notions of *symbiosis* and *ambiguity* are dealt with (Bleger, 1967). Third, the concept of *setting* is examined as described in *The Psychology of Behaviour* (Bleger, 1964 [1963]). In the fourth section, his ideas on the setting in the analytic process are addressed (Bleger, 1967). Finally, we introduce case material that illustrates how the above theoretical concepts are still relevant in clinical practice.

I Río de la Plata: Psychoanalytic context in the 1950s and 1960s

The predominance of psychoanalysis in the Argentine psychotherapeutic field was remarkable and widely recognized in the period 1955–1966. This situation was simultaneous with the professionalization of psychology and evidenced by projects such as those of Bleger and Pichon-Rivière. The intersections between psychoanalysis, psychiatry and psychology were varied and multiple, which led to clinical practice grounded on these allied disciplines.

Bleger became highly representative insofar as he exemplified such multidisciplinary confluence. He was an instance of the "exodus" of psychiatrists to psychoanalysis in the 1950s and 1960s. He was also the most recognized psychoanalytic psychology professor at the recently founded School of Psychology at Buenos Aires University (Dagfal, 2012).[4]

The historical development of psychoanalytic ideas in Río de la Plata was characterized not only by its attachment to the theories of Freud and Klein, but also by a controversial position in regard to them; these authors considered the analyst-patient interaction, along with the analysis of the intrapsychic, anticipating with their conceptions about the *bipersonal* and *intersubjective fields*, breakthrough ideas that would be echoed in the writings of international psychoanalysts many years later (Baranger, Baranger and Mom, 1982),

Klein's (1980 [1946]) contributions on the intrapsychic world were enriched in this context with the ideas of link (*vínculo*)[5] by Pichon-Rivière (1988 [1971]), *complementary and concordant countertransference* by Racker (1960) and *dynamic bipersonal field* by Baranger and Baranger (1969 [1961–1962]), as well as by Álvarez de Toledo (1993 [1954]) ideas about *doing with words* and the reciprocal effect between patient and analyst—an issue discussed by Oxford philosophers years later (Austin, 1971 [1962], Vinocur Fischbein, 2013). The outcome of these papers resulted in significant changes in the situational and interactional dynamics of psychoanalytic treatments.[6]

Bleger's contribution was to show the divergence between the classical Freudian "archaeological" model (Breuer and Freud (1973 [1893–1895]) and analysis focused on "genetic continuity" (Isaacs, 1948), which highlighted the *here and now* of the psychoanalytic situation.

II The role of symbiosis and ambiguity in Bleger's writings

Bleger argued that research into *symbiosis* implied the exploration of a wide field that encompassed a range of interconnected disciplines: from normal psychology to psychopathology, from individual psychology to group, institutional and community psychology. This led him to investigate the subject of ambiguity, not only in pathology, but also in normalcy and everyday life.

The connection between both themes—symbiosis and ambiguity—was based on a first hypothesis about the nature of the nucleus that constitutes or persists either in the link (*vínculo*) or in the symbiotic interdependence: it is a nucleus whose essence is ambiguous.

The examination of the phenomenon of symbiosis shows that it includes the dynamics of an object with complex characteristics, which includes indiscriminate good and bad parts, as well as those parts of the Ego that are involved in its own experiences. The mobilization of this object promotes extreme and massive anxieties of a catastrophic and confused nature, against which only the most primitive defences become active. Bleger defines this object as an *agglutinated nucleus*, which is the outcome of the primitive undifferentiated remnant that persists in a "mature" personality and manifests itself in symbiosis, both in the phases of normal development and in pathology. This hypothesis can be interpreted as a personal reviewing of Klein's theory about the existence of an initial Ego.

The maintenance of an agglutinated nucleus of an ambiguous nature—through which the link of close symbiotic interdependence between two or more people is constituted, or persists—fulfils the purpose of keeping controlled and immobilized the more immature or psychotic parts of personality (Bion, 1984 [1967]). The author characterises ambiguity both from the perspective of the observer and from that of the human being who suffers from it. If considered from the perception of countertransference as experienced in the psychoanalytic field, the ambiguous person is envisaged as someone whose behaviour generates doubts, uncertainty or confusion. If viewed from the individual who manifests this phenomenon, ambiguity means undifferentiation and identity deficit. To be precise, it is a discrimination deficit between Ego and non-Ego.[7]

The corollary of this hypothesis leads him to assert that the primitive state of undifferentiation is already a particular organization of the Ego and the world, a distinct structure, in such a way that it always includes the individual and his environment as undifferentiated entities. Consequently, our identity and sense of reality are one of the many possible organizations of these and cannot be read as deficits or distortions of identity and/or the sense of reality, but as another organization to "be studied *per se*".

Bleger sets forth a second hypothesis that refutes the assertion that the earliest stages of the human being are characterized by isolation, from which the *infans* gradually structures its social nature by assimilating culture. On the contrary, this author maintains the existence of primitive undifferentiation as the starting point of subjective development.[8] The corollary of his hypothesis can be understood as expanding his conception of ambiguity. When this state prevails, the demarcation or discrimination of differing or diverging terms has not been achieved. Human beings do not experience conflict regarding the situation that could affect them as being incompatible. Contradictory behaviours or attitudes are not mutually exclusive; they are just different and can coexist or alternate. This would be the basic feature of the *glischro-caric position* or of *syncretism* that is perpetuated in ambiguity, either because of immaturity or regression.

Bleger even puts forward a third hypothesis that challenges the generalized belief that psychological phenomena are originally mental, and that they do not display themselves because they pre-exist unconsciously. Bleger suggests that this belief has to be replaced by a different conceptual model. He maintains that mental phenomena are behaviour modes, which appear even later than other phenomena, since the first undifferentiated, syncretic structures are fundamentally bodily relationships (Bleger, 1967, p. 11).

In our view, the concepts described above have been crucial contributions of Bleger's theory, who partially questioned Klein's theory, arguing that primary undifferentiation precedes the psychic mechanisms of projection and projective-introjective identification. Thus, Bleger acknowledged his contemporaries' relevant innovative ideas, that is, Pichon-Rivière's *prenatal (fetal) stage* and Rascovsky's *theory of a fetal psyche*, described as an autistic condition that precedes the oral stage.[9]

III On the concept of setting

In 1963, Bleger anticipated his methodological concern with the notion of settings as essential, implicit tools to study phenomena. The settings do not constitute only "principles" or "mental models of thought", but reflect how the researcher is philosophically positioned and related to certain aspects of social reality and the object being studied. The validity of these tools depend on their "right" place in the dialectical process of phenomena. He depicts the various settings used by contemporary psychology and criticizes the fact that different schools are set in their own one-sided settings, which leads to false ideological implications.

The *historical setting* does not simply consist of the description, recollection or reconstruction of a chronological series of events, behaviours, and circumstances. Bleger points out that in all cases it means investigation of a sequence of behaviours and/or events, taking into account the situation in which they are reported, or remembered, considering these manifestations as current behaviours. This idea involves relationships, or some type of logical links, between different behaviours, different moments, and different manifestations in the course of time, as well as causal or significant links and inferences between behaviours that are repeated over time in an individual's life history.

Bleger explicitly asserts that the historical setting has been and is the one traditionally used by the clinical method, giving preference to childhood history as a connection between meaning and causality. This implicitly evokes the Freudian differentiation between psychic reality and material reality.

Essential to the author's position is the relationship that he establishes between the historical and the historical-genetic framing, although he distinguishes them from an evolutionary one.[10] However, he objects to the non-distinction between the historical and the genetic framing, embodied in the historical-genetic method of psychoanalysis, in which the genetic aspect implies not only examining the origin of a phenomenon, but also its continuity. The historical-genetic perspective partially overlaps with the evolutionary and dynamic framings, which stand out for their discontinuities, which are the result of the accumulation of gradual changes. Complex phenomena develop by progressing from simple to higher levels, which gradually become more complex and contain them.

> … Neither evolution nor regression explain the genesis or the cause of a given behaviour or a symptom; they only provide us with the guidelines in which the phenomena occur, and if—as in the case of the disease or the symptom—they constitute the reactivation of levels of integration and, therefore, can be considered as archaic behaviours, that is, *it is only the present situation that confers the motivation and the meaning of the appearance of these archaic behaviours.*
>
> (Bleger, 1964 [1963], p. 105) (Our translation and emphasis)

This quote leads us to consider the essential importance of the situational setting, based on K. Lewin's (1952) field theory, which strongly influenced the Argentine psychoanalysts of that period. This perspective focuses on a phenomenon as a result of a present field, that is, of all the coexisting and reciprocally dependent factors at a given moment. If a phenomenon occurs at a given moment, its causes are present, there and then. The situational examination is contrasted with historical, genetic and evolutionary ones.

Although Bleger maintains that there is a dialectical interaction among different settings—according to which the present is transformed into the past and this in turn operates in the present—he also heralds the importance that the Río de la Plata conceptions were beginning to acquire concerning the two-person/bipersonal dynamic field and retroactivity (Baranger and Baranger, 1961–62, Baranger, Baranger, and Mom, 1987).

Every situation contains a historical narrative: past experiences are included in the present field and organize the *here-and-now*. Hence, the use of a situational setting has expanded psychological research under experimental conditions, thus becoming a tool to transform the psycho-analytic session into an experimental situation of inquiry.[11]

Returning to the issue of genetic continuity, Bleger argues that it serves the exploration of behaviour as a process, and integrates, or dialectically systematizes, previous ones. He particularly cites the contributions of Isaacs (1950 [1948]) that closely link observational methods and psycho-analytic technique with three fundamental principles: They are: (a) attention to details; (b) observation of context; (c) study of genetic continuity. These involve the study of the emotional relationship between analysand and analyst (transference). Specifically, Bleger upholds the idea of the situational frame, which appears clearly in such formulation, under-pinning a specific approach to psychoanalytic clinical material. The situational frame also refers to the idea of a context considered in a synchronic cut of what was provided by the patient in the *here-and-now* of the session.

In our view, although the author establishes a gradual link between past and present and their dialectical interaction, this aspect is relegated for the sake of the technical application of a pure, and strict, here-and-now, which restricts the possibility of replacing linear temporality by an also dialectical concept of causality and a "spiral" model of temporality: the future and the past condition and signify each other in the structuring of the present (Baranger, Baranger and Mom, 1987).

IV On the psychoanalytic frame

In his classic work, Bleger (1967) examines the psychoanalytic frame or setting as a conceptual tool to approach the analytical process, to assess the different clinical situations in the transference-countertransference field. The setting constitutes the stable structure of the dynamic process, but it is not a process in itself. The setting is at the service of appraising the differences between the variable elements; it includes the person of the analyst, the environmental factors and the technical strategies necessary to carry out the treatment.

In Bleger's words:

> The frame is maintained and tends to be maintained (actively, by the psycho-analyst) as invariable; and while it exists as such it seems to be non-existent or it does not count, just as we become aware of institutions or relationships only when they are missing, are blocked, or have ceased to exist.
>
> (Bleger, 1967, p. 512)

A few lines below he points out:

> Thus, the frame is constant, and is therefore decisive in the phenomena of the process of behaviour. In other words, the frame is a *meta-*

behaviour, and the phenomena we are going to distinguish as behaviour depend on it. It is what remains implicit, but on which the
explicit depends

(ibid., p. 512)

Unlike Bleger's proposal—which emphasizes the invariant characteristics
of the frame—our aim is to focus on the infringements of the frame or
setting. According to our conception, *breaches in the treatment setting*
involve the repetition in different areas of specific behavioural expressions,
thus becoming an axis of the process. We hypothesize that this entails the
reiteration of very early experiences unable to generate verbal and com-
municable thoughts regarding their genesis within the primary environment, preceding word acquisition and Ego—non-Ego discrimination.

From the patient's idiosyncratic breaches in the treatment setting, it is
possible to infer the type of "behaviour setting" that they bring along related
to their primitive symbiotic relationship with their core family group and
their very first interpersonal relationships, which have contributed to create
an omnipotent infantile nucleus characterized by ambiguity.

These behaviours reappear in the transference-countertransference field,
as part of a culture that leaves indelible marks on the organization of the
self and the Ideal. They make up the agglutinated nucleus represented by
ambiguity as the expression of the primitive, undifferentiated psychological organization. Breaches also confront us with cleavages of the primary
nuclei, these are psychotic aspects that function as *bulwarks* of the infantile
symbiotic aspects (Baranger and Baranger, 1964).

The individual has not yet achieved the possibility of finding contradictions, divergent attitudes, ideas or beliefs. All of them may be compar-
able or equivalent to him; so, they may coexist—Bleger's *glischro-caric*
position or syncretism (1967, p. 168)—which will give rise to a peculiar
type of Ego identity or organization, characterized by a multiplicity of
non-integrated nuclei, a "granular self", whose source and clinical manifestations are confusing (Bleger, 1967, p. 169).

It may be possible to read Bleger's original hypothesis as a significant
forerunner to Green's thought in the depiction of borderline personality:

> [...] Variability of Ego boundaries is not perceived as an enrichment of
> experience, but as loss of control, as the last defensive resource against
> implosion, disintegration or loss. This Ego envelope, this ineffective
> shell, protects the vulnerable Ego, which is rigid while lacking cohe-
> sion. *Internal cleavage reveals that the self is made up of different nuclei that
> do not communicate. These nuclei of the self may be described as archipelagos*
> (Green, 1990 [1972]), p. 113) (Our translation and emphasis).

Infringements to the frame have led us to study how they become a phenomenon that can be considered analogous to that of a symptom. As it is

repeated in different situations, it becomes a helpful sign to appraise the vicissitudes of the therapeutic process. This ambiguous modality is only ego-syntonic for the patient, whereas the psychoanalyst will try to establish the capacity to discriminate in his interpretive work.

V Clinical illustration

The clinical material of a patient who underwent treatment with one of us, is appropriate in elucidating Bleger's ideas about the setting, as well as his thoughts about ambiguous personality and symbiotic dependence. The different meanings of a phenomenon are displayed—ranging from an identity trait to an alarm signal. Its gradual modification showed the therapeutic effect of psychoanalysis. His behaviour was initially attributed to the inherent culture of his social group, as an aspect of the Ego Ideal; only after analysing it could the patient become aware of its actual extent.

At the time of consultation, Mr. T was a fifty-year-old man. This presentation corresponds to the fourth year of his psychoanalytic treatment, of two weekly sessions. He was referred by his couple therapist. He was married and had two children, a boy and a girl. He consulted about family conflicts, mainly the impossibility of improving his upsetting marital relationship. Moreover, he held a conflicting bond with his eldest son. The youngster was highly critical of his father's relationship with his paternal grandfather. Mr. T and his brothers shared a family business led by the elderly man, who decided the economic withdrawals of each of his sons, without taking into account the individual characteristics of each of their families. In other words, the grandfather managed the cash flow of the business and the company's funds, by withholding the ownership papers.

From the beginning of his treatment, Mr. T's associations highlighted his close and ambiguous link with his father. It could be assumed as being a symbiotic bond, since father and son monitored each other closely, thus keeping immature and aggressive aspects of their personality under control, which brought about the cleavage of their more evolved aspects. Mr. T longed to differentiate himself, but in fact he was extremely dependent on his father. Outwardly, the patient and his father manifested themselves as being very active and autonomous, but this was only a reactive way of sustaining their identity.

Bleger accurately portrays these patients as follows:

> Sometimes they feel demanded, enclosed, urged or persecuted by events, things or people, and there is a deficit in the perception or insight of the meaning of actions, which they do not feel to be their doers but their victims. They feel like they are just doing what others wish.

> (Bleger, 1967, p. 199, our translation)

Mr. T's identity derived from and was maintained in deeds, as he carried out his tasks in the family business. He lacked his own initiatives and complied with either his brother's or his father's mandates; a situation that in turn revealed the lack of distinctiveness among family members. He did not show himself to be an autonomous individual, since in his basic structure a state of coalescence predominated. Insofar as he was able to maintain this state, he was protected from the appearance of aggressive impulses and persecutory experiences. In line with Bleger's conceptualization, it may be stated that his ambiguity kept the psychotic part of his personality—his indiscriminate primary nuclei—split from the more evolved psychoneurotic aspects, in that he displayed primitive identifications denoted by a prominent Ego–non-Ego undifferentiation.

Mr. T attributed part of his distress to his wife's lack of financial cooperation, because she did not contribute money to the family finances. He also complained that she did not listen to his claims. However, Mr. T frequently appealed to his wife for assistance in balancing his daily expenses, but she was reluctant to hand over her money. Mr. T was not aware of his participation in triggering the situations that caused his discomfort in these conflicts, because his wife had repeatedly given him money on the condition that he returned her loans later, a promise he had not fulfilled. He did not either take into account the fact that he actually controlled her expenses, since he did not want her to buy her clothes with the money he contributed to the household. In his opinion, these were superfluous expenses; he argued that she had lots of outfits and they were always made a mess. He constantly tried to impose his ideas regardless of her wishes. In this way, he acted out what happened with his father without noticing such similarity at all.

His portrayals about his wife's disorder and the amount of superfluous outfits were analysed as a metaphor for his mind, as a chaotic mixture of affections, objects, places and functions, even though he apparently maintained a certain organization in his daily life, carrying out what he was ordered to do in his business. As mentioned, a further cause of suffering for Mr. T was his son's rebellious attitude. Mr. T's disquiet was caused by the young man's job as a DJ at a nightclub characterized by marginality, homosexual and transsexual prostitution and drug trafficking.

At the beginning of his treatment, the contents of his discourse consisted in endless complaints about the fact that he suffered from lack of recognition for his efforts in life. Although he relentlessly expected to be confirmed as an autonomous being, deep down he wanted his wife and children—as well as his parents and brother—to function all together in accordance with the satisfaction of his own desires.

An event that wholly affected the transference relationship elicited our ideas at the basis of this account. On one occasion, ten minutes after his scheduled session had started, he phoned to inform his analyst that he had had a last-minute difficulty at work, and if he tried to attend his session, he would be so late that it would be more convenient to reschedule. As the treatment agreement stated that he would only be able to reschedule his sessions when changes were asked for in advance of the arranged hour, after evaluating the request, his analyst did not accept it and the patient was told goodbye until the next programmed session.

When Mr. T attended the next appointment, he did not mention the loss of the previous session at all, he acted as if the telephone conversation had not existed and began the session reporting that on Monday he had left his painting class late and realised that he would get delayed to session. As his son was downtown, Mr. T called him to invite him to have lunch together. It was just then that he decided to phone his analyst to ask for another session. Regarding his request he would make, he told his son: "… and if he lets it slip by … he lets it slip by."

The patient's account conjured up an episode from previous months. On that occasion he had reported that he had tickets to go to a recital. These tickets were valid for attending on a Friday night, and indeed, he went along with his wife. The next day he invited his son to attend the concert with the same tickets, clarifying that getting into the theatre depended on the usher's alertness: "We try … *if we get away with … we get away with* …". Thus they succeeded in attending the show.

These elliptical expressions were the key that allowed us to observe through a linguistic use a kind of behaviour that would lead to infer a certain psychic structure, through linking these idioms in the transference-countertransference relationship. The first part of the statements, "*if he lets it slip by …*" and "*if we get away with …*", with no further clarification of his thinking, disavows the underlying unconscious conflict; a conflict that hides the omnipotence of a specific desire. As will be seen later, the conflict is created by a desire to submit and an indiscriminate attitude towards the transgression of a parental mandate; namely, to obtain all the possible benefits of each situation.

Faced with the omnipotence of desire, there would be two possible ways of dealing with it, either relinquishing his omnipotence or accepting a passive position. The outcome being that the patient would feel himself to be a victim of the desire of the other, someone else would become responsible for the act, while he remained blameless and immersed in a manic situation of triumph. He no longer desires to transgress, but has to abide and submit to what the other (his father or his analyst) imposes on him.

Let us remember that the primitive transgressions driven by desire are related to the Oedipal conflict. If a subject tries to flee from Oedipal desires, his drives undertake a regressive path. Libidinal regression leads from activity to passivity. Thus, the individual becomes the object of the desire of the other, and also substitutes the regressive way of love for hatred. He is no longer someone who desires his mother, but someone subjected to paternal imposition and, therefore, wrapped in hatred for the father, or any other figure who holds authority. He accepts what is imposed on him and his defiant and reactively transgressive attitude becomes evident.

His analyst pointed out that Mr. T's admission to the recital was a contract between him and the artists; using it twice was a violation of this contract. He was surprised at the interpretation that showed him the existence of a deception in attempting to pass one thing off for another. Mr. T replied: "In my business this is continuously done." The immediate effect that each contractual proposal produced on the patient was a reaction of disavowal, which entailed the fantasy of an imposition on his wish. For example, although he paid for his sessions, he never did it according to what had been agreed. The established terms and expiration dates were "ignored" by him. His lack of compliance made him feel that the work schedule was extremely rigid and consequently he felt annoyed. He argued that he always complied. This was partly true, because somewhat belatedly, he did pay for his sessions.

The ambiguous zone created between payment and non-payment prompted his analyst to maintain a firm attitude concerning the differentiation and clarification of situations in order not to impair the frame that would make the analysis feasible. Putting the frame to the test was an element constantly at stake in the transference, inasmuch as the patient persisted in boycotting the established work guidelines. In this sense, his argument was what he called "the cultural factor", with which he established a false connection between "cheating" and "being a man".

Mr. T was able to gain insight into this fact, when in the middle of a session while talking about his weight gain he said: "I used to wonder: how do I get fatter if I just eat a cookie?" He admitted that now he would have to say: "Well, it's just a cookie, but I'm also eating a lot of bread." Now he was able to complete the text of his ellipsis with what he had previously obliterated.

In our opinion, utterances like "move on to something else", or "if it passes off … it passes off", verbalise the denial of painfully recognizing being a participant in a conflicting field, where there is always something missing. It depends on the place where he is positioned—either as performer, or being subjected to someone who benefits from this practice—to consider any action as legal (accepted) or illegal (rejected).

The situations of violence that took place paved the way for his enactments. What was "sanctioned" by his father, who did not admit objections, caused him pain. It should be noticed that as a verb "sanction" has a double meaning, it is used both to connote the imposition of a penalty as well as to ratify or enforce a law. This confirms Bleger's ideas on ambiguity; that is, for Mr. T, two opposite situations could coexist simultaneously, without this being a contradiction.

On one occasion, Mr. T clarified that if clients placed an order, but they did not have enough stock of the required colour, they would send a similar colour instead: "It's the same if the client does not claim … *if it passes off, it passes off* … and if they don't realize, all the better." The story about the delivery of goods, the colours that were in stock and their being different from those requested, served as material for the analysis of discrimination; sending supplies of a similar colour did not comply with what had been requested. Substituting goods of a similar colour for the correct one implied a contractual breakdown; it meant transgressing. These interpretations caused him to be puzzled and disoriented. He stated that he had not thought that the difference of colours mattered at all, since this had been his usual way of carrying on his work.

This episode signalled the beginning of a period characterized by attempts at discriminating life elements that had remained undifferentiated. He used to deny that he could be a participant in what he complained about. His usual utterances became a crucial axis of therapeutic work, not only focused on his commercial activities, but also in behaviours that took place in daily family life, which had become the source of confusion accompanied by persecutory anxiety. He reluctantly acknowledged that he had cheated his wife and that his habit of selling second-class merchandise was not really a sign of his virility, but a deception. His environment had encouraged rather than censured that attitude, while celebrating his skill in producing sales.

Mr. T slowly began to realize that hidden aspects of his personality, which had been silenced over time, were being actualized by his children. During one session he said:

> The "if it passes off … it passes off" is a relationship between three things, the first is having had bad schooling. These are the twists one has. Another one, what I think and do not say, the omissions, and the third one is the favours, taking charge of the dependencies that I have on others. It's my education; I was born with it, because it was always present in my parents' house. This is a knot that must be untied. At home there was a double standard. It is still there, I used it all my life, it is vital […]. It transcends the walls of my house, those of my parents' and is innate to my inheritance.

He went on to say:

> I always defended these situations. My dad had two sayings. [*He pauses and says that he has forgotten them. Then he adds*] One was: *if one hand hurts to any of us, it hurts to us all.* I always disagreed with my family's sayings, just like today that I've forgotten them. There was a point where I gave in to my dad's system and that's the system in which I live … I cannot differentiate degrees in the scale of values; I can't have my own mental scheme.

His surrender to his father as the representative of a superego instance intended to provide shelter in the notion that it was a cultural issue, something innate and unquestionable. He had to continue with his tradition, otherwise he lost his identity. This ideology allowed him to continue operating within the field of masochistic pleasure. Hence, the process of analysis intended to deactivate those "bulwarks" experienced as means of supporting his self-esteem and fragile cohesion.

As Bleger states:

> For the patient, "something" that had always been in a certain way and should always go on being that way was broken, and he did not recognize that it could be otherwise. He demanded the repetition of what he had experienced, of what "had always been like this", a requirement or condition that he could maintain in the course of his life, through an Ego restriction or constraint of his social relationships, by means of continuously managing these relationships, with a strong dependence on his objects.
>
> (Bleger, 1967, p. 246). (Our translation)

In successive sessions, he posed a series of questions: *How do I stop this? How do I get this out of everyday life? Do you realize that this part of my culture?* He interestingly associated his relationship with his parents with his own conflicts with his son. He gradually became aware of the problem of repetition.

In the vignette about the "bad schooling" and his "education", he showed his newly acquired aptitude to ponder on the consequences of his actions, he recovered the possibility of thinking before acting and could foresee the possibility of harm. Somehow, he tried to avoid the unnecessary risks of repeated enactments. What had been interpreted by the analyst became a tool for reading his current reality. The "if it passes off ... it passes off" was no longer the expression of an evacuatory act, but was transformed into a metaphor about those situations which he had not been able to think of before:

> You have to call things by their name instead of hiding them. An excess of silence generates violence. When things are not called by their name, it is Babel and you go nuts. Distrust emerges and from there one gets to violence.

Mr. T's crucial amendment of his interpersonal relationships and his way of experiencing other fellow beings indicated the relevance of his psychic change. His defences were also modified; he stopped denying facts and began to value the perception of himself, while acknowledging different outlooks.

Concluding remarks

When the most primitive and archaic aspects of the personality are deposited in the frame, the generated breaches reveal its syncretic facets in the transference. We have aimed at highlighting how this symbiotic way of living and structuring the world is realised.

We consider that in accepting in the transference-countertransference interplay, the "attacks to the frame" in their different modalities, it is possible to retrieve via the analytic link the study of the repetition of archaic aspects of syncretic nuclei, thus paving the way out of ambiguity and allowing the distinction between good and bad; namely, the passage to the paranoid-schizoid position.

Although many years have elapsed since our participation in Bleger's classes and lectures, writing this paper has allowed us to rediscover how his thinking remains contemporary in our therapeutic practice as implicit theories, although today we may have deepened them with new theoretical readings and perspectives.

Notes

1 Full Member, Asociación Psicoanalítica Argentina. jefischbein@gmail.com
2 Full member, Asociación Psicoanalítica Argentina. susyvinfisch@gmail.com
3 The translation into English of Bleger's paper read at the Second Argentine Psychoanalytic Congress, Buenos Aires, June 1966, established the term "frame" for the original Spanish *encuadre*. However, Bleger also used "setting" in his paper, *Psicoanálisis del encuadre psicoanalítico* (1967) Therefore, we are using these terms interchangeably.
4 He was not only Marxist and Kleinian, but also Pichon-Rivière's most prominent disciple. As a teacher Bleger made use of the "general theory of behaviour" by Daniel Lagache, the ideas of Georges Politzer on "concrete psychology", the "existential phenomenology" of Jean-Paul Sartre and the "topological and vector psychology" of Kurt Lewin.
5 Pichon-Rivière (1988 [1971]) defines *vínculo* as a complex structure involving an individual, an object, and their mutual interrelationship with processes of communication and learning.
6 While clinical practice was handled as drama, theory was still formulated in dynamic terms. Consequently, it became necessary to adapt the theory to clinical demands, introducing the social dimension implied by the psychoanalytic session understood as a two-person relationship, where a given situation made the behaviours of patient and therapist surface as necessary (Dagfal, 2012).
7 In Bleger's understanding the most frequent mistake is to attribute the countertransference confusion directly to the structure of the phenomenon that produces it.
8 This position implies a shift in child developmental research; namely, instead of focusing on how the child attaches to the external world, we must focus on modifying a type of undifferentiated relationship, so as to achieve the development of his/her identity and sense of reality.
9 The author also points out that his position bears a certain relationship with concepts formulated by other Argentine contemporaries, such as that of

"living-dead" object (Baranger and Baranger (1969 [1961–1962]), or that of "lethargic nucleus" (Cesio, 1958).

10 The genetic frame refers to the study of phenomena based on their origins and assumes that every phenomenon or object has a first origin before which it did not exist. It is clear that this assumption is absolutely untenable, since certain starting points are in general taken for evolutionary studies, though not in an absolute way.

11 However, the situational frame does not always entail establishing the causality of the behaviour under study, since what is remembered may also refer to present issues, not grasped or made explicit as such.

References

Álvarez de Toledo, L. (1993 [1954]): El análisis del 'asociar', del 'interpretar' y de 'las palabras'. *Revista de Psicoanálisis APA, 11*(3) and *50*(2).

Austin, J. (1971 [1962]). *How to Do Things with Words*. Edited by J.O. Urmson. Oxford: Oxford University Press.

Baranger, W. and M. Baranger (1961–1962) La situación analítica como campo dinámico. *Revista Uruguaya de Psicoanálisis, 4*(1), Montevideo: Asociación Psicoanalítica del Uruguay.

Baranger, M. and W. Baranger (1964). El "insight" en la situación analítica. *Revista Uruguaya de Psicoanálisis, 6*(1): 19–38.

Baranger, W. and M. Baranger (1969 [1961–1962]). La situación analítica como campo dinámico. In: *Problemas del campo psicoanalítico* (pp. 129–164 and pp. 217–219). Buenos Aires: Ediciones Kargieman.

Baranger, M., W. Baranger, and J. Mom (1982). Proceso y no proceso en el trabajo psicoanalítico. *Revista de Psicoanálisis, 39*(4): 527–549.

Baranger, M., W. Baranger, and J. Mom (1987) The infantile psychic trauma from us to Freud: Pure trauma, retroactivity and reconstruction. *International Journal of Psycho-Analysis, 69*: 113–128.

Bion, W.R. (1984 [1967]). *Second Thoughts. Selected Papers on Psychoanalysis*. London: Karnac.

Bleger, J. (1964 [1963]). Encuadres para el estudio de la conducta. In: *Psicología de la conducta*. Buenos Aires: EUDEBA.

Bleger, J. (1966). *Psicohigiene y psicología institucional* [Psychohygiene and the psychology of institutions]. Buenos Aires: Paidós.

Bleger, J. (1967). Psycho-analysis of the psycho-analytic frame. *International Journal of Psycho-Analysis, 48*(4): 511–219.

Breuer, J. and S. Freud (1973 [1893–1895]). *Studies on Hysteria*. S.E. Vol. 2. London: The Hogarth Press.

Cesio, F. (1964). El letargo. Una contribución al estudio de la reacción terapéutica negativa. *Revista de Psicoanálisis, 21*(1): 19–27.

Dagfal, A. (2012). *José Bleger y los inicios de una 'Psicología Psicoanalítica' en la Argentina de los años '60*. Buenos Aires: UNLP/UBA. Available at: http://www.elseminario.com.ar/biblioteca.

Green, A. (1990). *El concepto de fronterizo in De locuras privadas* (pp. 88–119). Buenos Aires: Amorrortu Editores.

Isaacs, S. (1948). The Nature and Function of Phantasy. *International Journal of Psychoanalysis, 29*: 73–97.

Klein, M. (1980 [1946]). Notes on Some Schizoid Mechanisms. In: *Envy and Gratitude and Other Works*. London: The Hogarth Press.

Lewin, K. (1952). *Field Theory in Social Science*. London: Tavistock Publications.

Pichon-Rivière, E. (1988 [1971]). *El proceso grupal. Del psicoanálisis a la psicología social*. Buenos Aires: Ediciones Nueva Visión.

Racker, H. (1960) *Estudios sobre técnica psicoanalítica*. Buenos Aires: Paidós.

Vinocur Fischbein, S. (2013) Luisa Álvarez de Toledo. Una analista de avant-garde. *Calibán: Revista Latinoamericana de Psicoanálisis*, *11*(2): 214–222.

5 On Bleger's view of the psychoanalytic frame

A critical approach

B. Miguel Leivi

More than fifty years have passed since José Bleger published his momentous paper, "Psycho-analysis of the psycho-analytic frame" (1967). Many articles have been written along those years; most of them have, after such a long period of time, surely fallen into oblivion or only retained a historical interest. But this hasn't been the fate of Bleger's paper; on the contrary, it has become a classical reference regarding the organization of the psychoanalytic clinical approach and, in particular, of the psychoanalytic setting.

Neither a museum piece to be preserved intact and revered uncritically, as if coated by an aged patina, nor a set of dogmatic injunctions that should be zealously obeyed, Bleger's article owes its classical character to the fact of its being open to engaging in an always renewed dialog with each of its readers, at any time. After all, that is what reading a classic is: an active and ever renewed exchange of ideas between a text and a reader in which, through coincidences, discrepancies, reflections, the reader can, in the last instance, find his own positions in the very process of reading. After the experience, neither the text nor the reader will remain the same. I can remember the surprise I felt when, re-reading in my forties *Rayuela* [Hopscotch], a novel by the Argentine writer Julio Cortázar, I discovered that the characters in the book were people in their forties, full of typical conflicts of that age; when I read it for the first time, at the end of my adolescence, it had seemed to me a book about adolescents.

The article owes its classical character to some central ideas that, well beyond the time of its redaction and also beyond the particularities of Bleger's theoretical and clinical approach, are in my opinion valid for any psychoanalyst, no matter his orientation inasmuch as he practices psychoanalysis. In particular, I would like to stress the value of resorting to psychoanalytic tools to analyze some problems that confront the psychoanalytic clinic, as Bleger does. Other statements are instead ancillary to the author's theoretical models, to his conceptions of the clinical work and also are, many of them, closely related to circumstances of time, place, local customs and traditions, and even to language particularities. These last ones are, of course, inherent parts of the clinical work but cannot,

DOI: 10.4324/9781003252252-7

unlike the first ones, claim a general and uncritical acceptance. Even so, Bleger's clarity and consistency in presenting his ideas and notions allow an enriching confrontation with other analytic approaches and also—considering that the analytic practice, besides its theoretical and technical principles, is always immersed in the multiple circumstances of its time and place—to differentiate between what should be considered inalienable principles of our practice, without which the result should no longer be called psychoanalysis, and what are contingent means that the analyst can resort to, in accordance with his and his patients' realities, without relinquishing an analytic approach in his clinical work.

Bleger's main proposal, the core of his article, "Psycho-analysis of the psycho-analytic frame", means applying psychoanalysis as a critical method to the very organization of our clinical setting, taking the psychoanalytic clinical work as the subject of a psychoanalytic inquiry; it means doing with the analytic frame what an analyst has to do in his clinical work, what his technical and ethical position demands of him: mistrusting certitudes, and always keeping a questioning attitude towards his own way of proceeding, not only when there are problems but also when things seem to go well, even *too* well. Following Bleger's valuable proposal, my intention in this paper is to apply this method to his article, to psychoanalyze his conception of the psychoanalytic frame, to submit his ideas to a critical reading from the perspective provided by some different theoretical and clinical ideas and also by different socio-historic circumstances.

How does Bleger characterize the psychoanalytic frame? Methodologically, as that part of the psychoanalytic situation, taken as a whole, that should be kept constant, immobile, in order that the variables—which constitute the analytic process itself—could be analyzed: "a process can only be investigated when the same constants (frame) are maintained" (Bleger, 1967, p. 241). This is, in his approach, a sine qua non condition, and for that reason the frame constants must be kept invariable (ibid., p. 243) and must be re-established if they have been broken or transgressed; in such a case, "our interpretation *always tends*[1] to maintain [the frame] or to re-establish it" (ibid., p. 242), because "any break of the frame that the analyst introduces or admits [...] disrupts fundamentally any possibility of a deep treatment" (ibid., p. 255).

As can be seen, Bleger equates the methodological constants that define the psychoanalytic approach with the frame; they are for him one and the same thing, and constitute a large set of elements that should all of them be kept constant: "the analyst's role, the ensemble of factors related to space (ambient) and time, and part of the technique (which includes the establishing and maintenance of time and fee arrangements, regulated interruptions, etcetera)" (p. 241). As the *etcetera* shows, the enumeration is not exhaustive, and could be extended. It is in fact larger, and also includes, as Bleger adds somewhat later, at least other factors, like handshaking at the beginning and at the end of the session (ibid., p. 255), or that "the analyst must not accept addressing informally (*tutear*) the patient" (ibid., p. 254).[2]

Bleger's notion of the frame differs from how Freud conceives the organization of the clinical setting, even when he does not speak about the frame; there is no such concept in his works. Resorting in some way to the model of chess, he clearly differentiates, in his Technical Writings, between what are the rules that give the "game" of analyzing its identity on the one side, and, on the other side, what are no more than optional resources, presented as *recommendations* that can at best be used or not, according to each analyst's criterion, to improve his analytic work (Freud, 1913, p. 123).

The first ones, the rules of the game, define what a psychoanalytic approach is, and are for that reason mandatory, even knowing that their "ideal" observance is impossible (ibid., p. 135n): on the patient's part, the fundamental technical rule of free association "that the patient *has to observe*"[3] (ibid., p. 134); on the analyst's part, an evenly suspended attention to everything that is communicated to him (Freud, 1912, p. 111) and an abstention of providing the patient the satisfactions he may demand (Freud, 1915, p. 165), which means conducting the analytic cure "as far as possible, under privation – in a state of abstinence" (Freud, 1919, p. 162). Nothing else. These are for him the only methodological constants that *must* be preserved as they are because their role is crucial in the psychoanalytic approach. Following Freud's metaphor, one could say that they are as defining of the psychoanalytic "game" as the movements of the different pieces are to chess; in case that, for instance, the complicated movement of the knight were altered, the game would become something different, but no longer chess.

The second ensemble of resources, set out by Freud as *recommendations*, is composed by a larger and not exhaustive set of *advices*, "petty details", optional and variable, that can, or cannot be followed:"I [do] not claim any unconditional acceptance for them" (Freud, 1913, p. 123), whose meaning derives "from their relation to the general plan of the game" (ibid.), defined, as has been said, by the fundamental rules. They can be used or modified according to "the extraordinary diversity of the psychical constellations concerned,[4] the plasticity of all mental processes and the wealth of the determining factors" (ibid.).[5] Any "mechanization of the technique" (ibid.) should be avoided. This second list of optional recommendations is comprised of many factors, some of which are included by Bleger among the unmodifiable constants of the frame: external or previous social relationships, arrangements of time and money, interruptions, other possible treatments that could be simultaneously needed, etc. Even the use of the couch is included by Freud in this set of recommendations, inasmuch as it depends to some extent on a personal preference of his.[6]

This distribution is due to Freud's methodological reasons, different, as can be seen, from Bleger's. Insofar as the analytic work aims at unveiling the unconscious of the analyzing subject—who is, essentially and above all, a speaking being—through the analysis of its distorted derivatives, the analytic setting is structured so as to make these unconscious emergences appear, as far as possible, mainly in the field of speech; the basic rules thus organize the peculiarities of the analytic dialog, distributing asymmetrically the places between both participants: he who speaks (free association), he who listens (evenly suspended attention). These are the rules that for Freud admit no variation,[7] because they are the fundamentals of the analytic method.

The other set of heterogeneous factors, and Freud does not completely enumerate these either, aim at improving the analytic work, at doing it more comfortably, more efficiently; sometimes, simply making it possible. Their value thus depends, in a subsidiary way, on how much they benefit the functioning of the basic rules. Inasmuch as they are not part of the fundamentals of the method, they can vary from analyst to analyst, from case to case, in one or another situation; at best, for reasons inherent to the analytic process, to favor it, but they can also vary to cope with extrinsic factors that operate in an unfavorable way on the analytic work. As far as the methodological bases are preserved, resorting to them makes it possible to work analytically even under adverse conditions. This perspective should, in my opinion, especially be taken into account, not only regarding the singularity of any analytic relation, but also the cultural diversity, the multiplicity of changeable socio-economic conditions and the geographic extension over which our analytic practice currently develops.

As has been said, for Freud analysis is a "game" that mainly takes place in the field of speech; so, the fundamentals are for him no different from those which regulate that particular speech relationship between the two participants in the analytic work. I think that no analyst, whatever his orientation, will reject this common ground; but perhaps for many of them that approach could appear insufficient, hence their need of superimposing on it other relationship models in order to provide it more consistency or more guarantees. The disadvantage is that this also causes new problems, and risks locking up the analytic work in a sort of Procrustean bed, deprived of the degree of flexibility allowed by Freud's approach.

In Bleger's case, the superimposed model, taken, one could say, from the natural sciences, seems to be considering the analytic relationship as if it were an experiment or a scientific exploration conducted by a researcher on an investigated object; to study it or to operate upon it, certain parameters must be immobilized, preserved invariable and constant, in order to only explore the factors that have been left as variables. The more elements are thus immobilized, muted, the lesser will they interfere with those being investigated, and the purer and deeper will be the research.

However, Bleger's reasons for thus conceiving the analytic frame are not only methodological; they also depend on his metapsychological model of the psychic development as applied to the clinical work. Just to mention it, because I'm not going to expand on this aspect of the paper, closely related to Bleger's clinical model, the frame has for him the same function that the symbiosis with the mother has for the infant: it serves as a holding, a framework that allows the development of the Ego (Bleger, 1967, p. 244); it contains "the most fixed and stable part of his personality, his 'phantom world', the delusional transference [...] or the psychotic part of his personality; a non-Ego that makes up the framework of the Ego and its identity" (ibid., p. 246). "The frame 'is' the most primitive part of the personality, it is the fusion Ego-body-world, on whose *immobilization* depend the formation, existence and discrimination (of the Ego, the object, the body image, the body, the mind, etcetera)"[8] (ibid., p. 248). From this point of view, it is easy to understand that *always*,[9] in a variable degree, any 'break' of the frame on the part of the analyst causes a *"catastrophic situation"* (ibid., pp. 248–249) and should be strictly avoided.

The need to maintain invariable the constants of the frame has thus a twofold source in Bleger's approach: a methodological one, to guarantee the possibility of a deep analysis of the variables, and a metapsychological one, to sustain the Ego and its identity and to avoid the aforementioned catastrophic situation produced by any break of those constants.

It should therefore be expected that the more the constants of the frame are preserved, the nearer the analytic situation can get to that ideal immobilization, thus avoiding any disruption and ensuring an adequate holding to favor the development of the Ego, the better and safer will the process develop through the profound analysis of its variables. Paradoxically as it may sound, this is not the case.

In fact, as Bleger says, his article aims at exploring, through observations taken from his ample clinical experience, not so much the ruptures of the frame but precisely the opposite situation: the problem raised by "the ideally normal maintenance of a frame" (Bleger, 1967, p. 242): "I want to examine the problem posed by those analyses where the frame is not a problem. But precisely to show that it is a problem" (ibid.). Bleger's open minded and non-dogmatic approach, so Freudian in this aspect of not glossing over the contradictions that may appear but, on the contrary, of exposing them openly and turning them into an object of an analytic exploration, is another of the valuable contributions that imbue this article its classical character.

This problem is widely exposed throughout the paper: a virtually "ideal" analysis, where the frame raises no problem, poses in fact, a dilemma that can become impossible to solve: the more the analytic situation approaches that ideal model, the more problematic it becomes; in the case where the frame is perfectly preserved, what is there immobilized constitutes "the most complete, less known and more unnoticed compulsion to repeat" (ibid., p. 247), containing in it "everything that doesn't show up and *will probably never be analyzable*" (ibid., p. 246);[10] it is "the most persisting, tenacious and unapparent bastion" (p. 245), "an 'addiction' that, if it is not systematically analyzed, can become a stabilized organization, the base of the organization of the personality" (ibid., p. 251).

The question, then, is how to get at this bastion to analyze it when it becomes unattainable due to the ideal preservation of the frame. Bleger says that "we only get to observe it [...] when [the frame] changes or is broken" (ibid., pp. 244–245); in that case, the frame ceases to be mute and its constants, turned into variables, could be analyzed; but such a change must not be introduced or allowed by the analyst; on the contrary, if something like that happens, his task is to reestablish the frame (ibid., p. 242). The author definitely asserts that *"the frame can only be analyzed within the frame*[11] [...], which must be neither ambiguous nor changeable or altered" (ibid., p. 255). These closing sentences of the article are not a conclusion of Bleger's research on the problem but a confirmation of his principles regarding the frame, to which he holds fast in the absence of a solution. The mentioned question on how this analysis can be done remains unanswered: "I can give no answer to that question. My interest is now to set out (to discriminate) the problem" (ibid., p. 246).

The problem is indeed clearly exposed, but what is less clear is to what extent this aporetic situation stems from the very conception of the frame as representing in itself the set of methodological constants, a frame that has been moreover broadened so as to include in it not only the fundamentals but every aspect of the analytic relationship, the undefined ensemble of Freud's optional recommendations, turned into constants of the frame. The analytic task is thus largely deprived of flexibility, of the resources that should allow it making room, as Freud advised, to singularity, to individuality, to the great diversity of circumstances and of changing conditions of any type, inasmuch as the fundamentals are preserved.

As has already been said, the methodological model proposed by Bleger: the technical constants, on the one side, and the variables of the process, on the other, seems to be taken from the empirical sciences, where it is the study led by a researcher on an investigated object. The crucial issue that this approach has to confront when it is applied to psychoanalysis is that a talking relationship between two subjects (isn't this, in the last instance, what an analytic relationship is?), does not easily lend itself to be reduced to a regulated relation between a subject and an object. As the French psychoanalyst Jean Clavreul (1978, p. 15) says, this is the problem of "the scientific objectivation: the impossibility of leaving any place to the question of the subject", which is precisely the main psychoanalytic task. Something in the subject will always resist that reduction; the more regulations are imposed on him for the sake of an ideal objectivity, the more will the subject affirm himself as a resistance to them. That resistance can be expressed openly, through different failures to fulfill the requisites of the frame, but also, on the contrary, as Bleger pointedly observes, through the most faithful compliance, as an "exaggerated obsessive observance" of it (Bleger, 1967, p. 241), which is perhaps the most successful resistance. In a certain sense, it could be said that the innovations introduced by Lacan regarding the constants of the frame, in particular, the non-fixedness of the duration of the sessions,[12] which have been, and still are, highly controversial, mainly aim at confronting this aspect of the resistance, the impasse it frequently produces in many analytic processes.

Bleger also applies, to further substantiate the relationship between process and frame, a difference of logical levels already used in other scientific areas, as, for instance, *language* and *metalanguage, communication* and *metacommunication*, etc. He says: "the frame, being constant, becomes decisive for the phenomena of the *process* of the conduct. In other words, the frame is a *metaconduct*, and on it depend the phenomena that we recognize as conducts"[13] (ibid., p. 244). In this aspect, the most obvious problem occurs when, "sometimes permanently, sometimes sporadically, the frame turns from background of a Gestalt into figure, that is to say, into process" (ibid., p. 242); it ceases then to be "mute", as it should be (ibid., p. 253). But, as has been seen, the silence of the frame when it is strictly complied with represents perhaps an even greater problem. The issue here does not differ from the one just considered: when dealing with speaking beings, what has been excluded from the process, muted and immobilized in the frame as metaconduct or metalanguage, invariably returns as conduct, as speech, and "joins in the conversation" (*Mitsprechen*) (Freud, 1895, p. 296) as part of the process. As Freud says in reference to Dora's repeated unconscious symptomatic action of putting her fingers into and taking them out of her bag, "he that has eyes to see and ears to hear may convince himself that no mortal can keep a secret. If his lips are silent, he chatters with his fingertips..." (Freud, 1905, pp. 77–78). Or, it could be added, also with the constants of the frame.

A wide temporal span separates the time when Bleger wrote his article from the present moment, the time of this exercise of reading it. Countless changes, gradual or critical, impossible to be enumerated even approximately, have occurred everywhere, in every field, social, cultural, political, technological, economical, etc. No society has remained unchanged; no individual has remained untouched by those metamorphoses. Along these years psychoanalysis has frequently been despised as unscientific, criticized as old-fashioned, questioned for carrying and reproducing ideological prejudices; its death has been announced or forecasted several times. As we can see, and also testify, psychoanalysis is still alive and in quite good health, even with all its problems and internal divergences; by contrast, many of those ill omens have fallen into oblivion. Is this survival due to its keeping equal to itself, to its adherence to a clinical practice that remains unmodified in spite of all the supervening changes and mutations or, on the contrary, to its capacity of making room to the myriad of singular and diverse situations it has had to face, while preserving faithfully its fundamentals, which strongly resonate with some trans-historical fundamentals of every subjective constitution, that transcend the epochal changes? As Lacan says, "Freud must be situated in a realistic and tragic tradition, which explains why its lights allow us to read and understand today the Greek tragic writers" (Lacan, 1981 [1956], p. 276), and, conversely, why the great classical tragedies, not only Greek, shed so much light on the subjective conflicts that psychoanalysis has to deal with in present times.

There is a long time span between Bleger's 1967 article and my present reading of it, a period during which much has happened and much has altered too, also in the same society we both belong to. It would, perhaps, be better said, in the society that dwells in our common place of living, which has gone through so many events and changes that one may wonder to what extent it can still be considered the same society. This offers an interesting perspective to evaluate the character of at least some of the constants of the frame proposed by Bleger, precisely those factors that should be considered as related to social uses and customs; in other words, to resume Freud's recommendations—largely referred precisely to contingent social conditions—as different from the methodological fundamentals of the psychoanalytic practice.

Psychoanalysis has been, and is still, in Argentina, and especially in Buenos Aires, very popular. For most people it is completely natural to tell to whichever person they choose that they are attending therapy, or consulting a psychologist or a psychoanalyst, with, by the way, a quite lax discrimination of the type of treatment they are involved in; it is up to psychoanalysts to introduce the necessary differences here. At the same time, our country has been, throughout the years, jumping from crisis to crisis, political, social, economic, and sometimes all these at once; there were also periods of cruel and bloody dictatorship. Analysts and patients have been obliged to take into account each one of those alterations, at times dramatic, and to consider the way each situation struck each person, in order to be able to go on with their work; they have needed to adapt to the rapidly changing conditions, in particular with respect to time and financial arrangements; otherwise, in most cases, the very continuation of the analyses would have become impossible. Keeping these frame constants immutable would have doomed most treatments to interruption.

Yet even in other aspects, not all of them as dramatic as the above-mentioned ones, many changes gradually occurred in social uses, customs and conventions that should also be taken into account regarding the question of the analytic frame. I will confine myself here in considering the way people greet each other, the way they address each other, and how to deal within analysis with these questions. Minor as they can appear, both aspects were covered by Bleger, as it will be recalled, among the constants of the frame.

Handshaking when meeting and parting has become, more than the regular and generalized way of greeting that it mainly was some fifty years ago, an expression of a more formal and distant relationship. For that reason, it is now less customary than it was. It has instead, gradually but consistently, become much more usual, as a way of greeting, to kiss on the cheek, no matter the age, the sex or the gender; it is even very common between men, something that sometimes amazes foreigners. There are no fixed rules thereon, and it does not necessarily mean closeness or express affection. A foreign patient of mine used to say that "Argentina is a land of devaluated kisses; people kiss for no reason, it is only a way of greeting and expresses no feeling", and so it is. How should an analyst behave in that respect in each session, when receiving or seeing off a patient? Should he adopt a uniform and regular way of doing it, let's say, invariably handshaking, or can he adopt, among the now common social use, the way proposed by the patient or that one that spontaneously appears between them? Because, after all, analyst and patient belong to the same society and share to a large extent the same social customs. If the aim of immobilizing the constants of the frame is muting them in order to exclude them from the process, why is one fixed way of greeting necessarily more silent than any other? Given the circumstances, especially if it is imposed, it can, on the contrary, become even noisier. It is, of course, not at all indifferent one way or the other, and the meaning it could acquire in the singularity of an analysis or in some particular situation of it should not be neglected by the analyst; but this shows how difficult, if not at all impossible, it is to exclude from the process any factor by immobilizing it as a constant of the frame. In any case, even muted, it cannot be left out of the analytic process; it will in some way join in the conversation, or it has to be joined into it and taken as a significant part of the process.

Something similar occurs regarding the way of addressing people. Social customs have also been gradually modified in this respect, and the informal way of addressing each other (*tutear, tuteo*) has become most common at any age, much more than the formal way, regardless of age or differences in status. This was something almost inconceivable fifty years ago. There are no fixed rules here either; the formal way, used in professional relationships, between unknown or elder persons, or sometimes by youngsters when addressing somebody elder, implies more distance or respect; but even in these cases the *tuteo* is not at all infrequent. The same previous questions can be put thereon: is it necessary to include this aspect among the constants of the frame? If the answer is "yes", then how? Should it remain as it was fifty years ago or should it adapt to the new conventions which, as already stated, are not at all uniform? Or, conversely, should the analyst use the way proposed by the patient or the one that spontaneously arises between them? Resorting only to the formal way does not have the same implications now it had when Bleger wrote his article, and may be felt as expressing something like coldness or distance, even rejection. With the aim of silencing this aspect of the relationship as a constant of the frame, it can become even noisier.

But it's interesting to consider in more detail the question of the *tuteo*, leaving aside the epochal changes, as it appears in one of the last clinical illustrations of Bleger's article. It was a control case, Bleger being the supervisor. The case had been taken to control because, after several years of analytic work, there was no progress, even when "the patient 'observed' the frame and, in that sense, 'there were no problems'". But, points out Bleger, "*patient and therapist treated each other informally [se tuteaban]*,[14] because the patient proposed it at the beginning of his analysis (and this was accepted by the therapist)" (Bleger, 1967, pp. 253–254). Bleger thus considered that "*the analyst's own frame was corrupted*" because, from his point of view, as already noted, the analyst should not have accepted the *tuteo* proposed by the patient (ibid., pp. 253–254). He considered that this was the reason for the stagnation in the treatment and, consequently, conducted supervision to correct that failure. It took many months to redress the *tuteo*, until it was abandoned by the therapist. That caused "an intense change in the analytic process and a breakdown of the precarious Ego of the patient [...]. Changing the *tuteo* through analysis showed that the case was not a phobic-obsessive character but instead a simple schizophrenia with a phobic-obsessive characterological 'façade'" (ibid., p. 254).

There are no more clinical data of the case. Even so, some questions can be formulated: if modifying the *tuteo* produced such a huge change in the diagnostic appreciation, should it not rather be considered that it was not the frame what had failed but, precisely, the diagnosis of the case? The lack of progress could then perhaps be attributed not to the irregular frame but to that diagnostic error, which implied mistaking a psychotic structure for a characterological case and inadequately undertaking a regular analysis with this patient.[15] The treatment showed no progress, it is true, but, with the agreed frame, which included a reciprocal *tuteo*, the patient was at least stabilized. Imposing a correction of the frame because of its corruption seems to have triggered a psychotic breakdown, contributing paradoxically to produce the very catastrophic situation that the strict preservation of the frame should avoid. From this point of view, would it not have been better, instead of correcting the supposedly failed frame, to reconsider the way in which the patient was being treated? Or even, in the last instance, would it not perhaps have been preferable to proceed with the agreed *tuteo*, albeit with no progress but also without breakdown, instead of forcing such a change, with its undesired consequences? These are no more than clinical speculations, but they bring up another clinical and technical alternative based on a different point of view regarding the questions of the structural differential diagnostic, on the one side, and the methodological constants on the other.

I am writing this paper in the middle of the Coronavirus pandemic, limited by a strict quarantine that impedes the usual in-person analytic sessions with my patients. As surely most analysts are doing all around the world, I'm working with my analytic patients, those who have accepted, by resorting to the virtual means now available: WhatsApp, Skype, phone, etc. This certainly is an exceptional situation, but unfortunately there is no lack of exceptional circumstances of any kind. It is of course impossible to think which could have been Freud's recommendations thereon, as impossible as to imagine Bleger's ideas regarding the frame in the present circumstances, but it is, however, clear that clinging to a strict and all-comprehensive conception of the frame would have made the continuation of the analyses completely impossible. Even the IPA has admitted online training analyses during the pandemic, something that had never been accepted before.

Online analysis is not of course an elective resource, at least for me, and the experience is quite different from in-person analysis. Many dimensions of the analytic exchange are surely lost; Freud would have never been able, for instance, to perceive Dora's chattering with her fingertips, inasmuch as they are left out of the screen image of the computer; other aspects bring new and unexpected dilemmas, as for example that one is never sure whether a silence is a silence or an interruption of the communication, and so on. The above-mentioned issues referring to that shaking of hands or with a kiss, obviously, are completely out of the question. Even so, if it is still possible to keep an analytic work going under such limited conditions, this is surely a demonstration that, in the last instance, the core of an analytic experience is essentially a particular speech exchange; in consequence, there can be analysis even amid so many unfavorable circumstances as long as the methodological fundamentals, which refer precisely to that exchange—free association, evenly suspended attention, rule of abstinence—can still be preserved.

It is quite impossible to foresee to what normality we will return once the pandemic is over, including our customary in-person analysis, but it is to be hoped that some experience should be drawn from our current work in the present circumstances. Exceptional situations usually strain and challenge admitted ideas and procedures; at best, they can leave behind important learnings and permanent changes. The question of the methodological fundamentals and the constants of the frame are issues that deserve being considered under the light of the experience we are living through, in order to better know where Ockham's razor should be applied. I have no doubt that Bleger's article will be a very important element in that future discussion, thus renewing its condition of being a classic.

Notes

1 Emphasis by the author.
2 In Spanish, as well as in other languages, like French, but not in English and other languages, there are at least two different ways of addressing another person: a more formal, respectful and distant one (*usted, vous*) and a more informal, familiar and near one (*tú* – or *vos* in some countries – *tu*), which is called in Spanish *tutear, tuteo*. Bleger considers that the formal way of addressing the patient (*usted*) is also a constant of the frame and is, for that reason, the only one to be used when addressing the patient, even if the patient uses *tuteo* to address the analyst.
3 My emphasis.
4 This obviously includes the individuality of the analyst himself.
5 As Lacan (1975 [1954], p. 16) says, "… they were, for Freud, an instrument, in the sense it is said of a tailor-made tool. Basically, he says, it is tailored to my hand, and this is how I hold it. Others would perhaps prefer a somewhat different instrument, more suitable to their hand …".
6 "I hold to the plan of getting the patient to lay on a sofa while I sit behind him out of his sight […] (this ceremonial) deserves to be maintained for many reasons. The first is a personal motive, but one which others may share with me. I cannot put up with being stared at by other people for eight hours a day (or more)" (Freud, 1913, pp. 133–134).
7 It should be remembered, for instance, his answer to the Rat Man when he asked Freud to be released from the obligation of telling all the details of his great obsessive fear: "I could not grant him something which was beyond my power. He might just as well ask me to give him the moon …"(Freud, 1909, p. 166).
8 Emphasis by the author.
9 Emphasis by the author.
10 Emphasis by the author.
11 Emphasis by the author.
12 "Time, far from being part of what the analysts call the 'frame', is part of the very process…" (Soler, 1984), p. 118).
13 Emphasis by the author.
14 Emphasis by the author.
15 As may be remembered, Freud (1913, p. 124) advised beginning with a short provisional treatment, "for a period of one to two weeks […] to decide whether it is a suitable (case) for psychoanalysis", precisely to avoid committing such a mistake.

References

Bleger, J. (1967). Psicoanálisis del encuadre psicoanalítico. *Revista de Psicoanálisis, 24*(2): 241–258.
Clavreul, J. (1978). *L'ordre médical*. Paris: Éditions du Seuil.
Freud, S. (with J. Breuer) (1895). *Studies on Hysteria*. S.E. Vol. 2. London: The Hogarth Press.
Freud, S. (1905). Fragment of an Analysis of a Case of Hysteria. S.E. Vol. 7 (pp. 7–122). London: The Hogarth Press.
Freud, S. (1909). Notes upon a Case of Obsessional Neurosis. S.E. Vol. 10 (pp. 155–249). London: The Hogarth Press.
Freud, S. (1912). Recommendations to Physicians Practising Psycho-Analysis. S.E. Vol. 12 (pp. 111–120). London: The Hogarth Press.

Freud, S. (1913). On Beginning the Treatment. S.E. Vol. *12* (pp. 123–144). London: The Hogarth Press.

Freud, S. (1915). Observations on Transference Love. S.E. Vol. *12* (pp. 159–171). London: The Hogarth Press.

Freud, S. (1919). Lines of Advance in Psychoanalytic Therapy. S.E. Vol. *17* (pp. 159–168). London: The Hogarth Press.

Lacan, J. (1975 [1954]). *Le Séminaire, Livre I: Les Écrits Techniques de Freud*. Paris: Éditions du Seuil.

Lacan, J. (1981 [1956]). *Le Séminaire, Livre III: Les Psychoses*. Paris: Éditions du Seuil.

Soler, C. (1984). Standards no standards. In: *Tercer encuentro internacional del campo freudiano: ¿cómo se analiza hoy?* (pp. 100–121). Buenos Aires: Manantial.

6 Of things that are not visible

José Bleger: A clinician for our times?

Howard B. Levine

Bion (1970) was very clear in asserting that the focus of psychoanalytic attention, "the realizations with which a psycho-analyst deals" (p. 7), emotions and states of mind, belong to a domain of "experience that is not sensuous" (p. 7) and so cannot be discovered directly by empirical observation. He continually asked the question: "… how are we to see, observe … these things which are not visible?"(Bion, 2005).

And even if "these things" come to be known, most often by intuition, there is an additional problem of finding the words with which to speak of them; a process that Bion (1962, 1970) called "publication".

There is a limitation to thought and language in regard to the infinitizing[1] dimension of Experience.[2] A portion of the latter is always untransformable and so there is an inevitable slippage or remainder left out as we move from O → K; between raw, unrepresented existential Experience and the psychic capacity to represent and delimit aspects of that Experience as "thought"; and then again in the transformational movement from thought into language: words that are addressed to another or verbalized to one's self within one's own mind, literally or metaphorically (what we colloquially call our "thoughts"). These *residues of the irrepresentable* present us with an epistemological problem: What do we know and how do we know that we know it? This problem has continued to intrigue and perplex philosophers as well as psychoanalysts and probably can never be resolved.[3]

As neophyte analytic psychotherapists-in-training and as analytic candidates, we are told to help our patients to free associate and "put their feelings into words". The purpose of this instruction is to try to help both patient and analyst gain access to what has been repressed. The latter has too often been referred to and equated with "the unconscious". In contemporary psychoanalysis, the concept of the unconscious has increasingly been seen to include far more than that which is repressed. This broader conceptualization of the unconscious, one that includes forces that are *unrepresented* in addition to thoughts—and perhaps feelings[4]—that are repressed, was already formulated by Freud (1923) in his conception of the Id. However, in the enthusiasm of applying the lessons learned from

DOI: 10.4324/9781003252252-8

the topographic theory to the treatment of neurosis and the enormous clinical gains that it offered, the implications of Freud's emendation to his theory have not always been systematically worked out or appreciated.

For many analysts and for many years, psychoanalysis has been essentially synonymous with the psychoanalysis of neurosis. So, for example, Leivi (Chapter 5, this volume) writes:

> Insofar as the analytic work aims at unveiling the unconscious of the analyzing subject—who is, essentially and above all, a speaking being—through the analysis of its distorted derivatives, the analytic setting is structured so as to make these unconscious emergences appear, as far as possible, mainly in the field of speech; the basic rules thus organize the peculiarities of the analytic dialog, distributing asymmetrically the places between both participants: he who speaks (free association), he who listens (evenly suspended attention). These are the rules that for Freud admit no variation,[5] because they are the fundamentals of the analytic method.

There is much in this characterization that is still valuable and still true. The very structure of the classical analytic setting, Freud's *talking* cure, is designed to channel Experience into language, in the service of Bion's "metabolization"—that is, containment via representation—and communication.

Parsons (1999), discussing Green's work, goes even further, suggesting: "The structure of the [classical] analytic setting is itself a representation of internal mental structure. It not only gives access to internal structure, it embodies it" (p. 64); "… the lying down, the frequency and the silence [of the analyst] are all examples of how the analytic setting is set up to embody the negation of ordinary reality" (p. 69). And he concludes: "If the analytic setting represents in its external structure the internal activity of negation, and if … negation is essential to the creation of psychic reality, this means that the structure of the analytic situation represents the process by which psychic reality is constituted" (Parsons, 1999, p. 69).

Parson's statement about setting is also a statement about elements in the *analytic situation* (Donnet, 2009) that are necessary, but perhaps not sufficient, to optimize the conditions in which an analytic process can take place. The term, analytic situation, combines the analytic action, the space-time in which it occurs, the offer of the mind, attitude and participation of an analyst and the rules and procedures that structure the nature of the encounter. What will prove decisive for any analytic situation is the degree to which the patient can use "the resources of the site" (ibid., p. 35), each in his or her own particular way, "through an experience of found-created" (ibid., p. 35). This Winnicottian reference is further amplified in Donnet's description that when analysis goes well, what develops is a pair-specific functional unity constituted by the ensemble 'analysand-analyst-situation'. That is to say, a binding unity between the patient's intra-psychic processes and their externalization on the stage of transference; but also between the mental processes of the two protagonists, to the extent of realising, through the interplay of transference and counter-transference, an activity of co-thought, a field (Baranger), a partial fusion, by bringing into play primitive identificatory processes, i.e., a shared area of play.

(Donnet, 2009, p. 35)

Thus, Donnet insisted that "… the analyzing situation takes the form of a structure integrating the analysand-analyst couple in its capacity for self-organization, as well as the dynamic processes of its disorganizations-reorganizations" (Donnet, 2009, p. 36).

Restating Donnet's and Parsons' comments in Bleger's terms, we can say that *the classical frame offered by the analyst* contains within its features an analogue to and embodiment of the psychic apparatus. It is serendipitously designed to embody, replicate and energize the transformational capacities of the neurotic-normal sectors of the psyche.

But this is a description of the classical setting used for the analysis of neurotic patients and the dynamic unconscious, that is, the represented, repressed sectors of the psyche. While it can take us a long way clinically, it can only get us so far. As Freud himself came to discover—see his metapsychological change from the first topography (the Topographic theory) to the second (the Structural Theory)—this is a goal that can only be striven for and at best, approached asymptotically. The difficulties, often futility, of trying to contain and work through the primitive agonies encountered in borderline and other patients whose difficulties are "beyond neurosis" or to work through the problems of "the psychotic part of the mind" are attested to in the refrain of the protagonist in T.S. Eliot's poem, *Sweeney Agonistes*: "It ain't no good, it ain't no good, I gotta use *words* when I talk to you." (Eliot, 1932, italics added).

Put another way, as psychoanalysis has attempted to expand its reach beyond the borders of neurotic organization to patients in what used to be called "the widening scope" of psychoanalysis, we have been challenged by the question: To what extent and in what ways are words useful, when the problem lies in the part of the mind that is not yet represented? How far do words reach, especially when we are dealing with forces that have not yet come into the domain of thought, much less language? This is the essence of the problem that I think Bleger (1967) was trying to address.

His classic paper opens up many different avenues of thought and moves in many rich and important directions, for example, the socio-cultural and institutional contributions to our identities and sense of self. At its core, however, is a clinical exigency that arises from the problems rooted in our earliest infantile[6] (pre-verbal) Experience. These are the problems that manifest themselves in phenomena such as borderline personalities, primitive narcissism, self-destructive behavior, negative therapeutic reactions, addictions, perversions, psychosomatics, etc. These phenomena led Freud (1923) to change his theory from one centered on representations (the Topographic Theory) to one (the Structural Theory) that tried to more clearly take into account his conception of the drives.[7] These are the issues and problems, the most difficult patients, that contemporary analysts continue to struggle with.

In designating *the frame* as the locus of each individual's silent symbiosis and the depository for the psychotic parts of the personality, Bleger was trying to say something about:

- how each of us attempts to stabilize ourselves
- where the most unstabilized and destabilizing parts of the psyche may be located
- what happens when that stabilizing structure is altered or threatens to break down.

He emphasizes that

> the frame *always* makes up a "ghost world", that of the most primitive and undifferentiated organization. In most instances, that ghost world holds in check the powerfully chaotic, unrepresented forces that are the residues of the earliest mis-attunements and failures of environmental provision. When the frame is threatened or ruptured, the symbiosis and containment may be fractured apart, these forces let loose and what was hidden, silent and "dumb" … reveals itself.
>
> (Bleger, 1967, p. 512).

If we look at the problems that result from a disrupted frame from the perspective of the analyst's wish to help the patient, then we see the patient behaving in ways that might be described as "attacks on" or "attempts to control" the analyst. However, looked at from the perspective of a desperate need to preserve or revivify an object or prevent destabilization and annihilation of the self, then we may have a different sense of what is driving the chaos. When dealing with the psychotic parts of the patient's mind, the question that analysts may have to ask of themselves is: What are the meta-conditions felt or actually needed by the patient to achieve sufficient symbiotic stability so as to guarantee the establishment and preservation of a sense of self and the vitality of self and object?

Although Bleger's paper alerts us to the dangerously disruptive consequences of alterations or threatened breaks in the frame, what he also brilliantly calls our attention to, and what I think is of the greatest concern to him, are "the cases in which the frame is being respected … [There,] the problem lies in the fact that the frame itself is the receiver of the symbiosis and that the latter is not present in the analytic process itself" (pp. 512–513). This, Bleger tells us, is the ultimate and most problematic resistance, 'the most powerful, endurable and at the same time least apparent, "bulwark".

What he is warning us about and calling attention to here are the many cases of intellectualized insight, pseudo-analysis, and analyses of *neurotic* processes that do not reach deeply enough into the unrepresented, pre-verbal, symbiotic core of the problem. His caution reminds me of a remark that Winnicott made in response to an analytic impasse that was brought to him for consultation. He said something to the effect that analyst and patient had a psychotic fish on a long neurotic line that neither one of them wanted to land. A similar remark was made by Horacio Etchegoyen, at a panel of the American Psychoanalytic Association which discussed an ego psychologically based analysis presented by Ed Weinshel: "The difference between us, Ed, is that our analyses begin where your analyses end." (Levine, 1992).

For Bleger, the anxieties, defenses and impulsive reactions that occur during weekend breaks, longer absences and once termination is decided upon, are related to threatened or actual ruptures of the frame that let loose the untamed forces that were held in check by a silent symbiosis. At that point, what had been hidden in the invariant of non-process, can make waves—often tsunamis!—that then become very much a part of a process and can go on to be observed and hopefully analyzed.

Taking this further, we can infer from Bleger's comments about how the analysis and its frame becomes an "institution" and how institutions in the social surround are used as stabilizing frameworks for the ordinary living of our lives,[8] that even outside of analysis, our socio-cultural surround provides us with suitable repositories for our psychotic parts, so that they can be contained, hidden and prevented from causing chaos and disruption. That is, as long as our usual socio-cultural and familial institutions remain in place. I will only briefly remind readers of the huge "institutional" disruptions caused by the COVID-19 pandemic at numerous levels. These reach beyond the enormous change in therapeutic setting from in-office sessions to telemetry to include the attenuation and loss of institutional contact in our daily lives required by social distancing and quarantine. Each change produced profound and variable responses in ourselves and in our patients.[9]

Bleger's formulation also raises the question of the *co-existence of multiple frames*, an aspect of his paper that has not always been appreciated. In the case of Mr. A, he notes that "It was only with 'unfulfillment' of his 'ghost world' that he [the patient] was able to see that my frame was different from his" (p. 513).

The disturbance produced by the analyst's "unfulfillment" of the expectations silently embedded in the patient's frame brought the disparity to light so that its consequences could be analyzed. That is, the discord produced by the discrepant goals moved this aspect of the patient's "ghost world" and its consequences from frame into process. What Bleger emphasizes, however, is not just the consequences of the disruption, but in regard to analyses in general, "how much this area does not appear and is therefore never likely to be analysed." (p. 513).

Bleger goes on to compare the problems of the silent symbiosis to character analyses, where "the character feature ... must be turned into a symptom in order to be analysed" (p. 513). He notes, however, that the problem in regard to the frame is infinitely more difficult, because its resolution often involves re-ordering "the groundwork on which the ego and the identity of the individual are built up" (p. 513). Although it may be growth obstructing and lead to maladaptive narcissistic strains, the silent symbiosis embedded in the frame is, at the same time, the patient's most effective—perhaps only—available defense against chaos. Is this not the problem of the patient's needing to face and accept the feelings aroused by the threat of true analytic movement that Bion (1962, 1970) called *catastrophic change*?

In further discussing the case of Mr. A, Bleger then makes the observation that "Patients with 'acting-in' tendencies or psychotic patients also bring 'their own frame', and *the institution of their primitive symbiotic relationship*; yet not only they, but all patients bring it too" (p. 515).

Here we have a formulation of *multiple frames*. If analyst and patient bring their own frames, then perhaps we should ask if they each bring multiple frames, conscious and unconscious? Is this a corollary or consequence of what, for example, Sandler (1983) has described as conscious and unconscious theories of analytic process and cure? Remember that Bleger has—rightly I think—included the *analyst's theory* in his description of the components of the frame. So, perhaps we should expect to encounter Freudian frames, Kleinian frames, Lacanian frames, etc. And also, my version of *my* Freudian frame; your version of *your* Freudian frame, etc.

To what extent has the classical frame, which works suitably in a general and generic sense for neurotic patients and parts of the mind, become concretized and fetishized into its own ritual and institution at the expense of flexibility sometimes needed to address the analytic needs of the non-neurotic patient and the psychotic portions of the mind, more broadly defined? How many patients have inadvertently found themselves locked into the Procrustean bed of an analyst's frame and the expectations that it has generated and so found themselves in a situation that does not fit optimally enough with their capacities or *their* frame? Do the ensuing misattunements and misfits recreate parallels to early infantile difficulties? How often do they threaten or actualize a too early destabilization of the containment of the patient's symbiosis leading to either adhesive compliance or chaotic eruptions of the forces of their psychotic parts jeopardizing the treatment from the very start?

As a final thought, I would like to return to Donnet's (2009) adumbration of the analytic situation, which adds the site and its resources to the process and frame to make up an essential ensemble on offer to the patient. A patient who begins analysis unable to make use of the resources of the site may nevertheless ultimately benefit from an analysis, if it takes place within a frame that allows for, values and includes an analytic logic of transformation and developmental facilitation.[10] Once analytic theory is extended in this way, then we can begin to understand the meaning of saying that in the treatment of patients whose problems lie at the limits of what we usually have thought of as analyzable, *the analytic process may have to take place internally and silently within the mind of the analyst for long periods of time.* A typescript of the manifest discourse of such a period in the treatment might seem "supportive" or "banal", even "non-analytic", because the patient has not yet arrived at a place where they possessed the functional capacity to use the resources of the site— free association, recognition of unconscious desires through use of the analyst as an object of transference, etc. And yet, the seemingly non-analytic interventions of the analyst may be being tracked internally and silently by the analyst within an analytic theory[11] and vision of a transformational or developmental analytic process that will eventuate in a more manifest form as the patient's capacities for representation and psychic elaboration develop and evolve. (In Bion's (1962) terms, as their alpha function strengthens and their capacity for containment grows more robust).

In regard to the question of whether or not we can rightly speak of an *internal frame* (Parsons (2007; L. Bleger, Chapter 1, this volume), I would suggest that certainly within each analyst—and hopefully, ultimately within each analysand—there should exist a space for dreams, imagination and intuition within which one can think analytically about whatever the patient is reporting or the analyst is experiencing. Green (1980, 2005) speaks of a *framing structure* and describes it as the result of the negative hallucination of the mother's *holding* in both a literal physical and a metaphorical "providing" sense. This structure is the internalized heir of Winnicott's *primary maternal preoccupation.* These are the earliest caretaking transactions that do go well, so well that Winnicott proposed that they appear to the infant as if they were created by the very wish or need itself and so support unstated assumptions of omnipotence and symbiotic fusion. When articulated with the details of the analyst's particular analytic theory, the framing structure enables the analyst to maintain an analytic attitude (Schafer, 1983) towards whatever the patient is doing or saying and allows for a presumptive, silent, running analytic account of the process within the mind of the analyst.

The title of Bleger's paper can now be seen to have a double meaning. The frame and its vicissitudes, the possibilities that it affords and the problems that it causes when threatened or disrupted are certainly in need of being analyzed. But in analyzing the frame and its place in our theory and practice, in clarifying the metapsychological status and meaning of the frame, in pointing out that it is far more than a matter of administrative details such as time, money and conduct, he has made a significant contribution to and deepened our understanding of the analysis itself.

Notes

1 See Bergstein, 2019.
2 I use the word Experience, written with a capital E, to indicate raw existential Experience, that is unknowable in its entirety by the human mind. In Bion's terms, Experience is in the domain of the infinite, (O), while that part of it that can become known, and that we colloquially call our "experience" and can be known, is in the domain of (K). See Levine (2013).
3 See Levine (2022) for a broad discussion of these issues, or Stanicke, Zachrisson and Vetlesen (2020) for a more focused discussion of Freud's Kantian epistemological heritage (*noumenon* vs. *phenomenon*).
4 I say "perhaps feelings", because Freud (1915) stated that only thoughts (ideationally saturated representations) were subject to repression and emotions (feelings) were not. The latter could be attenuated—perhaps suppressed and kept from being consciously felt—if their accompanying feelings were kept out of consciousness. Not every analyst seems to agree with this description and so it is a matter of continued debate whether or not feelings may also be directly subject to repression.
5 It should be remembered, for instance, his answer to the Rat Man when he asked Freud to be released from the obligation of telling all the details of his great obsessive fear: "I could not grant him something which was beyond my power. He might just as well ask me to give him the moon ..." (Freud, 1909, p. 166).
6 The word, "infantile", is most apt here, because it comes from the Latin, meaning "without speech".
7 As Green convincingly describes it, the major development in Freud's revision of theory was the change from "one model, at the centre of which one finds a form of thinking (desire, hope, wish), to another model based on the act (impulse as internal action, automatism, acting) ... the analyst now not only has to deal with unconscious desire but with the drive itself, whose force (constant pressure) is undoubtedly its principle characteristic, capable of subverting both desire and thinking" (Green, 2005, p. 47).
8 See his citation of the work of Elliot Jaques (1951) who says that "social institutions are unconsciously used as a defence against psychotic anxiety" (Bleger, 1967, p. 514).
9 For a series of detailed discussions of these matters and others related to the pandemic, I would refer readers to *Psychoanalysis and Covidian Life: Common Distress, Individual Experience*, ed. by H.B. Levine and A. de Staal (London: Phoenix, 2021).
10 See for example, Levine (2010), where I advocate for a two-track psychoanalysis, transformational as well as archeological and Levine (2022), where I explore these and related issue at length. But these writings are just one of many variations on the theme of enlarging the scope and reach of psychoanalytic treatment.
11 For example, as interpretations *in* the transference rather than *of* the transference. See Sechaud (2008).

References

Bergstein, A. (2019). *Bion and Meltzer's Expedition Into Unmapped Mental Life.* Abingdon and New York: Routledge.

Bion, W.R. (1962). *Learning From Experience.* London: Heinemann.

Bion, W.R. (1970). *Attention and Interpretation.* New York: Basic Books.

Bion, W.R. (2005). *The Italian Seminars.* London: Karnac.

Bleger, J. (1967). Psycho-analysis of the psycho-analytic frame. *International Journal of Psychoanalysis, 48*(4): 511–519.

Bleger, L. (2022) What is the setting after all? (Chapter 1 this volume).

Donnet, J-L. (2009). *The Analyzing Situation.* London: Karnac.

Eliot, T.S. (1932). *Sweeney Agonistes: Fragments of an Aristophanic Melodrama.* New York: Faber & Faber.

Freud, S. (1909). Notes upon a Case of Obsessional Neurosis. S.E. Vol. *10* (pp. 155–249). London: The Hogarth Press.

Freud, S. (1915). The Unconscious. S.E. Vol. *14* (pp. 166–204). London: The Hogarth Press.

Freud, S. (1923). The Ego and the Id. S.E. Vol. *19* (pp. 109–124). London: The Hogarth Press.

Green, A. (1975). The analyst, symbolization and absence in the analytic setting (On changes in analytic practice and analytic experience)—In memory of D.W. Winnicott. *International Journal of Psycho-Analysis, 56*: 1–22.

Green, A. (1980). The Dead Mother. In: A. Green (1997). *On Private Madness* (pp. 142–173). London: Karnac.

Green, A. (2005). *Key Ideas For A Contemporary Psychoanalysis. Misrecognition and Recognition of the Unconscious.* Trans. A. Weller. London and New York: Routledge.

Jaques, E. (1951). *The Changing Culture of a Factory.* London: Tavistock Publications.

Leivi, B.M. (2022). On Bleger's view of the psychoanalytical frame: A critical approach. (Chapter 5, this volume).

Levine, H.B. (1992). Freudian and Kleinian Theory: A Dialogue of Comparative Perspectives. Panel reported by Howard B. Levine. *Journal of the American Psychoanalytical Association, 40*: 801–826.

Levine, H.B. (2010). Creating analysts, creating analytic patients. *International Journal of Psycho-Analysis, 91*: 1385–1404.

Levine, H.B. (2011). Construction Then and Now. In: *On Freud's "Constructions in Analysis"*, ed. S. Lewkowicz and T. Bokanowski with G. Pragier (pp. 87–100). London: Karnac.

Levine, H.B. (2013). The Colourless Canvas: Representation, Therapeutic Action, and the Creation of Mind. In: *Unrepresented States and the Creation of Meaning*, ed. H.B. Levine, G. Reed and D. Scarfone (pp. 42–71). London: Karnac/IPA.

Levine, H.B. (2020). Reflections on therapeutic action and the origins of psychic life. *Journal of the American Psychoanalytical Association, 68*: 9–25.

Levine, H.B. (2022). *Affect, Representation and Language: Between the Silence and the Cry.* Abingdon and New York: Routledge/IPA.

Levine, H.B. and A. de Staal (eds.) (2021). *Psychoanalysis and Covidian Life: Common Distress, Individual Experience.* London: Phoenix.

Parsons, M. (1999). *Psychic Reality, Negation and the Analytic Setting.* In: *The Dead Mother*, ed. G. Kohon (pp. 59–75). London: The New Library of Psychoanalysis.

Parsons, M. (2007). Raiding the inarticulate: The internal analytic setting and listening beyond countertransference. *International Journal of Psycho-Analysis, 88*: 1441–1456.

Sandler, J. (1983). Reflections on some relations between psychoanalytic concepts and psychoanalytic practice. *International Journal of Psychoanalysis, 64*: 35–45.

Schafer, R. (1983). *The Analytic Attitude*. New York: Basic Books.

Sechaud, E. (2008). The handling of the transference in French psychoanalysis. *International Journal of Psycho-Analysis, 89*: 1011–1028.

Stanicke, E., A. Zachrisson, and A.J. Vetlesen (2020). The epistemological stance of psychoanalysis: Revisiting the Kantian legacy. *The Psychoanalytic Quarterly, 89*: 281–304.

7 Thirst for infinity and the analytic frame

Reflections on Bleger and Matte-Blanco

Riccardo Lombardi

Bion (1984 [1970]) brought about an important shift in focus concerning psychoanalysis of the Repressed Unconscious described by Freud (1915) to the Unrepressed Unconscious, by reformulating the opposition conscious/unconscious in terms of finite/infinite. The perspective of the Unrepressed Unconscious was more systematically developed by Ignacio Matte-Blanco (1998 [1975], 1988), who concentrated his research on the logical characteristics of the unconscious, reformulating in a more concise manner Freud's description in *The Interpretation of Dreams* (1900) and in the essay, "The Unconscious" (1915).

Before discussing the relationship between Bleger's research on the psychoanalytic frame and the deep mental functioning described by Matte-Blanco, I think it is useful to present some of the essential characteristics of his thinking.

Symmetry and infinity in Matte-Blanco's thinking

Matte-Blanco therefore surpasses the traditional distinction between conscious and unconscious in order to focus on the logical functioning, reducing the various characteristics of the Freudian Unconscious (the absence of both mutual contradiction and negation, displacement, condensation, timelessness and the replacement of external by internal reality) to two basic logical principles: the generalization principle and the symmetry principle, with a view in order to making Freud's discovery more directly accessible in terms of clinical technique. The principle of symmetry, which characterizes the functioning of the unconscious, acts, according to Matte-Blanco, like an acid that removes all differentiations, so that all elements become identical and indistinguishable. The operation of the principle of symmetry is particularly evident in our most difficult patients; it is very like what von Domarus (1944) and Arieti (1974) have described as "paleological thinking." The functioning of the consciousness is characterized by the asymmetry principle which allows the introduction of distinction and discrimination. The two Symmetry and Asymmetry principles

DOI: 10.4324/9781003252252-9

always co-exist within the mind and they combine in various ways according to higher or lower levels of mental integration.

For Matte-Blanco, the concept of feeling implies, in addition to symmetrical relations, the concept of infinite sets: emotional experience is, in fact, typified by its engrossing and infinitizing nature, as a result of which the object is invested with all the characteristics of the class to which it belongs. In point of fact, the infinite occupies emotion! Dealing clinically with profound emotions is not without its difficulties and dangers, but it does have enormous potential for mental growth.

The finite and the limit, or boundary, are the direct opposites of the infinite. I think that the limit, or boundary, is the key concept of contemporary psychoanalysis to the extent that it dynamically opposes the formless infinite of primitive mental states (Lombardi, 2018).

Departing from this opposition between the absence of limits, which characterizes the deep mental functioning, and that limit which allows the mind to function in creating distinctions, we can imagine a connection between Matte-Blanco's perspective and Bleger's study of the analytic frame.

The frame and space-time limits

Bleger's study of the analytic frame introduces an element that has become increasingly important in psychoanalysis with progressive broadening of the treatment to serious cases where extreme fragmentation and lability of the space-time categories align the mind with the parameters of Unconscious functioning. In this context, I will utilize the expressions of the analytic frame as the equivalent of analytic setting and vice versa.

When the difficult patient brings intolerance to boundaries to the point of losing themselves in a formless infinity (Lombardi, 2015), the analytic frame can provide the necessary conditions that allow access to space-time parameters. The function of setting is therefore not to be misinterpreted as an expression of analytic authority, and hence the Superego, but rather as an important element related to the activation of the functions of the Ego. For this to happen it is useful to regard the setting not as a "rule" for its own sake, but rather for the important functions that this parameter carries out in an experience such as analysis, which involves the unconscious: the work on the unconscious therefore cannot be separated from a frame, that allows the approach with areas free from distinction, without risking being overwhelmed by the absence of limits characterized by the unconscious. This emphasis on the structure is particularly useful with patients with serious representative deficiencies, where access to traditional mental elaboration becomes almost impossible.

If Bleger, in an "object relation" perspective, underlines the correlation between the role of the frame and that of the mother, I would like to underline the connection between the analytic frame and the structure of the unconscious with respect to the clinical implications that are thereby derived thanks to Matte-Blanco's contribution (Matte-Blanco, 1998 [1975], 1988).

Bleger writes:

> Symbiosis with the mother (immobility of the non-ego) enables the child to develop his ego. The frame has a similar function: it acts as support, as mainstay, but, so far, we have been able to perceive it only when it changes or breaks. The most powerful, endurable, and at the same time least apparent, "bulwark" is, then, the one that lies on the frame.
>
> (Bleger, 1967, p. 513)

The emphasis on the symbiosis with the mother introduced by Bleger refers to levels connoted by an absence of differentiation: in the patient's subjective world, a subject differentiated in time and in space does not yet exist, making the recognition of alterity impossible. The symbiosis with the mother described by Bleger corresponds to that which I described as utilizing Matte-Blanco's perspective (Lombardi, 2015), Symmetrical Transference: the principle of symmetry impregnates the transfer with functions that, according to the different phases of evolution of the patient, may be of a constructive or destructive nature. In the constructive sense, in particular, the symmetrical transfer allows us to work within the analysand's more archaic zones and deepest conflicts with themselves. The push towards the infinite can be, however, pursued by the patient with an emotional intensity capable of violating the realistic parameters of space-time, sometimes at the cost of obstructing destructively the relationship with one's own life (Lombardi, 2018), or even annihilating it by means of suicide, which presupposes the fantasy of access to a situation without limits—as often occurs in many adolescent suicides. The psychoanalytic frame then plays a fundamental role in the clinical work with these patients, counteracting and balancing the dangerous force of the principle of symmetry.

When the symbolic working through appears almost impossible due to the analysand's limited representational resources, the Setting becomes the last "bastion", as Bleger would have said, in defending the access to space-time and to a mental world. At times the acting-out against the analytic frame is able to elicit aspects of the psychotic zone of the personality which would otherwise be precluded from representation. As Bleger points out: "I must emphasize, however, that the maintenance of the frame was what led to the analysis of the psychotic part of his personality [...] how much of this area does not appear and is therefore never likely to be analysed." (Bleger, 1967, p. 513). The analytic frame defined in the initial analytic contract, connoted by parameters such as time and money, can be utilized by the analyst then as an instrument of containment of the patient's omnipotent and infinite pushes, defending the relationship with the limits of space-time, as a condition of access to the mental functioning.

A clinical case story

I would like to take into consideration the case of Mara, a 40-year-old patient who requested analysis out of fear that the trembling of her hands would be noticed and for occasional panic attacks. I, however, did not observe any trembling and medical tests did not reveal any disorders. Regardless, the patient complained that the problem was unbearable and had tried several psychotherapies, none of which had produced any results.

We began a program of three sessions a week on the couch, clarifying from the outset the usual conditions of the settings that implied a commitment to the continuity of the sessions and the requirement of payment, even if missed. Quite soon the patient showed signs of intolerance because she felt disappointed in not seeing an immediate improvement in her symptomology. Neither the realization that the analytic working-through could not be immediate, nor acknowledgment that it demanded a realistic period of time, helped her to respect the time she needed. Mara lived out of the city and had to drive an hour to reach my office. She liked to drive fast and when she got to 160–180 Km/h she would experience the pleasant sensation of being on a cloud suspended over the ground. When I warned her of the dangers of speeding, she laughed at me, because she thought it was a pointless concern on my part. Realizing my impotence and alarmed by a suicidal component in this analysand that I had underestimated, I told Mara that if she wanted to die in a road accident, I was not able to save her because only she was responsible for her own safety.

In contrast to her speeding, Mara's analysis itself moved forward slowly and with difficulty, not helped by her tendency to skip sessions. Her communications in the session were slow and often led to a silence that was impervious to my solicitations. One day she confessed to me, "If it were for me, I would be silent all the time. I really don't like coming here, and even less making the effort to talk. I want to go away, travel around. I'm tired of my family, it's all too much effort." Having already attempted in vain to stimulate her trust, I spoke to her of her hatred, which I suggested made her mentally distance herself, not least in order to skip sessions, when instead, hatred could be verbalized and thought out. Her reply to my comment was nothing more than a silence that seemed to be icier than usual.

At this point the patient disappeared for a week. When I tried to contact her the following week by telephone, she did not reply. At the end of the second week, Mara called me at her appointment time and informed me that she had decided to discontinue the analysis and that she would only pay the sessions in which she had been present, but not those she had skipped, sending the payment by mail. I replied that if that were her decision, it was important that she discuss it with me in person. Mara replied that she had already stated that she wanted to go away. I answered that it was however necessary to terminate the contract which had been stipulated in person. At this point Mara accepted the invitation to come and speak with me.

I received the analysand by acting as if it were a normal analytic session, waiting for her to lie on the couch. After some hesitation, Mara lay down and told me that she wanted to discontinue, because she couldn't see any results. I pointed out that results need a realistic time frame, and moreover, her tendency to retreat into herself and slow down the analytic exploration with silence only made things more difficult. The patient declared that her decision was final, even though she continued to remain on the couch. I added that her decision came at the very time when her emotions of hatred were beginning to appear, even if the confrontation with those emotions risked resulting in a concrete interruption. Let's follow the dialogue that ensued:

MARA: "I don't get it! What do you mean by thinking about hatred? That's just how I am, and I don't see how I can change. If it were for me, I would walk out right now, in this very moment. I'm feeling aggression."

LOMBARDI: (considering the patient appeared willing to remain on the couch to speak with me) "If you acknowledge your hatred and your violence but still remain here instead of getting up and leaving, it means you have already found a way to think of your hatred, instead of averting it."

MARA: (astonished) "Is that it? Are you sure?"

LOMBARDI: "I'm absolutely sure. If, however, you get up and leave right now, you will miss the opportunity of beginning to think about your emotions."

MARA: (after a long silence and with a muffled voice) "I had a dream the week after I went away. I was certain I would never come back. I don't feel like telling you about it. (silence) It's a real effort for me … I was in a marathon in my parents' town: I had to beat everybody. (pause) Some of my friends are really smart: those I envy I make friends with to make the envy disappear. I am friendly and I seduce them. (pause). In the dream I find myself in a house in which there was one room after another. I go from one to the next, closing the doors behind me. I am blind. At a certain point I hear my mother's voice: I hear her but I don't see her. Then my mother calls me by my nickname she used to use and I felt very moved. When my mother calls me, then I see her. I cry and I realize that I can actually stop to rest, that I can't keep running for ever.

LOMBARDI: What name did your mother call you?

MARA: I don't want to say.

LOMBARDI: (surprised at the contrast between the collaborative opening-up as evidenced by the sharing of her dream and then her refusal) Your preoccupation with competition and envy drives you to want to win and triumph over me, just like you triumph over your own real sentiments. In this sense you maintain your blindness rather than acknowledging your real feelings of hatred. If on the other hand you acknowledge your hatred, you will also be able to acknowledge your maternal love. In that way you will be able to remain in analysis in order to learn to live with your real sentiments of hatred and love without running away.

MARA: (after a long silence and with a steady voice) I can accept returning to analysis but I have no intention of paying for the skipped sittings, because "they didn't happen." You shouldn't have waited for me.

I told her that I didn't agree, because if I had not remained faithful to our contract, waiting for her at her sessions, we wouldn't have been there. Making the skipped sessions disappear was like making her hatred disappear, which instead was important to recognize as real. Seeing that the patient was determined not to give in, I proposed to continue, waiting to see what the next sittings would reveal.

In the following sessions it was possible to analyze her suicidal impulses which led her to fast driving that put her life at risk. In a dream Mara and her mother were speeding towards the edge of a cliff, just like in the movie *Thelma and Louise*: we could see that her dangerous speeding on the highway corresponded to her fantasy of pursuing absolute freedom (*Thelma and Louise*): an infinity with no limits that did, however, in the movie, corresponded to a fatal car accident.

In a subsequent session Mara recounted a dream in which she was in analysis, lying on the couch, but her studio had no walls and as such she was surrounded by the open country. The patient however noted a white line, like the ones used to mark boundaries on a soccer field, which corresponded to the effective border of the analysis room. And so it was possible to interpret to her that along with her tendency to eliminate boundaries, at the same time, there was evidence of her new ability to recognize the boundaries that exist in analysis and within herself. After having acted out her hatred for boundaries in analysis, and having this interpreted to her, she was now able to think of limits, including those of the analytical context, as something with which it was possible to coexist.

After this phase of elaboration, Mara paid for the missed sessions that had occurred during her interruption and was more collaborative. Her analysis lasted five years, concluding, after another very difficult phase before the ending of analysis, with her gratitude for the benefits she had received.

Conclusions

Mara's case is an example of the difficulties in managing an analysis in the context of a patient's serious representative deficit and thought defects, which led her to stagnate in silence. The symptoms described by the analysand of trembling hands and panic attacks seemed to indicate a dissociation of the mind from the body (Lombardi, 2017), so that the rejected body continued to send signals of its existence through trembling and uncontrolled explosions in the panic attacks.

The evolution of the phases of the analysis passed through a confrontation with her tendency to act-out. In the analytic dialogue, the patient clearly showed her "defect of thinking" (Bion) about hatred when she stated: "What do you mean by thinking about hatred? That's just how I am and I don't see how I can change". The patient symmetrizes "herself" (Mara) and "her feeling" (hatred), so that they become "the same thing": through this symmetrization, Mara's capacity for thinking is paralyzed. When I pointed out to her that she was able to remain on the couch, instead of getting up and leaving (hence respecting the analytic frame), the patient shows an unexpected capacity for listening and thinking. My intervention introduces an asymmetrization between the patient's feelings and her total person, so that she can hate but, at same time, can remain still instead of leaving. The patient's confrontation with the analytic frame (not leaving the session meant respecting the frame) became an important source of "asymmetry", that catalyzed the working-through, so that Mara started to realize she could think about hatred while remaining on the couch, instead of acting hatred out.

The analytic frame revealed itself to be essential in stimulating the analysand's dream too, as an expression of her unconscious collaboration. The dream was able to represent Mara's 'muscular' marathon (acting-out), where she went from one room to another, closing doors behind her in endless flight. In her dream, the patient discovers her actions lead her to be blind, becoming able to pass from a non-representative level to a representative one, and recognizing competition, triumph, envy, as well as the denial of separation and its loss. Despite this revolutionary access to representation and to thought ("and so I see", Mara said), the patient refused to pay for the missed sessions. The following dream allowed for some progress in the analytic work, showing how the denial of her hatred and reality limits led Mara to risk suicide (*Thelma and Louise*), in order to triumph over her human limitations.

In other words, Mara was ready to destroy her analysis and commit suicide just so that she could affirm her longing for an infinity that cancelled all real limits, which Mara was able to learn to tolerate in order to abandon the infinitizing symmetry of the unconscious (Matte-Blanco).

The dream of the analytic office without walls, in which she acknowledges the real borders of the room by a white line that marks them, shows the recognizing of the analytic frame/boundaries (Bleger), in parallel with the assumption of the asymmetrical limit that characterizes the capacity of thinking (Matte-Blanco). In this dream, the coexistence of infinity (the view of nature outside the studio) together with the finite (the white line that marks the boundary) shows the working through of the relationship between the infinite and the finite together with an acceptance, no longer claustrophobic and oppressive, of the analytic setting.

In this clinical example, Bleger's and Matte-Blanco's perspectives converge, showing that the working through of the formal parameters in analysis—primarily in the frame and the limit—can become a main springboard towards mental growth.

References

Arieti, S. (1955). *Interpretation of Schizophrenia*. New York: Robert Brunner.

Bion, W.R. (1984 [1970]). *Attention and Interpretation*. London: Karnac.

Bleger, J. (1967). Psycho-analysis of the psycho-analytic frame. *International Journal of Psycho-Analysis, 48*: 511–519.

Freud, S. (1900). *The Interpretation of Dreams*. S.E. Vols 4/5. London: The Hogarth Press.

Freud, S. (1915). The Unconscious. S.E. Vol. 14. London: The Hogarth Press.

Lombardi, R. (2015). *Formless Infinity: Clinical Explorations of Matte-Blanco and Bion*. New York: Routledge.

Lombardi, R. (2017). *Body-Mind Dissociation in Psychoanalysis: Development after Bion*. New York: Routledge.

Lombardi, R. (2018). Entering one's own life as an aim of clinical psychoanalysis. *Journal of the American Psychoanalytic Association, 66*: 883–911.

Matte-Blanco, I. (1998 [1975]). *The Unconscious as Infinite Sets: An Essay in Bi-logic*. London: Karnac.

Matte-Blanco, I. (1988). *Thinking, Feeling, and Being: Clinical Reflections on the Fundamental Antinomy of Human Beings and World*. New York: Routledge.

Von Domarus, E. (1944). The Specific Laws of Logic in Schizophrenia. In: J.S. Kasanin (ed.), *Language and Thought in Schizophrenia: Collected Papers*. Berkeley: University of California Press.

8 Understanding early experiences

Bleger's contribution to the undifferentiation of early states

Bernd Nissen

After the flight and expulsion of important psychoanalysts from the German-speaking area as a result of fascist and National Socialist tyranny, the long phase began in which psychoanalysis was dominated by the English language, in the US under the ego-psychological paradigm, in England, and after the decline of ego-psychology, eventually worldwide under the paradigm of Kleinian psychology. Thus, important concepts fell into oblivion in the English-speaking world (e.g. *Nachträglichkeit* ("afterwardness"), poorly translated as "deferred action"; see Dahl, 2010). Of greater consequence, however, was that psychoanalytic research activities from other countries met with little receptive resonance and did not find their way into an 'interlingual' discourse. The consequences were two-sided: English-speaking psychoanalysis could not process and further develop innovative challenges, and the stimulation of these concepts in other languages, through an animated discourse with the central paradigms remained, for the most part, marginal.

With the decline of the Kleinian paradigm, the international psychoanalytical community discovered studies from many different regions in the world, and the "South Americans" in particular, have attracted great attention for some years (see, for example, *International Journal of Psychoanalyis* (2017), Education Section and Key Papers, vol. 98, no. 1). Indeed, many individual papers had already been translated (e.g., Bleger, 1967, 1974, and Baranger, Baranger, and Mom 1988), but it was the growing influence of the interpersonal/intersubjective and relational school (e.g. Stolorow and Atwood, 1992) and of field theory (e.g. Ferro, 2003, 2006, 2009) that changed the situation. These schools, which diverge enormously from each other, strongly invoke the "pioneer psychoanalysts of the Rio Plata region" (Levine, 2017), seeing the laying of theoretical foundations of intersubjective psychology in these papers (see, for example, Arbiser, 2017; Scharff, Losso, and de Setton, 2017). But even if the current followers, for example, Stolorow and Ferro, adopt selected views of Latin American pioneering, it has to be noted that they have not taken over the socio-critical, especially the dialectical context of the ideas.[1] Translations of important individual contributions (Baranger and Baranger, 2008, [1961–

DOI: 10.4324/9781003252252-10

62], Bleger, 2012 [1969]), and the works of M. and W. Baranger (2009) and of Bleger (2013 [1967]) followed. The ground-breaking works of Pichon-Rivière, which had a great impact on all the South American thinkers, were published, belatedly, in 2017.

Bleger was one of the thinkers who developed many ideas, terms, and concepts thus opening up perspectives which, in part, attracted attention in psychoanalytic research only years, indeed decades later. One focus of contemporary psychoanalysis lies in the investigation into nameless, unrepresented, autistic/autistoid states, of traumatic condensations, breakdowns and so on. For this field specifically, Bleger submitted a number of terms that to me appear to be helpful for a deeper under-standing of such psychic structures and dynamics, namely terms from the series: undifferentiation/syncretism, glischro-caric position, ambiguity, ego–non-ego, agglutinated nucleus, symbiosis, frame/setting (*encuadre*), and body schema/body image.

Critical classification of Bleger's key terms

The problem, or rather my problem with these terms, is that even though they are psychoanalytic or rather, fully compatible from a psychoanalytic perspective, they were integrated by Bleger into an institutional, social-psychological/sociological reference system, so that when studying them, some vagueness and confusion occur. To name but a few of these terms: field theory, 'Gestalt', behaviour, institution, dramatics, identity.[2] This uncertainty is exacerbated, it seems to me, by the fact that Bleger chooses a theory of science that originated in Marxist positions of the 1960s and 1970s as a metatheory,[3] which to me does not appear compatible with psychoanalytic positions. Notably, in a paper published in 1969 (2012), Bleger distances himself, with a Marxist theory of science, sharply from Freud, whom he accuses of a naturalistic-deterministic, unipersonal psy-chology in which the analysand was examined like an object in natural science.[4] Bleger goes on to maintain that psychoanalysis is trapped in a historico-genetic, dynamic, and logical rigidity Bleger (2012 [1969], p. 994) —and hence fails to see the human being: "Dramatics is an understanding of human beings and their behaviour in terms of events that refer to the very life of human beings considered as such, whereas dynamics attempts to reduce dramatics to an interplay of forces, to such an extent that from a theoretical point of view these forces and instincts dominate and even determine human events." (Bleger, 2012 [1969], p. 996. See also Etch-egoyen (2013, p. xiii), who links forces (Triebe) with Newtonian physics.)

In 1958, Bleger wrote (as quoted in Etchegoyen, 2013, p. xiii): "In other words, to explain the difference between the dramatic and its dynamic transposition, it could be said that in the former the drives derive from the object relations, while Freud argued in his dynamic theories that object relations derives from the interplay of drives."[5]

In the tradition of Pichon-Rivière, and probably also against the background of massive social upheaval during that time, Bleger attempts to unite a dialectical (Marxist) theory with psychoanalysis. This also changes the concept of drive. In the dramatic position, the dialectical forces constitute the object relationships from which drives then derive, so that dimensions such as "alienation" and "need" come into focus. But with it the term/concept "drive" runs the risk of being reduced to what Freud calls "Reiz/stimulus": "By an 'instinct' ('Trieb' BN) is provisionally to be understood as the psychical representative of an endosomatic, continuously flowing source of stimulation, as contrasted with a 'stimulus' ('Reiz' BN), which is set up by *single* excitations coming from *without*. The concept of instinct is thus one of those lying on the frontier between the mental and the physical." (Freud, 1905, p. 168) For Freud, "instincts are mythical entities, magnificent in their indefiniteness" (Freud, 1933, p. 95).

Kleinian psychoanalysis is also founded on instinct, as Isaacs shows:

> a. Phantasies are the primary content of unconscious mental processes.
> b. Unconscious phantasies are primarily about bodies, and represent instinctual aims towards objects.
> c. These phantasies are, in the first instance, the psychic representatives of libidinal and destructive instincts; early in development they also become elaborated into defences, as well as wish-fulfilments and anxiety-contents.
> d. Freud's postulated 'hallucinatory wish-fulfilment' and his 'primary introjection' and 'projection' are the basis of the phantasy life.
> [...]
> i. Unconscious phantasies form the operative link between *instincts* and *mechanisms*..."
>
> (Isaacs, 1948, p. 96)

It seems to me that ultimately, Bleger does not adequately integrate his dramatic theory into the key psychoanalytic concepts and theories, such as the unconscious and preconscious/conscious, cathexis, transference resistance (to name but a few from Freudian analysis), or unconscious phantasy, projective identification, transference-countertransference, enactment (to name but a few from the Kleinian theory), and in this way add it to the psychoanalytic reference system.

Without this integration, formulations such as "understanding of human beings and their behaviour in terms of events that refer to the very life of human beings considered as such" or "the drives derive from the object relations" run the risk of taking on a completely different meaning. With terms such as institution, behaviour etc. and particularly with the focus on the experience of a specific, actual situation by a person without a psychodynamic depth dimension, they eventually fall more within the social-psychological field theory (see Köhler, 1968, Metzger, 1999, and particularly, Kurt Lewin) than within psychoanalysis. The field theory assumes that from a given arrangement of psychologically relevant forces (vector forces), individual behaviour emerges in the respective situation (see Lewin, 1951; for a good introduction, see also Hall and Lindzey, 1970) —and these forces are shown in the behaviour in actual life and in the object relations. Without the concept of the unconscious and that of the unconscious phantasy, the "here and now" and the "object relation" acquire a completely different meaning.

The problems which result from the shifting of the scientific reference framework are even greater with the above-mentioned Marxist, meta-theoretical integration:

> This alienation and de-dialectisation occurred in psychoanalytic theory and in many other theories in other fields of investigation; not only the so-called human sciences but in scientific knowledge as a whole.
>
>   Reconsidering these last statements, it could be said without forcing the facts in any way that, just as neurosis is invariably a phenomenon of human alienation, theory has been structured in a way that reflects in its own structure the same alienation and the same de-dialectisation of the neurotic process.
>
> (Bleger, 2012 [1969], p. 997)

Even if no one would advocate such scientific theoretical positions today, it should be noted that Bleger considers that Marx's concept of alienation plays a crucial role—both for neurosis and for the scientific theoretical concept. Here, there is at most, only room for the concept of the descriptive unconscious, the dynamic, suppressed, structural unconscious can hardly be connected.

Since Bleger, on the other hand, investigated the series of terms listed above (undifferentiation etc.) mainly from a psychoanalytic perspective, a mixing of scientific reference systems emerges, which may lead to serious confusion.[6]

Early mental experiences in Bleger's works

Undifferentiation

Bleger's terms, such as symbiosis, undifferentiation/syncretism, glischro-caric position, ambiguity, ego–non-ego, agglutinated nucleus, revolve among others, around the early forms of experience, experience forms which are of key importance both for the psychoanalytic concept and theory formation as well as for issues concerning treatment techniques. Yet they represent precisely the areas in which we have to engage metapsychology which, as Freud said, is a "witch", but without which it is not possible: "Without metapsychological speculation and theorizing—I had almost said 'phantasizing'—we shall not get another step forward" (Freud, 1937, p. 225).

I think we need to assume that in earliest experiences there are very different emotional occurrences, involving highly diverse forms for processing them (see also Loch, 1991). These psychic processing forms (i.e. the earliest digestion) are arguably often autoerotic and dreamingly self-absorbed, as well as hallucinatory wish-fulfilling. They may in sensory experience suggest a oneness, but also be objectal, projectively identificational. It was Freud who dealt intensively with these early experiences, trying to capture them in terms such as "autoeroticism", "hallucinatory wish-fulfilling", "primary narcissism", "primary identifications", which, however, were never clearly defined. At the end of his life, Freud paraphrases: "'... I am the breast.' Only later: 'I have it' ...'" (Freud, 1938b, p. 299).

We can now read Freud's comment as an attempt to capture the oneness intrapsychically in a paraphrase, though he does not quite succeed—for "I" and "breast" are there. Even if we omit the verb ("am") and read I = breast, a paradoxical contradiction remains. Or is it precisely about this paradoxical contradiction? Must the at-two-ment be concealed in the at-one-ment?

The paraphrase "I am the breast" denotes an experience *after* the realization of the preconception "breast", so that in the presence moment (O) the infant is "there", the mother is "there" and the relationship is "there"—a complex, multiple existence which must now *become* in a transformative process. In the aforementioned presence moment, time and space are therefore also "there", out of which the times and the three-dimensional space will arise. Out of the existence of child, mother, relationship, the first psychic qualities emerge, which are bound in the conception and stabilize the conception. The conception sinks and becomes a preconception, thus, for the infant, the anticipation of the breast, which has already experienced a simplest satiation (memory trace). Processes of hallucinatory wish-fulfilling may emerge. Nevertheless, after the realization in the infant's experience with the initialization in O, still no (psychically stable) differentiation ego/self—object has occurred, which has yet to become. States of undifferentiation continue to appear, paraphrased: ego/I = breast.[7]

Bleger now investigates this (primitive) undifferentiation (or syncretism) and ambiguity: "However, for the person who experiences or manifests the ambiguity, it is neither doubt nor uncertainty nor confusion. It is *undifferentiation*, which means *a deficit in discrimination and identity, or a deficit in differentiation between ego and not-ego*" (Bleger, 2013 [1967], p. 163). Later he writes: "... this ego–non-ego undifferentiation constitutes *a different* type of organization of *the personality and of reality*." (p. 176) With this personality organization, introjection and projection and introjective-projective identifications cannot yet be detected (pp. 185ff).

Bleger therefore sees primitive undifferentiation as an organization of the personality and the ambiguity as a functional form in this organization in which exclusionary states naturally exist alongside each other.

> The primitive undifferentiation is not actually *a state* of undifferentiation but a different structure or organization that always includes the subject and the subject's environment, though not as differentiated entities. The remnants of the nuclei of this primitive undifferentiation in a 'mature' personality is responsible for the persistence of symbiosis …
>
> (Bleger, 2013 [1967], p. 4)

Glischro-caric position

Bleger gives this primitive structure the name "glischro-caric position", which is prior to the Kleinian paranoid-schizoid position. Ogden (1989) later called this position an autistic-contiguous position and investigated it in detail (see also Nissen, 2006). In this position there is "… no real object relation between the objects and the ego nuclei … differentiation has not occurred between the object and the part of the ego that is related to it" (Bleger, 2013, p. 74). Bleger speaks of an agglutinated nucleus. Ambiguity and fusion (not confusion!) are dominant in these dynamics. In the very beginning, Bleger postulates, "the first undifferentiated, syncretic structures are fundamentally bodily relations" (Bleger, 2013, p. 5).

Although he does not state it explicitly, Bleger is referring here to Freud's reflections: "The ego is first and foremost a bodily ego; it is not merely a surface entity, but is itself the projection of a surface" (Freud, 1923, p. 26). The English version includes an explanation: "I.e. the ego is ultimately derived from bodily sensations, chiefly from those springing from the surface of the body. It may thus be regarded as a mental projection of the surface of the body, besides, as we have seen above, representing the superficies of the mental apparatus" (Freud, 1923b, p. 26, fn. 1). He attributes a special status to the body: firstly, one's own body is the place from which internal and external sensations can spring simultaneously. Secondly, "Getast", Freud's expression, (in English inappropriately translated as "touch" (p. 25; GW, dt. 253)) is followed by two sensations, namely touch and be touched.

My understanding of Freud is that he obviously attaches a special importance to the surface of the body. The "Getast", touching and being touched, being held in love, is captured by the consciousness, and memory traces are stored, an interdependent, circular process evolves. The surface of the body, perceived from the difference between touching and being touched, is eventually projected psychically into the emerging psychic apparatus and constitutes the ego.

In my view, however, this process is likely to be extremely complicated. The glischro-caric position includes different forms of experience, which—

from the infant's perspective—range from a oneness (ego = non-ego) to a differentiation (ego ≠ non-ego). The glischro-caric position is therefore not a closed monadic system (as Mahler (1968) postulated) but the infant is, by virtue of transformations in O (Bion, 1970) T → O, *in the world*. But this world is initially experienced sensuously, its ego (subjectivity) preserved by the presence moment (O) in the mother.

We thus have an interlocking of sensuous impressions and sensations, which comprise a oneness as well as a non-oneness, and preconceptions (conceptions) of self, mother, relationship, which are there and have yet to become. The sensuous impressions and sensations can only be *qualified* in the relationship (with Bion: raw-elements → α-element), and the preconception can only be *realized* in the presence moment. This process of transformation O → K is, to my knowledge, not really understood (see Nissen, 2015). Bion tries to capture it with his concept of "constellation":

> The facilitation of "constellation"[8] must in turn be seen as a step in the process of at-one-ment (the transformation O → K). In practice this means not that the analyst recalls some relevant memory but that a relevant constellation will be evoked during the process of at-one-ment with O, the process denoted by transformation O → K.
>
> (Bion, 1970, p. 33)

When a realized preconception becomes a conception, sensuous elements in the relationship become psychically qualified and can be perceived by the consciousness. These qualified, psychic elements are then available as a memory trace in the hallucinatory wish- fulfilment. In it, the differentiation between ego and non-ego/ego and breast is not yet present, also because the conception of the "breast" in the mother's absence cannot be thought by the infant and is only preserved as thinkable as a thought in the mother. This means that the child experiences a realization and feels a conception which is not yet available to the child as a thought in the absence of the object. The conception has not yet become a thought.

For the infant, this hallucinatory cathecting *is* being breastfed, hence indistinguishable from the real, experienced event of satisfaction – but it is no realization (Nissen, 2019; see Bion's considerations on hallucinosis, 1970, pp. 36ff). The 'hardness' of reality will teach him to begin to distinguish between the real breast and its hallucinated, perceptual identity, as unpleasure increases. "Such hallucinations, however, if they were not to be maintained to the point of exhaustion, proved to be inadequate to bring about the cessation of the need or, accordingly, the pleasure attaching to satisfaction" (Freud, 1900a, p. 598).

The preconception, the anticipation of the breast, hence that of realization, rises again and sensuous impressions which are not self-generated are added to the qualification.

One could now say that in this rhythmical process of the qualification of internal and external impressions and sensations and of the realization of preconceptions, a differentiation of self and object, self and environment, develops, yet to me the process seems more complicated.

Ambiguity

Let us consider our standard situation. An infant is hungry and cries: It has many internal and external sensations and impressions which are not psychic, hence, raw elements. They are unpleasurable states. Beyond this sensuous level, something is added to this cry: the pre-conception of the breast, that is, the diffuse anticipation of an object. Bion thinks the pre-conception "α-elementarily." In my understanding, for Bion, a pre-conception is an α-element version of an unknown expectation (see Bion 1963, p. 93). The preconceptional α-elements are therefore not sense impressions and sensations transformed by the α-function but exist before all experience, yet still require reality (realization) in order to become initialized and effective. The α-elementary pre-conceptional expectation pervades the urging sensuous states of agitation, which take on a pre-objectal direction. The unconnected raw sense impressions and sensations gather in the α-elementary structure of the preconception. Thus the unpleasure is given a direction, the cry becomes (for the mother) a call.

The mother, the anticipated object, comes, picks up and breastfeeds her child. Here a presence moment occurs, in which mother, infant and the mother-child-relationship are there/exist.

In breastfeeding there are new sensations and impressions: being held, gentle voice, drinking, being touched and touching, pleasurable sucking, retreat of unpleasurable sensations etc. These are pleasurable states. For the infant the pre-conception has become the conception, for the mother it has become the thought.

The mother with her α-function is able to qualify both the unpleasurable and pleasurable states. Bion conceives this process as follows:

> the infant, filled with painful lumps of faeces, guilt, fears of impending death, chunks of greed, meanness and urine, evacuates these bad objects into the breast that is not there. As it does so the good object turns the no-breast (mouth) into a breast, the faeces and urine into milk, the fears of impending death and anxiety into vitality and confidence, the greed and meanness into feelings of love and generosity and the infant sucks its bad property, now translated into goodness, back again.
>
> (Bion, 1963, p. 31)

He thus assumes a transformation of the "bad" states into bearable "good ones". But is this true? Bleger is more cautious here: with his concept of ambiguity, he assumes that states can exist alongside each other without contradiction. Therefore, the mother can qualify the non-pleasurable and the pleasurable sensations as well as capture the moments of transformation. The result is a high differentiation of the conception, even if the way the infant experiences it is undifferentiated. The phenomena of unpleasure can be called emptiness, anxiety, threat, greed, anger, despair; those of pleasure love, tenderness, satisfaction, satiety, well-being; those of transformation happiness, relief, reassurance, etc. These mental qualities find their place in the conception, are connected in it and the conception is thus stabilized and intuitively graspable.

Bion writes:

> The point that demonstrates the divergence most clearly is that the physician is dependent on realization of sensuous experience in contrast with the psycho-analyst whose dependence is on experience that is not sensuous. The physician can see and touch and smell. The realizations with which a psycho-analyst deals cannot be seen or touched; anxiety has no shape or colour, smell or sound. For convenience, I propose to use the term 'intuit' as a parallel in the psychoanalyst's domain to the physician's use of "see", "touch", "smell", and "hear".
>
> (Bion, 1970, p. 7)

But we can "see", "touch", "smell", and "hear" anxiety; at the same time, Bion maintains that psychic qualities cannot be perceived sensuously. He refers back to Freud's comment that consciousness is "a sense-organ for the perception of psychical qualities" (Freud, 1900a, p. 615; also, Freud, 1915e). How can this contradiction be resolved?

Consciousness in undifferentiation

There can be no doubt that consciousness perceives *sensuous* qualities, but sensuous qualities are not *psychic* qualities (Bion 1965, p. 107; Bion, 1970, p. 28)! Sensuous qualities only become psychic qualities when they are connected in the underlying preconception/conception (more appropriate would be the Freudian expression "primal phantasy"). The sensuous perception of anxiety, for example, only becomes a psychic quality when the depth dimension of the primal fantasy is included. The anxiety that the breast will not come is different from the anxiety that it could be bitten off, all the more the anxiety when castration is feared. A sensuous perception of the psychic quality is not possible as the α-elementary preconception is not sensuous and, after the realization, disappears again. They can only be "intuited". Hence, "The psycho-analyst and his analysand are alike dependent on the senses, but psychic qualities, with which psycho-analysis deals, are not perceived by the senses but, as Freud says, by some mental counterpart of the sense organs, a function that he attributed to consciousness" (Bion, 1970, p. 28).

Yet this is where the concept of consciousness (which, like the concept of the unconscious, hardly appears in Bleger) comes into focus. Freud almost despairs at this concept: Consciousness is "by a fact without parallel, which defies all explanation or description" (Freud, 1938b, [GW, 1940a], p. 157) ("unvergleichliche, jeder Erklärung und Beschreibung trotzende Tatsache" (Freud, GW, 1940a, p. 79)). Freud defines consciousness firstly as the organ which can perceive sensations and impressions of the sense organs from the periphery as well as pleasure and unpleasure from the inside of the apparatus (Freud, 1900a, 1915e). It is a *perception consciousness*. Bion postulates a mental function, he calls it the α-function, "to convert sense data into α -elements", which, when mentalized in this way, are compatible "and thus provide the psyche with the material for dream thoughts, and hence the capacity to wake up or go to sleep, to be conscious or unconscious" (Bion, 1962, p. 308). Here Bion encounters the difficulty that either the consciousness depends on the alpha function or he needs two consciousness concepts. In fact he does operate with two consciousness concepts, namely a consciousness which, if an α-function is available, perceives psychic quality and faces an unconscious, and one which, in the absence of an α-function, faces untransformed sensorial impressions that while they can be felt are in a sense prior to anything that can be qualified as psychically conscious or unconscious. They are not psychic but actual raw elements. From this he derives his theory of thought disorders. It is precisely Bion's second consciousness concept that we need to take as a basis for the infant's outlined, undifferentiated experience (which Bleger captures brilliantly with his term "granulated"). It is a pure perception consciousness which is not yet conscious of any self, not self-conscious. The impressions and states can be recognized and felt, but they cannot be known psychically (see Bion, 1970, p. 30). This consciousness does not clash with undifferentiation, as Bleger observes.

Yet how does a consciousness come into play which can perceive *psychic* qualities, or has developed and can use an α-function? Perhaps we can ask the question in a different way: How can we imagine a presence moment (T → O) in which a thought of the absent breast emerges so that the absent breast as a present one is "there" (cf. also Beland, 2015)?

I don't know the answer, yet I could imagine that it is linked to the following dynamics. With Bleger we can take the process O → K to mean, for example, that alongside the states of hunger, states of satiety persist. When hunger is felt again, hallucinatory images first set in which do not satisfy the infant's need, so that unpleasurable sensations which have already been qualified start to spread. Although qualified and "somehow" attached to the breast, the infant cannot think it. According to Freud (and Klein), it tries to evade or excrete them.[9] Both fail. Yet necessity forces the infant (in contrast to qualified elements of satiety when the mother is present) into an awareness of and having to relate to these states. If it succeeds in linking this relating to the absent "present breast", a presence moment occurs in which the absent breast becomes the past and future present breast. A thought emerges in which time evolves into past, future and present, and space becomes a three-dimensional space in which the place where the breast was appears (Bion, 1965, 1970). Then the necessity arises to develop the apparatus for the thinking of thoughts: "Nevertheless there are grounds for supposing that a primitive 'thinking', active in the development of thought, should be distinguished from the thinking that is required for the use of thoughts. The thinking used in the development of thoughts differs from the thinking required to use the thoughts when developed" (Bion, 1963, p. 35; cf. also Bleger's (2013, p. 205) distinction between "thinking" and "mentation").

If this development is successful, the infant has the breast (Freud). Then, the self–object differentiation has arisen out of the undifferentiation, whereas the undifferentiation remains unchanged in the agglutinated nucleus and in the glischro-caric. The psychic skin is likely to play a major role in this differentiation since self and object have many encounters in the "Getast".

Undifferentiation and unintegration

Bick addressed similar questions from a different perspective. In 1968 she published, after Bleger had published *Symbiosis and Ambiguity* and other preliminary works, reflections on skin function and on the relationship between integration and unintegration: "In its most primitive form the parts of the personality are felt to have no binding force amongst themselves and must therefore be held together in a way that is experienced by them passively, by the skin functioning as a boundary" (Bick, 1968, p. 484).

Tustin then showed that if this holding-together function fails, autistic reactions develop which "divert attention away from this mother, who is spurned in favour of self-generated sensations which are always available and predictable, and so do not bring shocks" (Tustin, 1986, p. 27). In a desperate search, the dangers of dissolution are resisted by formations which center the sensations (a lamp, a voice, a smell or others) and can thus, at least momentarily, be experienced "as holding the parts of the personality together" (Bick, 1968, p. 484).

If the binding force, the binding function is absent or fails, "the concept of a space within the self cannot arise" and an unintegrated state "as a passive experience of total helplessness" will appear, which must be distinguished from disintegration as a consequence of excessive splitting (Bick, 1968, p. 484; see Nissen, 2008).

While Bick focused on the psychic skin function, or the second skin under the vertex of integration and unintegration, Bleger shows under the vertex of undifferentiation that the skin, surface and ego boundaries are more fluid, more situative and more vague than when we experience it in our self-perception. In consciousness, the body image may orient itself particularly to the psychic skin, but in the pre-unconscious, it is more extended.

Psychoanalytic setting

With investigations into the psychoanalytic setting, Bleger transposes the results of his reflections on undifferentiation, symbiotic attachment and ambiguity into the analytic situation (Bleger, 2013 [1967], pp. 228–241).

Every psychoanalytic situation constitutes a process "which is what we study, analyse and interpret" and includes a setting, "which is a 'non-process' in the sense that it provides the constants within whose framework the process takes place" (Bleger, 2013 [1967], p. 241).

Bleger starts from the earliest mother-child-relationship, which in the infant's experience results in a most primitive fusion with the mother's body. Being held results in a fusion of the two bodies, the undifferentiation which is expressed in "I am the breast" or in the tension ego–non-ego. The natural presence of the breast becomes a non-ego, which is the background and basis for the formation of the ego.

Bleger now introduces the concept of the institution:

> A relationship which lasts for years, in which a set of norms and attitudes is kept up, is nothing less than a true definition of *institution*. The frame is then an institution within whose bounds certain phenomena take place which we call behaviour … What became evident to me was that each institution is a portion of the individual's personality; and it is of such importance that identity is always, wholly or partially, institutional …
>
> (Bleger, 1967, pp. 511f)

> However, in addition to this interaction between individuals and institutions, institutions always function (in varying degrees) as boundaries of the body schema (body image)[10] and as the fundamental nucleus of identity.
>
> (Bleger, 2013, p. 230)

A three-step derivation: 1. The frame is an institution; 2. Each institution is part of the individual's personality – and so each frame becomes part of the personality; 3. The institution and thus the frame function as a kind of boundary of body image. Institution, frame and body image are "mute" yet not non-existent. The common characteristic is that of symbiosis. Bleger thus derives that ultimately the analytic frame is present in the same way the mother's body used to be present and that an undifferentiation remains unchanged between the body of the subject and (the objects) of the environment.

In my opinion, it is very difficult to interpret one of the key theses in the text clearly: "The frame is part of the patient's body image; it *is* the body image in the part that has not been structured and differentiated. It is thus something different from the body image itself; it is the body-space and body setting non-differentiation" (Bleger, 1967, p. 517).

In the 2013 translation, we read:

> The setting forms part of the patient's body schema. It *is* the body schema in the part where this has not yet been structured and discriminated. This means it is something different from the body image in the narrow sense of the term: it is the undifferentiation of body and space, and of body and environment.
>
> (Bleger, 2013 [1967], pp. 238ff)

In Spanish, the last part of the sentence reads: "es la indiferenciación cuerpo-espacio y cuerpo-ambiente".[11]

Bleger (2013 [1967], p. 241) maintains that the frame/setting is "the depositary of the psychotic part of the personality". Here Bleger adopts Bion's view of the psychotic part of the personality. Bion, however, did not explore the failure of projective identification, which he observed himself, any further. This task was taken on by Tustin and Meltzer. In my view, disorders in the earliest undifferentiation correspond to autistic/autistoid disorders; psychotic disorders are already based on an object reference (but this is a further development, which had not yet taken place in Bleger's time—or the studies were taken up only after a long delay, such as Liberman's (1958) "transference autism", which Gomberoff, Noemi and Pualuan de Gomberoff (1990) then integrated into their concept of "analysis as an autistic object").

With his investigations of the setting, Bleger succeeds, in my opinion, not only in capturing and depathologizing early forms of experience but also in making the vagueness of the psychic body image accessible. For many people, for example, their home is so highly cathected, as if it were part of the "ego". If there is a burglary, this cathexis can be felt ad hoc (with Bleger, the frame has been violated) and it is experienced by many as very close to the body, like an "intrusion into the body". The psychoanalytic setting too becomes in the (regressive) process during which unconscious things become visible a support. The setting/the frame must therefore be stable. Major changes, also of a spatial kind, can be very irritating (ranging from normal irritation to imminent breakdown). A female patient of mine, who suffered from a severe autistoid disorder, upon entering the consulting room noticed instantly that a bright orange book was missing from my bookshelf. On the couch, she kept glancing at the empty space. When I gently confronted her with my observations, she said: "it looks like a gaping, dark wound". Here it became apparent that the consulting room had also become a second skin—and can arguably serve as an example of when the setting/frame (here, the consulting room) *has* become a body schema.

Yet I am at odds with the fact that Bleger defines encuadre in the social-, institution psychological/sociological and behavioural frame. When Bleger, for example, maintains that "the frame is part of the patient's body image" (Bleger, 1967, p. 517), the statement is unfounded from a psycho-analytic point of view. The psychoanalytic frame/space is *cathected* in all manner of forms and with unconscious phantasies, and this cathexis has an impact on the patient's psychic system and *can* also operate in the body ego. It is therefore not the frame that becomes part of the body image/ schema but the cathexis. In Bleger's formulations we are in a social-, institution-psychological reference system in which its concepts come into effect.

I think that before analyst and analysand meet for the first time, pre-conceptions of the analytic relationship and situation already exist. When someone decides upon psychoanalytic treatment and is prepared therefore to engage in a highly frequent relationship (three to five sessions a week) for many years, they sense intuitively that there will be regressive pro-cesses and unconscious forces. The pathogenetic dynamics are also located in the preconception. So there must be anxiety and hope that this venture is given a framework with clear agreements and rules. The analytic rela-tionship and situation are therefore highly cathected. The analyst too, this may be hidden from us by routine, is afraid of every new treatment. It requires courage and every interpretation will demand courage. So on both sides there are highly complex preconceptional expectations. The situation has similarities with the preconceptional encounter between mother and child. When the preconception is realized, the analyst is there (exists), the analysand is there (exists) and the analytic relationship is there (exists).

This means that the psychoanalytic relationship requires, indeed forces, a frame. There is a primacy of the analytic relationship prior to the frame, not vice versa. The frame serves, allows the process—and must be geared to this. The negotiation of the frame is asymmetrical since the analyst is experienced and is well aware of the power of resistances and change-resistant, destructive forces. The analyst knows what acting out is neces-sary, something Freud (1914g) already described as a crucial informative source. Psychic processes need to be shown in *statu nascendi* [in a state of nascency], and cannot be slain in absentia or in effigy (see Freud, 1912a, 1912b, 1913c, 1914g), meaning the transference becomes so fierce that the pathogenic complex in *statu nascendi* pushes into the relationship and threatens to unfold in vivo. Then a conviction forms in the patient that the transference object (analyst) *becomes* the feared or loved object in the complex (concerning this "become", see particularly Bion, 1965, 1970).

This means the frame must be such that all these forces can be shown and can be processed—and cannot block, sabotage or destroy the analytic process. For Bleger too, maintenance of the frame is of the greatest importance for the frame/setting can only be analyzed within the frame/setting (Bleger, 1967, p. 518, 2013, p. 241).

This means we cannot define the frame in a social-institutional-functional-operational way. Bleger's claims that the frame becomes part of the personality and functions as a kind of boundary of body image or is part of the patient's body image, should be defined from within the analytic relationship. With such a perspective it becomes understandable why different facets of the frame are cathected as "background".

Bleger's psychoanalytic attitude

From what has been said above, it becomes clear that Bleger adopts a psychoanalytic attitude in which he meets the analysand with great respect and deep humanity. For him, we need to see analysands as subjects who operate on the basis of their developed structure and organization. The focus of his investigations is always the experiences of the patient, taking into account the difference between analyst and analysand:

> … *our* identity and *our* sense of reality are not *the* identity and sense of reality but only one of their many possible organizations. Therefore, we need to recognize that what differs from our own ways, structure and organization is not *always* a defect or a distortion but often a *different organization* that we need to study in its own right.
>
> (Bleger, 2013 [1967], p. 4)

Characteristic of Bleger's attitude is not to pathologize forms of existence and experience but to see the human being, to give them space to show themselves in free association and to communicate and to listen to them with evenly suspended attention (e.g., Freud, 1912a; see also Nissen, 2018a, Nissen, 2018b; Barratt, 2017), to abandon memory, desire, understanding (Bion, 1970, p. 129). With this approachable, open, respectful attitude it is possible to recognize the other in their *personality*. We need this attitude precisely because the unconscious has such power, a power that lies beyond our sovereignty/control, capable of being pleasurable-unpleasurable, destructive-constructive, loving-hating for the self (and the object). In the presence moment, in the O, which in the analytic process cannot be thought without F (Faith), there is no knowing person, and both, analyst and patient, must suffer. Yet the process remains asymmetrical (see Ogden, 2001, p. 11; Nissen, 2015; see also Ogden, 2004), a position which Bleger also indirectly adopts in his work on the frame (Bleger, 2013 [1967], pp. 240ff).

Consequently, he demands, quite rightly in my view, a separate nosology (and a separate diagnostics, I would like to add), for psychology and social psychiatry:

> For we cannot and should not continue to work in psychology and dynamic psychiatry with the concept of illness as an entity, but as organizations or structures of behaviour and personality, dynamically interrelated to each other, mobile and changing; otherwise we would go back to Kraeplin's conception, one of whose fundamental defects is precisely this conception of nosological 'entities'.
>
> (Bleger, 2013, p. 224)

This postulate, formulated here for psychology and psychiatry in the context of behaviour and personality, has in my view, the same validity for psychoanalysis.

The analyst must therefore share in the patient's experience, become immersed in their world. "The analyst does not maintain", as Lorenzer writes, "a contemplative distance to the patient in order to watch – as if from a theatre box – his drama. He must get involved in the play ..." (Lorenzer, 1983, p. 34), generate a flow of communication from unconscious to unconscious (Freud, 1900a; 1915e), get involved in the projective identifications and entanglements (Feldman, 1992, 1999; Hinz, 2002). Only this direct scenic interplay constitutes the analytic relationship and creates a common transference space in which understanding, to which in O both parties are subjected, becomes possible! But getting involved does not mean abandoning analytical neutrality and abstinence (see Steiner, 2006). Only in neutrality and abstinence is the analytical attitude assured. Evenly-suspended attention (Freud, 1912a) can only be achieved through strict self-discipline. Bion also emphasises again and again the strict self-discipline that is necessary to renounce the known, desires and memories and to concentrate attention on the unknown (for my understanding of the analytical attitude see Nissen 2015, 2018b, 2021).

Conclusion

Further developments in psychoanalysis in the last sixty years have achieved results independently of Bleger that coincide with many of Bleger's reflections—which we can quite certainly take as evidence of the scientific nature of psychoanalysis. Bleger gained important insights into psychic dynamics and structures, including those that have not yet been substantially understood. The concepts undifferentiation, ambiguity, glischro-caric position open a vertex through which we can deepen our understanding of current issues and research topics in psychoanalysis, particularly concerning "unrepresented states". As far as I can see, Bleger's reflections on the psychoanalytic setting, which refer back to these early forms of experience, still await development. I have attempted to demonstrate some aspects of this, knowing that it can only be a rough outline.

What impresses me most about Bleger is the way he approaches people, adopting an attitude with which we simply understand without judging, without categorizing, also allowing forms of existence to exist which appear strange to us, and without abandoning or renouncing us. It sounds so simple and natural—and yet it is the hardest thing, not only in our profession but also in our lives.

Notes

1 I thank C. Moguillansky for this hint.
2 The definition of institution without the concept of "purpose" does not seem convincing to me either (Bleger, 2013, p. 230). Whether the concept "identity" is a psychoanalytic one, is undecided despite long discussion; yet Bleger tends to use it institutionally.
3 See the positivism dispute and the Popper–Adorno controversy. In the Marxist theory of science, science has not only the task of describing and explaining reality, but reality has to be interpreted in a judgmental way.
4 This claim is not made any more valid by its having been repeated for decades. Freud does not pursue a "one-person psychology" and after his "Entwurf einer Psychologie", in *The Interpretation of Dreams* he clearly moved away from the monistic epistemology even though, honest scholar that he was, he always despaired at how to think a dualism: "The unconscious is the true psychical reality; in its innermost nature it is as much unknown to us as the reality of the external world, and it is as incompletely presented by the data of consciousness as is the external world by the communications of our sense organs." (Freud, 1900a, S. 613) ("Das Unbewußte ist das eigentlich reale Psychische, uns nach seiner inneren Natur so unbekannt wie das Reale der Außenwelt, und uns durch die Daten des Bewußtseins ebenso unvollständig gegeben wie die Außenwelt durch die Angaben unserer Sinnesorgane." (Freud, 1900a, S. 617f)) The workings of the unconscious described by Freud (e.g. 1900a; 1915e; see also Matte-Blanco, 1998) do not allow any 'naturalistic' investigation method. Freud's writings on treatment techniques also show the exact opposite. Yet the object of investigation remains the unconscious of the patient.
5 But a careful reading of Freud reveals that he never holds such a binary dichotomy tenable for psychoanalysis (see note 4).
6 Something similar can be observed when transferring terms from infant research, attachment research or neuroscience into psychoanalysis.
7 In my view, it is very important to think these processes not in a linear but in a circular-paradox way!
8 "I use the term 'constellation' to represent the process precipitating a constant conjunction."
9 Since internal and external are not yet differentiated, excretion takes place into the non-psychic body, i.e. the organism (Nancy, 2019, introduces, with reference to common German usage, *die drei Größen* (the three factors): organism, body, *Leib*). Thus the tension/threat remains present, but cannot be discovered (similar to traumatic/autistoid encapsulations, which are clearly felt but can never be found).

10 There is a translation problem. The word in German is 'Körperschema': which can mean either body schema or body image.
11 In my view, the best translation of this unclear passage was provided by E. Vorspohl, who translated Churcher into German in 2015: "die Nicht-Differ-enziertheit zwischen dem Körperraum/der Körperausdehnung und der Umwelt des Körpers" (in Churcher 2016, p. 65; in English, roughly, the undif-ferentation of body-extension and environment of the body).

References

Arbiser, S. (2017). Enrique Pichon-Rivière's conception of reality in psychoanalysis. *International Journal of Psychoanalysis, 98*: 115–127.

Baranger, M., and W. Baranger (2008 [1961–62]). The analytic situation as a dynamic field. *International Journal of Psychoanalysis, 89*: 795–826. [La situacíon analítica como campo dinámico. *Revista Uruguaya Psicoanálisis, 4(1)*: 3–54].

Baranger, M., W. Baranger and J.M. Mom (1988). The infantile psychic trauma from us to Freud: Pure trauma, retroactivity and reconstruction. *International Journal of Psychoanalysis, 69*: 113–128.

Barratt, B.B. (2017). Opening to the otherwise: The discipline of listening and the necessity of free-association for psychoanalytic praxis. *International Journal of Psychoanalysis, 98*: 39–53.

Beland, H. (2015). *Transformation in O – Pragmatisches Lernziel für den analy-tischen Alltag. Oder: Die Zukunft einer Illusion?* Unpublished. Vortrag auf dem Bion-Symposium zu Ehren von Erika Krejci, 25 April 2015, Forum am Park, Heidelberg.

Bick, E. (1968). The experience of the skin in early object-relations. *International Journal of Psychoanalysis, 49*: 484–486.

Bion, W.R. (1962). *Learning from Experience.* London: Tavistock Publications.

Bion, W.R. (1963). *Elements of Psycho-Analysis.* London: Heinemann.

Bion, W.R. (1965). *Transformations.* London: Tavistock Publications.

Bion, W.R. (1970). *Attention and Interpretation.* London: Tavistock Publications.

Bion, W.R. (1992). *Cogitations.* London: Karnac.

Bleger, J. (1967). Psycho-analysis of the psycho-analytic frame. *International Journal of Psychoanalysis, 48(4)*: 511–519.

Bleger, J. (1974). Schizophrenia, autism, and symbiosis. *Contemporary Psycho-analysis, 10*: 19–25.

Bleger, J. (2012 [1969]). Theory and practice in psychoanalysis: psychoanalytic praxis. *International Journal of Psychoanalysis, 93*: 993–1003. [Teoría y práctica en psicoanálisis: la praxis psicoanalítica. *Revista Uruguaya Psicoanálisis, 11*: 287–303].

Bleger, J. (2013 [1967]). *Symbiosis and Ambiguity: A Psychoanalytic Study,* edited by J. Churcher and L. Bleger. Translated by S. Rogers, L. and J. Churcher. New Library of Psychoanalysis. London: Routledge. [*Simbiosis y ambigüedad: estudio psicoanalítico.* Buenos Aires: Paidós].

Bleger, L. and J. Churcher (2013). Editorial Introduction (pp. xvii–xlv). In: J. Bleger (2013).

Churcher, J. (2016). Der psychoanalytische Rahmen, das Körperschema, Tele-kommunikation und Telepräsenz. Implikationen von José Blegers Konzepts des "encuadre". *Psyche – Zeitschrift für Psychoanalyse und ihre Anwendugen, 70(1)*: 60–81.

Dahl, G. (2010). The Two Time Vectors of Nachträglichkeit in the Development of Ego Organization: Significance of the Concept for the Symbolization of Nameless Traumas and Anxieties. *International Journal of Psychoanalysis*, 91: 727–744.

Etchegoyen, R.H. (2013). *Preface* (pp. xii–xvi). In: Bleger, J. (2013).

Feldman, M. (1999). Projektive Identifizierung. Die Einbeziehung des Analytikers. *Psyche – Zeitschrift für Psychoanalyse und ihre Anwendugen*, 53: 991–1014.

Feldman, M. (1992). Splitting and Projective Identification. In: R. Anderson (ed.), *Clinical Lectures on Klein and Bion*. London: Routledge.

Ferro, A. (2003). *Das bipersonale Feld*. Gießen: Psychosozial-Verlag.

Ferro A. (2006). *Mind Works: Technique and Creativity in Psychoanalysis*. New Library of Psychoanalysis. London: Routledge.

Ferro, A. (2009). Übertragung und Transformationen im Traum. In: B. Nissen (ed.), *Die Entstehung des Seelischen*. Gießen: Psychosozial-Verlag.

Freud, S. (1900a). *The Interpretation of Dreams*. S.E. Vol. 4. London: The Hogarth Press.

Freud, S. (1905). *Three Essays on the Theory of Sexuality*. S.E. Vol. 7. London: The Hogarth Press.

Freud, S. (1911). Formulations on Two Principles of Mental Functioning. S.E. Vol. 12. London: The Hogarth Press.

Freud, S. (1912a). Recommendations to Physicians Practising Psychoanalysis. S.E. Vol. 12. London: The Hogarth Press.

Freud, S. (1912b). The Dynamics of Transference. S.E. Vol. 12. London: The Hogarth Press.

Freud, S. (1913c). On Beginning the Treatment. Further Recommendations on the Technique of Psychoanalysis. S.E. Vol. 12. London: The Hogarth Press.

Freud, S. (1914g). Remembering, Repeating and Working Through. S.E. Vol. 12. London: The Hogarth Press.

Freud, S. (1915). *The Unconscious*. S.E. Vol. 14. London: The Hogarth Press.

Freud, S. (1923). The Ego and the Id. S.E. Vol. 19. London: The Hogarth Press.

Freud, S. (1926). The Question of Lay Analysis. S.E. Vol. 20. London: The Hogarth Press.

Freud, S. (1927). Fetishism. S.E. Vol. 21. London: The Hogarth Press.

Freud, S. (1933). *New Introductory Lectures on Psycho-Analysis and Other Works* (1932–1936). S.E. Vol. 22. London: The Hogarth Press.

Freud, S. (1937). Analysis Terminable and Interminable. S.E. Vol. 23 (pp. 209–254). London: The Hogarth Press.

Freud, S. (1938). Moses and Monotheism. S.E. Vol. 23 (pp. 139–208). London: The Hogarth Press.

Freud, S. (1938). Splitting of the Ego in the Process of Defence. S.E. Vol. 23. London: The Hogarth Press.

Freud, S. (1938b). Findings, Ideas, Problems. S.E. Vol. 23. London: The Hogarth Press.

Freud, S. (1980). *Briefe. Edited by Ernst und Lucie Freud* [Letters. Edited by Ernst and Lucie Freud]. Frankfurt am Main: S. Fischer Verlag.

Gomberoff, M.J., C.C. Noemi, and L. Pualuan de Gomberoff (1990). The autistic object: Its relationship with narcissism in the transference and countertransference of neurotic and borderline patients. *International Journal of Psychoanalysis*, 71: 249–259.

Hall, C.S. and G. Lindzey (1970). *Theories of Personality*, 2nd edn. New York and London: John Wiley & Sons.

Hinz, H. (2002). Wer nicht verwickelt wird, spielt keine Rolle. *Jahrbuch der Psychoanalyse, 44*: 197–223.

Isaacs, S. (1948). The nature and function of phantasy. *International Journal of Psychoanalysis, 29*: 73–97.

Köhler, W. (1968). *Werte und Tatsachen*. Berlin: Springer.

Levine, H. (2017). Introduction: Pioneer psychoanalysts of the Rio Plata region. *International Journal of Psychoanalysis, 98*: 111–113.

Lewin, K. (1951). *Field Theory in Social Science: Selected Theoretical Papers*. New York: Harper.

Liberman, D. (1958). Autismo transferencial. Narcisismo, el mito de eco y narciso. *Revista de Psicoanálisis, 15*(4): 369–385.

Loch, W. (1991). Variable und invariante Objektbeziehungen im psychoanalytischen Prozeß. *Jahrbuch der Psychoanalyse, 28*: 9–49.

Lorenzer, A. (1983). Sprache, Lebenspraxis und szenisches Verstehen in der psychoanalytischen Therapie. *Psyche – Zeitschrift für Psychoanalyse und ihre Anwendugen, 37*: 97–115.

Lorenzer, A. (2006). *Szenisches Verstehen. Zur Erkenntnis des Unbewussten*. Marburg: Tectum Verlag.

Mahler, M. (1968). *On Human Symbiosis and the Vicissitudes of Individuation, Vol. I*. New York: International University Press.

Matte-Blanco, I. (1998). *Thinking, Feeling, and Being: Clinical Reflections on the Fundamental Antinomy of Human Beings and World*. New Library of Psychoanalysis. London: Routledge.

Meltzer, D. (1975a). The Psychology of Autistic States and of Post-autistic States. In: D. Meltzer, J. Bremner, S. Hoxter, D. Weddell, and I. Wittenberg (eds.), *Explorations in Autism*, (pp. 6–29). Strath Tay: Clunie Press.

Meltzer, D. (1975b). Dimensionality in Mental Functioning. In: D. Meltzer, J. Bremner, S. Hoxter, D. Weddell, and I. Wittenberg (eds.), *Explorations in Autism* (pp. 223–239). Strath Tay: Clunie Press.

Metzger, W. (1999). *Gestalt-Psychologie. Ausgewählte Werke*. 2nd edn, edited by M. Stadler and H. Crabus. Frankfurt: Kramer.

Nancy, J-L. (2019). *Körper*. Vienna: Passagen Verlag.

Nissen, B. (ed.) (2006). *Autistische Phänomene in psychoanalytischen Behandlungen*. Gießen: Psychosozial-Verlag.

Nissen, B. (2008). On the determination of autistoid organizations in non-autistic adults. *International Journal of Psychoanalysis, 89*: 261–277.

Nissen, B. (2015). Faith (F) and Presence (O) in analytic processes: An example of a narcissistic disorder. *International Journal of Psychoanalysis, 96*: 1261–1281.

Nissen, B. (2018a).The debate on frequency: Can low-frequency psychoanalysis be free-floating? *International Journal of Psychoanalysis, 99*(5): 1212–1220.

Nissen, B. (2018b). Frei-schwebend zum Ereignis. Der Prozess zur Deutung. *Psyche – Zeitschrift für Psychoanalyse und ihre Anwendugen, 72*(9/10): 847–868.

Nissen, B. (2019). From Word to Deed. Why Psychoanalysis needs Laypersons. In: P.C. Sandler, and G. Pacheco Costa (eds.), *On Freud's 'The Question of Lay Analysis'*. London and New York: Routledge.

Nissen, B. (2021). Das Erleben von Auflösung. *Jahrbuch der Psychoanalyse, 82*: 217–222.

Ogden, T.H. (1989). On the concept of an autistic-contiguous position. *International Journal of Psychoanalysis, 70,* 127–140.

Ogden, T.H. (2001). *Conversations at the Frontier of Dreaming.* Northvale, NJ: Jason Aronson.

Ogden, T.H. (2004). The analytic third: Implications for psychoanalytic theory and technique. *The Psychoanalytic Quarterly, 73,* 167–195.

Pichon Rivière, E. (2017). *The Linked Self in Psychoanalysis: The Pioneering Work of Enrique Pichon Rivière,* edited by R. Losso, L.S. de Setton and D.E. Scharff. New International Library of Group Analysis. London: Karnac.

Scharff, D.E., R. Losso, and L.S. de Setton (2017). Pichon Rivière's psychoanalytic contributions: Some comparisons with object relations and modern developments in psychoanalysis. *International Journal of Psychoanalysis, 98:* 111–113.

Steiner, J. (2006). Interpretative enactments and the analytic setting. *International Journal of Psychoanalysis, 87*(2): 315–320.

Stolorow, R. and G. Atwood (1992). *Contexts of Being: The Intersubjective Foundation of Psychological Life.* Hillsdale, NJ: Analytic Press.

Tustin, F. (1972). *Autism and Childhood Psychosis.* London: The Hogarth Press.

Tustin, F. (1981). *Autistic States in Children.* London: Routledge & Kegan Paul.

Tustin, F. (1986). *Autistic Barriers in Neurotic Patients.* London: Karnac.

9 Revisiting José Bleger's ideas in times of pandemia

Alberto Pieczanski

Introduction

Despite Bleger's short life (1957–1972)—there were only eighteen years between the presentation of his APA membership paper and his death—he became one of the most influential pioneers of psychoanalysis in Argentina and a key player in developing a psychological culture in society and in academia. His works show that his main areas of interest encompassed psychoanalysis, groups, institutions, and a desire to define and formalize the thinking processes that characterize each field and how they relate to each other.

Bleger's ideas are not easy to categorize, and they do not constitute a system. He would probably be happy with that since he intended to include and contrast many perspectives on each subject. This becomes self-evident when checking the bibliography at the end of every one of his papers. Revisiting his writings, particularly "Psycho-analysis of the psycho-analytic frame" (Bleger, 1967), can help us think about how psychoanalytic treatments have changed due to the global COVID-19 pandemic.

These days I find Bleger's *Symbiosis and Ambiguity* a necessary anchor of sanity in my life as a psychoanalyst insofar as it provides me with a setting to think about what my colleagues and I are doing and how to think or detect what may consciously or unconsciously inform my behavior, as well as its potential to promote development or impair it.

While psychoanalysis has significantly evolved over the last century, the ongoing pandemic has prompted a broad range of clinical, technical, and institutional changes at a pace previously unknown.

Bleger's ideas can assist us in thinking about how and why we decided on the changes that have been implemented by analysts in order to continue their clinical work and institutional activities.

It may also help us figure out whether the thinking process that fueled those changes was informed—or not—by the principles of psychoanalytic theory and technique.

DOI: 10.4324/9781003252252-11

Bleger explains the principles that guide his study of the frame in the following terms:

Winnicott (1956, p. 387) defines "setting" as "the summation of all the details of management. For reasons that will become clearer further on, I suggest that we apply the term "psychoanalytic situation" to the totality of phenomena included in the therapeutic relationship between the analyst and the patient. This "situation" comprises phenomena that constitute a process that is studied, analyzed, and interpreted. Still, it also includes a frame, that is to say, a "non-process," in the sense that it is made up of constants within whose bounds the process takes place.

(Bleger, 1967, p. 511)

The core idea that explains Bleger's theoretical and the logic of his technical approach is the view that the frame is the "natural" depository and container of the most primitive psychic modes. Together with interpretation, it operates like Bion's (Bion, 1970, p. 108) description of the maternal alpha function and reverie. This containing function allows the analytic dyad to explore the most primitive aspects of our inner world without psychotic fragmentation or development into autism.

When describing the frame, Bleger (1967, p. 511) writes that it refers to "... to the constants of a phenomenon, a method or technique". In an attempt to be more specific, he says:

The frame is maintained and tends to be maintained (actively, by the psychoanalyst) as invariable; and while it exists as such it seems to be non-existent or it does not count, just as we become aware of institutions or relationships only when they are missing, are blocked, or have ceased to exist. (I do not know who it was who said about love and children that we only know they exist when they cry.) What is the meaning of the frame when it is maintained, when "it does not cry"? In all instances, it is the problem of symbiosis, which is "dumb" and only reveals itself when it breaks or is on the verge of rupture. This is what happens, too, with the body image whose study started with pathology, which first proved its existence.

Similarly, as we speak of the "ghost member," we must accept that institutions and the frame always make up a 'ghost world,' that of the most primitive and undifferentiated organization. What is always there is never noticed unless it is missing.

(Bleger, 1967, p. 512)

As with every other model, Bleger's coexists with the clinical reality, the real session, whose frame, while adhering to the model's general principles, accepts a certain flexibility that is specific and different for each patient–analyst dyad. He refers to that when he says: "This is perhaps what Rodrigué had in mind when he once referred to the patient whose history nobody has written, and nobody will ever be able to write" (Bleger, 1967, p. 511).

Etchegoyen, while asserting the validity and the importance of keeping the setting as invariable in the analytic situation, ends his discussion by saying: "However, this rule is not absolute. Sometimes it is appropriate to take into account certain desires of the analysand since the setting must be firm but also elastic ... and it should never be made with the idea that based on this type of modification, we are going to obtain structural changes in the patient" (Etchegoyen, 1991, p. 520).

According to Bleger (2013), those early configurations belong to a developmental phase before the paranoid-schizoid position named the glischrocaric position [*Glischros*: Viscous, *Karion*: nucleus]. In this early mode of object relations, splitting does not yet occur, and all internal and external objects form an undifferentiated set.

There is disagreement about the existence of the glischrocaric position as a normal developmental phase. Robert Caper thinks that

> Psychopathology of the type requiring psychoanalytic treatment is connected to persistent unconscious omnipotent fantasies (delusions). It is not the result of a regression to a normal primitive mental state, since, in a normal primitive mental state, such delusions and their resultant inhibitions, symptoms, and anxieties are gradually and spontaneously overcome through learning from experience.
>
> (Caper, 1998, p. 548)

However, one can use Bleger's ideas even if the inner world configurations he describes are not part of normal development. In my view, symbiosis and ambiguity exist. Their derivatives show up in most patients' material if we are ready to identify them, and agreeing or not with Bleger or Caper may be like trying to establish which comes first, the chicken or the egg.

The frame, then, is the container (Bion, 1970, p. 72) that, like maternal reverie, allows the analytic exploration to proceed. In this way, it protects the patient from anxieties related to fragmentation and disintegration, as conscious or unconscious phantasies and, in other cases, as real possibilities allowing the more developed parts of the personality to engage in the analytic dialogue. This theory's inevitable conclusion is that more severe pathologies require an analyst solidly convinced that he understands the danger of exposing vulnerable patients to an unstable, inconsistent setting. This conceptual model stands in stark contrast with those who believe that the psychoanalytic technique cannot treat very disturbed patients.

Regarding the socio-cultural impact on the structure and content of our inner world (setting in its broader sense), it is relevant that Bleger was one of those pioneers of Argentinian psychoanalysis who opened the door to the inclusion of group and social psychology to the psychoanalytic field.

In Argentina, Pichon-Rivière pioneered the psychoanalytic study of groups and society as an integral part of psychoanalysis. He was inspired by Fairbairn, Klein, and Bion's psychoanalytic ideas, among others, and used sources outside the psychoanalytic field, such as Kurt Lewin (Lewin, 1939). Lewin was a Gestalt psychologist and developed Field Theory to explores patterns of relationships between the individual and his environment.

Bleger, in a very unconventional way for his time, did not draw a line between psychiatry, psychoanalysis, group, social psychology, and culture.

A quote from Bleger (1963, pp. 47–48), may clarify Pichon's perspective: "… all human phenomena are, inevitably, also social … because the human being is a social being. Moreover, psychology is always social, and it also makes it possible to study an individual as a unit".

Unfortunately, a combination of factors makes Pichon's contributions mostly only available to Spanish-speaking analysts because his strength was extemporaneous delivery to his students, and he wrote comparatively very little. Some of his papers were circulated among colleagues but never published, let alone translated. Student notes constitute the sources we can now access regarding his ideas. One of the many Pichonean concepts implicit in this chapter, and Bleger's conceptual chest of tools, is Internal Group. Pichon-Rivière did not write specifically and extensively about it, but in an article called: 'Freud, Point of Departure of Social Psychology' (1971), we can gain hints at what he thought.

> We may observe according to the contributions of the School of Melanie Klein, that these are social relations which have been internalized, relations that we call internal Links that reproduce group or ecological relations in the ambit of the Ego. Those linking structures, which include the subject, the object, and their mutual interrelationships, are shaped based on extremely early experiences. It is the reason for excluding from our model the concept of Instinct. It replaces it with the concept of "Experience." Likewise, the entire unconscious mental life that is the realm of Unconscious Phantasy must be considered the interaction between internal objects (the Internal Group) in permanent dialectic interaction with the external world.

Liberman (1970–72) calls the social milieu that encircles the setting and informs it: the meta-setting.

The Barangers' field theory (Baranger, Baranger, and Mom, 1983) are also, in my view, an integral part of Bleger's model, mostly when dealing with any socio-cultural phenomenon—such as the pandemic—that radically and globally modifies meanings, behaviors, and understanding of many aspects of the human predicament.

The analytic situation in the pandemic

As a result of the COVID-19 pandemic, changes have taken place in society and in psychoanalysis that may be on their way to becoming a new normality that will remain in place after vaccines or a cure are developed to a greater or lesser degree.

This paper was written eight months after the start of the global COVID-19 pandemic. Its spirit is the one Bleger describes in his article on the frame: to explore the setting changes and use those changes and the way they were implemented to understand their meaning and relationship to psychoanalytic theory and practice. His paper, for our purpose, will be the ideal, standard, constant model of the psychoanalytic situation, and the conscious and unconscious meaning of the technical changes will be understood in relation to Bleger's ideas, operating as the constant, implicit presence. The use of this methodology follows from Bleger's assertion that: "The frame (in our case, his paper) is constant, and is therefore decisive in the phenomena of the process of behavior. In other words, the frame is a meta-behavior [The prefix meta describes a set of premises that applies to another set of rules.], and the phenomena we are going to distinguish as behavior depends on it. It is what remains implicit, but on which the explicit depends" (Bleger, 1967, p. 512). He then adds: "The problem is similar to what physicists call an ideal experiment, that is to say, a problem that does not occur fully and precisely in the way it is being described or stated, but it is of great theoretical and practical use" (Bleger, 1967, p. 512). The socio-cultural dimension is, therefore, a meta-setting that informs and becomes embedded in the frame.

When talking about the environment, it should be emphasized, as I mentioned before, that Bleger adheres to the notion that the social dimension is essential to psychoanalytic understanding and should be present in our theory and technique. This view is particularly relevant in times of global cultural upheaval and collective anxiety.

For Bleger, regarding the setting, patients and analysts perform fundamentally different roles. (asymmetry) It is the analyst's role to preserve the setting actively. The meaning of the frame in the analyst's inner world is one component of a conglomerate of conscious and unconscious theories (unconscious phantasies) that contains the analyst's understanding of psychoanalysis. The analytic process as an internal object needs to be reasonably established in the analyst's inner world for him to have a chance to understand and interpret the conscious and unconscious meaning of a frame modification since, as we stated, it becomes impossible outside the context of a preserved and stable frame. Changes in the setting, irrespective of their manifest justification, always can elicit primitive mindsets and anti-therapeutic defensive organizations. Anti-therapeutic defensive organizations can frequently establish themselves as part of the analytic situation. The Barangers called this configuration the 'bastion' (Baranger and Baranger, 1983).

Let's see why.

As a system and process, a psychoanalytic relationship consists of several parameters, some of which are symmetrical between patient and analyst, and some are asymmetrical. Amongst the symmetrical, the abstinence rule, for example, is specifically designed to facilitate the analytic process and should be observed by patient and analyst.

The "crying frame" alters the balance between "putting oneself in our patients' shoes" and keeping the necessary separation in order to preserve our own mind, provide interpretations, and develop insight. The analyst's active role in safeguarding the frame is an integral part of the necessary asymmetry.

In the pandemic, I observed that multiple symmetrical internal organizations started to inform the analytic situation. One being that patients and analysts are exposed to a life-threatening situation and perceive each other as concretely dangerous (that is, potentially infectious). The idea (and fact) that patients and analysts become life-threatening objects to each other is likely to activate in both primitive modes of experience, those that Bleger calls symbiotic and ambiguous, that belong to the agglutinated nuclei (Bleger, 2013). Those primitive psychotic object relationships can significantly alter the analyst's painfully acquired ideas about psychoanalysis and its technique.

One of my patients, unconsciously perceiving the proposed setting change as a threat to the good analytic bond, accepted the move to telephone sessions enthusiastically. As soon as we started, we went into an impasse where the sessions were reminiscences of different moments in our analytical work over the years. I became increasingly bored and had nothing to say. The acceptance of the change was a way of both keeping me alive and ensuring that he contributed to my income. Unconsciously, he "understood" my recommendation as a way of not losing income that he was willing to support. Our adaptation to the pandemic's limitations was interpreted by him as an expression of my narcissistic anxiety about my well-being and had very little to do with continuing the analysis. Working through the idea that I was in a panic, while trying to survive both physically and financially, allowed us to think more freely about what he wanted to do and what worked best. Eventually, the analysis was interrupted until in-person sessions could safely resume. I believe we will ultimately continue. Time will tell.

To resolve the complex issues linked to this new paradigm, psychoanalysts largely, and swiftly, began to work online and by telephone. Looking at this behavior from the perspective of Bleger's paper, it might be valuable to infer what might have been the thinking that led to this rapid change. In other words, what was the balance between adapting to protect the analytic process and the fear of contagion since features of the COVID-19 virus turned the members of the analytic dyad into mutual, dangerous persecutors. This balance, particularly its unconscious components, will ultimately decide the content and emotionality of the interpretations and their therapeutic or anti-therapeutic effect and the changes in the frame necessary to continue the therapy. The internal and external survival threats informing the transference–countertransference are compounded by the analyst's possible loss of income and anxieties about the future. Furthermore, we have to face the fact that we are dealing with circumstances that most analysts have never before experienced, irrespective of their seniority.

The meaning and implications of our decisions will only start to emerge when we study post-pandemic clinical data. At that moment, thinking might also be complicated because analysts and psychoanalytic institutions will be dealing with the trauma we have all been exposed to.

Still further complicating the study of these issues, there are other aspects of the meta-setting that should be addressed, like the fact that there are many colleagues who plan to work only online once the pandemic is over, and publications and professional meetings that portray themselves as providers of advice on technique, are taking for granted that working online is not just a temporary necessity, but a legitimate, newly "standardized" variation of psychoanalysis.

I would now like to look at the tools of online work. It is evident in Bleger's paper that the tools of our trade—the frame being one of them—are signifiers that convey to a patient our core ideas—mostly implicit—about the process, its implementation, and the aim of the analysis. Consequently, we should be reasonably sure that the meaning and nature of the technique, tool, or technology we use is consistent with our purpose.

The circumstances that led to the rapid adoption of electronic means of communication to conduct a session (audio or video) were a behavioral modification manifestly triggered by the speed of transmitting the virus and the mortality rate. The circumstances did not allow much space for reflection and evaluation of the pros and cons, alternative solutions, or gradual change.

The use of digital screens may be a good starting point since it seems that video has been widely accepted as an option. Digital screens play an intricate role in human communication. They have culturally been understood as allowing closeness by eliminating physical distance and the illusion of human contact. However, virtual reality does not physically bring people together, but the software creates that illusion.

My comments also apply to texting, emailing, and social media communication, with the added factor that those electronic means also allow the corruption of the time boundaries established in the analytic contract for each session because many patients and analysts use them to communicate in between sessions, implicitly colluding in a phantasy of a world without geographic or time boundaries, a most anti-therapeutic (psychotic) phantasy. These phantasies have been extensively explored by psychoanalysts for more than a hundred years and belong to clinical conditions like mania, perversions, and psychosis.

I would like here to indulge in a linguistic-psychoanalytic digression.

The word "screen", psychoanalytically speaking, looks like an excellent example of the return of the repressed. The *Oxford Dictionary* tells us that as a noun, it is a "fixed or movable partition used to divide a room, give shelter … or provide *concealment*" (the emphasis is mine). As a verb, the first quoted meaning is: "a thing providing concealment or protection." As practitioners of the science of the Unconscious, we should pay close attention to this signifier whose use, while intended to shelter us from the patient as a spreader of the virus, may also serve, as an unintended consequence, to shelter us emotionally and cognitively from our patients. The technique aims to create the best possible conditions for containing and understanding. The tools we use may potentially bring a level of inconsistency which is challenging to overcome even if those aspects of the experience are correctly interpreted.

If implicit in the frame is the idea that actual geographic distance *is not* an obstacle to psychoanalysis, then it may be that the issues we are discussing are informed by the manifestation of ambiguity and symbiosis in our analytic identity. The illusion of closeness in digital communication promotes illusions that can quickly become delusions.

The conflict between the yearning for close contact with the accompanying sensual components and the bodiless and odorless illusion of presence generated by computer software can make vulnerable patients lose touch with the reality of separation and reinforce the substitution of reality with virtual reality.

The experience I am trying to describe is more problematic when the analyst has to deal with pathologies in which hatred of reality dominates the patient's inner world (Bion, 1957).

The overlapping of unconscious phantasies—psychic reality—and acting out (perversions, addictions, acting-out), or external events that a patient cannot control, like the ongoing pandemic, become a part of what John Steiner (1993, p. 14) describes as a *psychic retreat*, "a refuge where the patient was relatively free from anxiety but where development was minimal".

While the catastrophic external situation or the acting out is active during the therapy, it has the effect of emptying the interpretation from its mutative function. My impression is that the nullification of an interpretation's transformative effect is more destructive when the action is initiated by the patient or the analyst in contrast with external events beyond their control.

The pathological organization described by Steiner can be usefully combined with Bleger's ideas, in the sense that the pandemic has shown that similar processes can be simultaneously active in the patient and the analyst when, for example, the analyst starts to function under the illusion of an uninterrupted analysis, refusing to accept the loss caused by the disruption of the meta-setting.

I think it is still premature to try to resolve the conflicts triggered by the rapid internal and external changes in patients' and psychoanalysts' lives. This chapter tries to orient our gaze towards the questions that we should ask ourselves, primarily to avoid anti-therapeutic behaviors or attempts to force patients to comply with what we offer instead of offering the therapy each patient needs.

Unfortunately, virtual "psychoanalysis" found its way into our daily practice in a somehow uncritical manner before the pandemic because analysts borrowed the model from already well established similar behaviors in our culture. We belong to a cultural psycho-social environment in which we can find almost anything in a virtual form: virtual sex, virtual classroom, virtual tourism, virtual dating, etc. In the future, we may conclude, as I did in the short vignette I presented here, that those patients who refused to continue their analysis online, as mine did, were trying to protect their painfully achieved progress in the analysis from a perceived destructuring change. In other words, they might have been trying to save the *'good analysis' and not retreating from it* as a superficial analysis might suggest, by accepting the temporary, or permanent, loss.

The loss of the analysis, as known to analyst and patient, is a reality that will have to be accepted and worked through by both. Loss can lead to depression and manic defenses, and, as Bleger tells us, it can activate psychotic parts of the personality. Being in touch with those possibilities is the first step in reparation required to preserve the good analytic experience. If we eventually go back to a frame similar to the pre-pandemic one, we need to be clear that it will not be the same. If we accept Bleger's ideas about the meaning of the frame and the vicissitudes of its disruption, we will then be dealing not with "returning to home sweet home", but with a new modification of the frame, potentially acting as a trauma that can rekindle primitive anxieties in the analytic dyad.

Our exploration should also include an attempt to answer why many colleagues feel more at ease working online, and many patients, too, prefer it. It occurs to me that part of this may be to avoid the frightening process triggered by the previous change.

At this point, I have no real answer to the questions I have raised. At first glance, they look like a textbook list of how psychoanalysis should not be practiced. However, I also remember Bleger mentioning a comment from another master and pioneer of South American psychoanalysis, Emilio Rodrigué, who said that the ideal analysis is that of the patient that no one analyzed or will never be.

References

Baranger, M., W. Baranger, and J. Mom (1983). Process and non-process in analytic work. *International Journal of Psychoanalysis*, 64: 1–15.

Bion, W.R. (1957). Differentiation of the psychotic from the non-psychotic personalities. *International Journal of Psychoanalysis*, 38(3–4): 266–275.

Bion, W.R. (1970). *Attention and Interpretation*. London: Tavistock Publications.

Bleger, J. (1963). *Psicología de la Conducta*. Buenos Aires: EUDEBA.

Bleger, J. (2013). *Symbiosis and Ambiguity*. London: Routledge.

Bleger, J. (1967). Psycho-analysis of the psycho-analytic frame. *International Journal of Psychoanalysis*, *48*(4): 511–519.

Caper, R. (1998). Psychopathology and primitive mental states. *International Journal of Psychoanalysis*, *79*: 539–551.

Etchegoyen, H. (1991). *The Fundamentals of Psychoanalytic Theory*. London and New York: Karnac.

Lewin, K. (1939). Field theory and experiment in social psychology. *American Journal of Sociology*, *44*(6): 868–896.

Liberman, D. (1970–72). *Linguistica intracción comunicativa y proceso psicoanalítico, Vol. 1*. Buenos Aires: Galerna.

Lisman-Pieczanski, N. and A. Pieczanski (1975). *The Pioneers of Psychoanalysis in South America: An Essential Guide*. London and New York: Routledge.

Steiner, J. (1993). *Psychic Retreats*. London and New York: Routledge.

Winnicott, D.W. (1956). On transference. *International Journal of Psychoanalysis*, *37*: 386–388.

Index

'α-function' 134, 136

Abstinentzregel (abstinence rule) 18

'adhesive equation' (Tustin) 62–63

'adhesive equivalency' 58, 66, 69, 73–74; and adhesive identification 62; in phantasy agglutinates the two physical bodies into one body 70; and the psychic processes of adhesive identification 60; symbiotic link of 68

'adhesive identification' (psychic process of) 58, 60–62, 73–74

'agglutinated nucleus' 42, 61, 63, 70, 82, 86, 128, 130, 132, 137, 153

agieren (Freudian concept) 27, 29

'alienation' (dimension) 129–130

Alizade, Mariam 33–36, 46

Álvarez de Toledo, Luisa 8, 81

ambiguity 1, 39–40, 43, 72–73, 81–83, 85–89, 91, 93, 128, 130–132, 134–135, 137–138, 148, 150; as being a function of undifferentiation 57; and Bleger's ideas on 90; characteristic of the most primitive organization of the personality (Bleger) 80; concept of 80; and symbiosis 39–40, 43, 57, 72, 81–82, 150

analysts 105, 154, 156; Argentinian 24; and patients 46, 104, 113–114, 141, 156; Spanish-speaking 151

analytic 31, 100, 123, 150; attitudes 45, 115; candidates 109; contracts 121, 154; dyad 48, 76, 149, 153, 156; experiences 106, 156; frame 75, 97, 100, 103, 119–121, 123, 125–126, 138; process 3, 1, 29, 58–59, 61–62, 97, 99, 102, 104–105, 110, 113–115, 141, 152–153; psychotherapists-in-training 109; relationships 3, 99, 101, 140–142; sessions 46, 106, 123; settings 15–16,

19, 23, 48, 99, 110, 120, 126; situations 1–2, 1, 17, 25, 27, 32, 59, 110, 115, 150, 152–153; situations 16, 23–24, 26–29, 31, 34–35; treatments 26, 33; work 17, 25, 64, 75, 98–99, 105–106, 125, 153

'analytical attitude' (idea) 33, 142

Anaximander of Miletus 14

anger 64–65, 67, 73, 135

anxieties 4, 17–18, 20, 25–27, 30, 32, 73, 134–135, 140, 150, 154–155; associated 18; collective 152; deepest 73; important 26; indiscriminate 17; massive 82; mobilizing symbiotic 18; narcissistic 153; persecutory 42, 91; primitive 156; psychotic 6, 25, 34–35; separation 26, 30

aplasic phantoms 43–44

Argentine 24, 151; analysts 26, 33; psychoanalysis setting 24, 151; psychoanalysts setting 84; psychotherapeutic field 81; and writer Julio Cortázar 96

avatars 47–50

aymmetry principles 119, 125, 152–153

Baranger, Madeleine and Willy 3, 1, 46

Barangers' field theory 151

behaviours 2–3, 12, 81–87, 89, 91, 128–130, 138, 142; archaic 84; contradictory 83; individual 130; process of 3, 85

Bick, Esther 58, 61, 63–64, 137

Biocca, Frank 49–50

Bion, Wilfred 18–19, 59–64, 109–110, 125, 133–134, 136, 139, 142, 149; argues that understanding provides hope for difficult analytic work 64; brings about an important shift in focus concerning psychoanalysis of the Repressed Unconscious 119; postulates a mental function and calls it the α-function 136; psychoanalytic ideas of 151; and the 'the psychotic part of the personality' 42

black holes 58, 61, 63, 65–67, 69, 76

Bleger, José 1–2, 6, 15, 17–20, 24–25, 27–28, 34–35, 39–46, 49–51, 57–64, 66–73, 75, 80–87, 96–105, 111–115, 119–121, 126–132, 136–143, 148–153, 156; ability to understand the multiple and simultaneous presence of psychic processes in all body relations 59, 81; approach guarantees the possibility of a deep analysis of the variables 100; asserts that the fame is constant 152; claims that the frame becomes part of the personality 141; clarity and consistency in presenting his ideas 97; coexistence of multiple frames 113; concept of undifferentiation 42; concept or one category of modified settings 46, 48–9; concepts presented in *The Fundamentals of Psychoanalytic Technique* 80; contribution to psychoanalytic thinking 15; definition of the psychoanalytic situation in his 1967 paper 24, 30; distances himself from Freud with a Marxist theory of science 128; ideas of 15, 80, 87, 90, 106, 148, 152, 155; and the paper "Psycho-analysis of the psycho-analytic frame" 24, 40, 96, 105–106, 112, 115, 153–154; postulates "the first undifferentiated, syncretic structures are fundamentally bodily relations" 132; and psychic equivalency 61; psychoanalytic situation 39; raises the question of the co-existence of multiple frames 113, 140; research on the psychoanalytic frame 101, 119; shows the divergence between the classical Freudian "archaeological" model and analysis focused on "genetic continuity" 81; study of the analytic frame 120; *Symbiosis and Ambiguity: A Psychoanalytic Study* 39–40, 43, 57, 72, 81–82, 137, 150; understanding of a psychic organization prior to the paranoid schizoid position 27, 57, 76

Bleger, Leopoldo 21–37

bodily relations 59, 64, 70–71, 73–74, 76–77, 132

body 41–44, 46, 49–51, 57–60, 62–63, 66, 68–74, 76, 125, 129, 132, 138–139; analyst's 9, 49, 62; biological 49; image 2, 6, 10, 43, 100, 138–141, 149; maternal 18; memory 61; natural 50; patient's 42; physical 49, 70, 76; rejected 125; relations 58–59, 63, 74; responses of 74; schema 24, 41–44, 49–51, 128, 138–140

Bollas, Christopher 19

boundaries 39, 43–44, 51, 73, 120, 124, 126, 137–138; analytic frame 126; ego 86, 138; fixed 45; healthier 75; losing 43; psychic 60; sensual 61; and social origins 42; time 154

Bouvet, Maurice 17

Bowlby, John 26

breast 131, 133–138

Bridge, Marie 34

Bullinger, André 49

Caper, Robert 150

cases 2–3, 9, 19, 23, 31, 83, 97, 99, 103–104, 112–113, 120; borderline 31; classical 31; difficult 31; extreme 9; psychotic 1

childhood 7–8, 19, 60

children 2–3, 9, 58, 60, 62, 87–88, 91, 131, 133–134, 140, 149

Churcher, John 34–36, 39–51

clinical work 12, 20, 36, 51, 96–97, 100, 121, 148

coexistence 1, 113, 126

communication 3, 18–19, 44, 51, 58, 61–62, 102, 106, 110, 122, 142; channels 18; differentiated emotional 62; digital 155; human 154; intercorporeal 44; intrusive 62; social media 154; somatic 62

complex prosthesis 49

conflicts 27, 29, 64, 73, 88–89, 92, 96, 121, 155–156; central 29; family 87; subjective 103; unconscious 45, 89

confrontations 97, 123, 125

consciousness 119, 132–133, 135–136, 138; concepts 136; perception 136

contradictions 30, 86, 90, 100, 119, 131, 135

Cortázar, Julio 96

couch 9, 23, 30, 33–35, 42, 49, 69, 98, 122–125, 139

counter-transference 35–36, 63, 74, 77; raises the question of the unconscious aspects of 36; somatic 63, 74

COVID-19 pandemic 20, 46, 106, 113, 148, 152
cyborg, idea of 49–50

de Gomberoff, Noemi 139
de Gomberoff, Pualuan 139
deficits 61, 64, 69, 72, 76, 82, 87, 125, 131
delusions 21, 61, 65, 67, 69–70, 150, 155; of oneness 61, 65, 70; psychic 59; transference 4, 100; unconscious 68
denial 1, 51, 90, 125
digital screens 154
discrimination 58, 64, 68, 70–71, 83, 91, 100, 119, 131; deficits 82; lax 103; non-ego 86
disorders 19, 63, 88, 122, 139; autistoid 139; pragmatic 19
dispensary 21–22, 24, 32
Donnet, Jean-Luc 115
dreams 22, 32, 115, 119, 123–126

Eekhoff, Judy K. 57–77
ego 3–6, 8–9, 41, 43, 70, 73, 82, 86, 88, 100, 113–114, 120–121, 128, 130–133, 138–139; boundaries 86, 138; functions 59; identity 86; integrated 42; internalized 8; and non-ego 24, 82; organized 6; patient's 10; precarious 105; primal 63; psychologists 29, 36; psychology 127; syncretic 6; syntonic 1, 87; tension with non-ego 138; vulnerable 86; weak 59
encuadre 15, 20, 24, 39–40, 45, 128, 140; José Bleger's concept of 39; misunderstanding between different versions of the term 16; as a predefined space to frame an image 14; as a scope e of exposure and development of the analytic process 16; Spanish term with two different versions in English 16
epistemophilic instincts 73
essays, 'The Unconscious' 109, 114, 119
Etchegoyen, Horacio 27
ethical security 18
existence 3, 6–7, 23–24, 28, 32, 40–41, 45, 69–71, 73–74, 82–83, 141, 143, 149–150; factic 8; multiple 131; physical 66

'factic ego' 8–9
Faimberg, Haydee 45

family 6–7, 14, 41, 87–88, 122; businesses 87–88; conflicts 87; institutions 12; life 4, 91; members 88
fantasy 7–8, 15, 28–29, 63, 90, 121, 124; aristocratic 28; hypochondriacal 28; inaccessible 28; patient's 29; persistent unconscious omnipotent 150; world 29
fathers 8, 22, 87–90, 92
Fenichel, Otto 2, 26, 80
Ferenczi, Sandor 35
fetal psyche (Rascovsky's theory) 83
fetus 57, 75
field theory 84, 127–130, 151
Fischbein, José E. 80–93
Fischbein, Susana Vinocur 80–93
Foucault, Michel 14
frame 1–12, 14–20, 24, 40, 45, 85–86, 90, 97–98, 100–106, 112–116, 120–121, 125–126, 138–141, 149–150, 152–156; analyst's 11, 114; classical 111, 114; constants 45, 97, 103; crying 153; internal 115; irregular 105; multiple 113–114; patient's 11, 45, 113; psycho-analyst's 10–11; setting (*encuadre*) 139, 141; situational 85; stable 152; temporal spatial 40
framework 14, 17, 19, 66, 100, 138, 140; classical 32; conceptual 14; ethical 18; immediate 66; reflexive 14; scientific reference 130
framing 19, 84, 115
France 30, 36
freedom 16, 20, 33, 36, 124; absolute 124; enveloping 33; expressive 16
Freud, Sigmund 18, 22–23, 25–27, 29–30, 34–36, 80–81, 98–103, 106, 109–112; and *Abstinentzregel* (abstinence rule) 18; definition of acting as a way of remembering 27; description of the unconscious in *The Interpretation of Dreams* and in the essay, "The Unconscious") 119; differentiation between psychic reality and material reality 84; emendation his theory have not always been systematically worked out or appreciated 110; expression "Getast" followed by two sensations, namely touch and be touched 132; and the expression "primal phantasy" 135; *The Interpretation of Dreams* 119; methodological reasons 99; neurotic structure leads him to "take for granted" the early mothering situation 23;

and the notion of agieren 27, 29; patients 23; recommendations refer to contingent social conditions 103; Structural Theory 111–112; study of separation anxiety and absence 30; and the Topographic Theory 112; "The Unconscious" 119

fusion 8, 18, 76–77, 132, 138; ego-body-world 6, 100; partial 111; primitive 11, 18, 138; somatic 73

Gallagher, Shaun 43
Gestalt psychology 39
'Getast' (Freud's expression) 132, 137
'ghost world' 3, 7–8, 12, 112–114, 149
'glischro-caric position' (Bleger) 42, 59, 61, 67, 70, 74, 83, 128, 132–133, 142
Glover, Edward 17
grandparents 7–8
Green, André 17, 24, 30, 49
Greenacre, Phyllis 19

hallucinations 63–64, 115, 131, 133
human beings 83, 128–129
hypochondriacal symptoms 4

identification 62–63, 70–71, 131; introjective 58, 62, 76, 131; primary 131; primitive 88; projective-introjective 83
identity 2, 4–6, 70, 82, 87–88, 98, 100, 111, 114, 128, 131, 138, 141; analytic 155; deficits 82; disorders 61; mature 9; monolithic 17; perceptual 59, 133; personal 41; separate 44; traits 87
illusion (of human contact) 154–155
impressions 7, 133–134, 136, 155
indifferenz (Freud concept) 18
infant research 44, 57
infants 23, 42, 57–58, 60, 67, 100, 115, 131, 133–134, 136–138
infinity 119, 121, 123–125; coexistence of 126; formless 120; in Matte-Blanco's thinking 119
inner world 60, 77, 149–150, 152, 155
instincts 128–129, 151; destructive 129; epistemophilic 73
institutions 2–3, 6, 8, 12, 20, 22, 35, 41, 43, 45, 80, 113–114, 128–129, 138, 148–149; analytical 30; definition of 2, 138; familial 113; family 12; psychoanalytic 80, 154; social 6, 41
'internal setting' 21, 33–36, 44–46
International Journal of Psychoanalyis 127

The Interpretation of Dreams 119
interpretations 2, 4, 10–11, 31–32, 61, 65, 67, 70–71, 77, 90–91, 97, 149, 153–155; analyst's 28; correct 30; transference 76
Isaacs, Susan 80–81, 85, 129

Kernberg, Otto 18
Klein, Melanie 16, 26, 42, 60, 69, 80–81, 136; believes the infant is born object related, with a primal capacity for differentiating self from other 58; conception of the integration of the self that guides thinking. 26; and the School of Melanie Klein 151; transference repeats the primitive object relationships 1
Kleinian 18, 25, 29; frames 114; paradigm 127; paranoid-schizoid position 132; psychoanalysis 129; psychology 127; theory 82–83, 129

Lacan, Jacques 102–103
Lacanian frames 114
language 3, 16, 27, 51, 57–58, 62, 71, 74, 102, 109–111, 127; English 127; particularities 96; verbal 19
Latin America 15, 36, 80, 127
'Le divan bien tempéré' 30
Leivi, Miguel 96–106, 110
Lemma, Alessandra 49–50
Les mots et les choses 14
Levine, Howard B. 109–116
Lewin, Kurt 84, 130, 151
Liberman, David 151
libidinal dimensions 43, 129
life 4, 7–8, 60, 63, 68–69, 72, 75, 77, 88, 91–92, 121, 124, 128–131; daily 51, 82, 88, 92; inner 50; sexual 22; unconscious mental 151
limitations 23, 48, 109; human 125; pandemic's 153
linguistic-psychoanalytic digression 155
Lombardi, Riccardo 119–126
Lorenzer, A. 142
losses 26, 34, 61, 68, 86, 89, 113, 125, 154–156
Losso, R. 127
love 2, 9, 17, 23, 25, 71, 73, 124, 132, 134–135, 140; analyst's 23; maternal 9, 23, 124

Macalpine, Ida 17, 29
Mahler, Margaret 26

maintenance 1, 4, 6, 17, 41, 48, 82, 97, 121, 141; normal 11, 100
Marxist 128–130; concept of alienation 130; theory of science 128
material world 68, 71
maternal care 23
Matte-Blanco, Ignacio 119–120, 126; contributions 121; perspectives 120–121, 126; thinking about symmetry and infinity 119
medical tests 122
medium 9, 44, 47–48
Meltzer, Donald 19, 58, 61–62, 64–65, 139
Meltzoff, A.N. 43–44
memory 4, 10, 66, 71, 133, 141–142
memory traces 131–133
mental processes 98, 111, 129
Merleau-Ponty, Marcel 43–44, 49
meta-behaviour 3, 6, 12, 152
meta-communications 3, 102
meta-ego 1–6, 8, 10–11, 59, 76
meta-setting 151–152, 154–155
metalanguage 3, 102
metapsychology 100, 116, 130–131
Milner, Marion 40, 46
mind 22, 25, 27, 33–34, 57, 59, 61–63, 69–74, 76, 109–111, 114–115, 120, 150, 153; analyst's 35, 76; extended 50; patient's 76, 112; psychotic part of the 111; separate 66
Minsky, Marvin 47
model 24, 30, 41, 98, 149, 151, 156; archaeological 81; clinical 100; conceptual 83, 150; paradigmatic 23; postural 43; spiral 85; superimposed 99; theoretical 96
modifications 20, 36, 46, 150; behavioral 154; gradual 87; new 156
Moguillansky, Carlos 14–20
money 1, 7–8, 22, 88, 98, 116, 121
mother-child-relationships 23, 134, 138
mothers 3, 8, 11, 23, 30, 58, 60, 115, 120–121, 124, 131, 133–137, 140
movements 47, 63, 75–76, 98; analyst's 63; analytic 114; bodily 43; compli-cated 98; potential 67; precipitate 63; transformational 109
mute 28, 45, 61, 101–102, 138; aspect 63; character 19
muteness 19, 27–28
mutual contradictions 119

narcissism 30, 60, 70; primary 42, 131; primitive 112
narcissistic strains 114
National Health Service 35
National Socialists 127
nature 26, 28, 40–41, 49, 59, 82, 110, 126, 154; aggressive 48; ambiguous 82; confused 82; destructive 121; infinitizing 120; primitive 58; scientific 142; social 83
'need' (dimension) 129
negative hallucinations 115
neurological work 43
neurosis 25, 110–111, 130
neurotic personality 6, 9, 25, 70, 111
Newton, Isaac 14
Newtonian physics 128
Nissen, Bernd 127–143
non-ego 3–4, 6, 8–9, 12, 24, 42–43, 121, 128, 130, 133, 138; discrimination 86; undifferentiation 88, 131
non-existence 2, 6, 12, 73, 85, 138, 149
non-oneness 133
'non-process' (frame) 1, 17, 24, 27, 39–40, 43, 113, 138, 149
nuclei 42, 82, 86, 132, 150; fundamental 138; non-integrated 86; omnipotent infantile 86; primary 86, 88; syncretic 93

object relations 31, 59, 62, 64, 70, 77, 128–130, 150; perspective 120; primitive 1, 153; real 42, 132
objects 3–4, 6, 24, 26, 30–31, 65, 73–76, 82–84, 88–89, 100–101, 112, 128–129, 131–134, 137, 139; anticipated 134; bad 134; external 73; internal 3, 151–152; investigated 99, 101; life-threatening 153; loved 140; maternal 75; primary 60
Ockham's razor 106
Oedipal conflict 89
Oedipus complex 20
office 35, 64, 70, 122; analytic 125; private 21
Ogden, Thomas 19, 59, 141
Old Testament 71
omnipotence 7, 30, 36, 89, 115
oneness 66, 68, 131, 133; absolute 71; concrete material 71; sensual 58; symbiotic 70
online analysis 106, 156
online work 106, 154, 156

organization 1, 8, 69–70, 80, 82, 86, 88, 96–98, 101, 131–132, 141–142; anti-therapeutic defensive 152; basic 7; levels of 59, 63, 68; narcissistic 10; neurotic 111; omnipotent 7; pathological 155; primitive 80; psychic 57; stabilized 8, 101; undifferentiated 3, 112, 149
organizational levels 73, 75–76

pain 17, 22, 26, 57, 68, 71, 90, 134
pandemic 51, 106, 148, 151–156; *see also* COVID-19 pandemic
panic attacks 122, 125
paradoxical contradictions 131
parameters 39, 99, 120–121, 153; formal 35–36, 126; realistic 121; space-time 120; technological 46
paranoid schizoid position 60
parents 4, 6–9, 57, 88, 91–92, 123; *see also* grandparents
Parsons, Michael 35–36, 46, 110–111, 115
pathology 2, 29, 31, 33, 82, 149–150, 155
patients 1–2, 4, 7, 9–12, 17–36, 41–42, 44–49, 58–59, 61–64, 69–77, 87, 89–90, 97–98, 103–106, 109–115, 120–125, 140–142, 149–150, 152–156; with "acting-in" tendencies 6; and ana-lysts 46, 104, 113–114, 141, 156; aris-tocratic 29; difficult 19, 112, 119–120; disturbed 59, 150; female 139; foreign 104; idiosyncratic 86; intrapsychic processes 111; neurotic 59, 76, 111, 114; non-neurotic 114; projects 1, 29; psychotic 6, 23, 25, 63, 114; of Sig-mund Freud 23; traumatized 62, 75; use of the unconscious phantasies of adhesive identification and adhesive equivalency 74; vulnerable 150, 155
perception 3, 34, 39, 49, 82, 87, 92, 135; individual's 3; sensuous 135
personal identity 41
personality 3–4, 6–9, 11–12, 41–42, 58–59, 75, 77, 80, 82, 87–88, 100–101, 121, 131–132, 137–139, 141–142; ambiguous 87; borderline 86, 112; individual's 2, 41, 138; infant's 57; mature 82, 132; organization of 3, 12, 131; patient's 9; psycho-analyst's 9
perspective 15, 19, 24, 26, 80, 82, 84, 93, 97, 99, 103, 112, 137; controversial 20; historical 29; infant's 133; mutual 19; new 15; varied 20

phantasy 63–64, 66, 68–70, 76, 129, 154; agglutinating the two physical bodies into one body. 70; life (Freud) 129; nature and function of 80; primal 135; undifferentiated symbiotic 65
phantom limbs 41, 43
phantoms 43–44
phenomena 1, 8, 11, 24, 29, 82–87, 102, 112, 130, 135, 138, 149, 152; human 3, 151; mental 83; psychic 57; psycho-logical 83; socio-cultural 151
phenomenology 34, 51
phobic characters 4, 10
physical existence 66
physicians 135
Pichon-Rivière, Enrique 15, 43, 81, 83, 128–129, 151
Pichonean concepts 151
Pieczanski, Alberto 148–156
Politzer, Georges 15, 50
preconceptions 131, 133–134, 140; α-elementary 135; realized 133
pregnancy 11
premature separation 60
prenatal research 57
primal 59–60, 62, 74, 77; areas 73; awareness 75; capacity 58; container 63; dissociation 65; fantasy 135; phantasy 135; trust 58
principles 48, 83, 85, 101, 121, 148–149; general 119, 149; guiding 33; inalien-able 97; logical 119; technical 97
problems 1–3, 14–15, 24, 41, 96–97, 100–102, 109, 111–115, 128, 130, 149, 152; clinical 36; epistemological 109; fundamental 4; human 30; new 99; theoretical 11; translation 16, 18
process 1–6, 9, 11–12, 23–24, 26–28, 31–33, 39–40, 59, 66–67, 74–77, 85–86, 96–97, 100–102, 104, 109–110, 113–115, 132–134, 138–141, 152–156; analytic 1, 3, 29, 58–59, 61–62, 97, 99, 102, 104–105, 110, 113–115, 141, 152–153; circular 132; dialectical 83; dynamic 85, 111; evolutionary 17; introjective 70, 75; introjective identi-fication 58–59; mental 98, 111; neu-rotic 113, 130; organizational 59; primary 18, 59; psychic 59–60, 140; psychoanalytic 19, 43, 48; psycho-analytical 9, 26; regressive 140; secondary 9; transformative 131
prognostic estimates 26

projective identifications 10, 19, 58, 60, 62, 67, 71, 75, 129, 139, 142
psyche 28, 50, 57, 59, 61, 64, 71, 111–112, 136; analyst's 33; fetal 83
psychiatry 81, 142, 151
psychic 58, 65, 67, 73, 76, 134, 136; adhesion 67; annihilation 60; apparatus 111, 132; capacity 109; change 45, 92; delusions 59; distinctiveness 61; dynamics 142; equivalency 59–61, 63–65, 67, 69–71, 73–76; life 22, 25, 61; qualities 131, 135–136; reality 28, 84, 110, 155; separateness 62; skin function 61, 63, 137–138; space 62, 71–72, 74
"Psycho-analysis of the psycho-analytic frame" (Bleger) 24, 40, 96, 105–106, 112, 115, 153–154
psychoanalysis 1–7, 9, 11, 17, 39, 96–97, 135, 148; Argentinian 24, 151; contemporary 34, 36, 109, 120, 128; defended as a medical practice 16; despised as unscientific and criticized as old-fashioned 102; practices 16, 96; psychoanalysts 9, 15, 40, 45–46, 80, 85, 87, 103, 109, 135–136, 148–149, 153–154, 156; Argentine 84; important 127; international 81; pioneer 127
psychoanalytic 33, 48, 97–98, 109; attitude 141; clinical work 36, 51, 85, 96–98, 128; community 15; concepts 23, 129–130; consultation 48; discipline 33; frame 1, 4, 6–8, 10, 12, 80–81, 83, 85, 87, 89, 91, 96–97, 99, 101, 103; meanings 1, 2, 12; methodology 80; movement 31; perspective 35, 128, 130; positions 128; practice 16–17, 103; research 127–128; setting 17, 39–41, 43–45, 47, 49–51, 96, 138–139, 142; techniques 27, 39, 85, 150; theory 130, 148, 152; tradition 15; treatment 8, 11, 31, 75, 77, 87, 140, 150
psychoanalytic field 82, 151
'psychoanalytic situation' 1, 6, 11, 30, 81, 97, 138, 149, 152
psychoanalytical: community 30, 127; societies 41
psychological organizations 11, 86
psychology 46, 81, 142, 151; community 82; contemporary 83; developmental 43, 49; Gestalt 39; individual 82; intersubjective 127; Kleinian 127; normal 82; social 151; unipersonal 128

The Psychology of Behaviour 81
psychotic 9, 23, 25, 58–59, 75, 86, 154; anxieties 6, 25, 34–35; breakdown 105; cases 1; disintegration 1; disorders 139; fragmentation 149; normalizing autistic experiences 59; part of the mind 111; part of the personality 4, 6, 8–9, 11–12, 17, 42, 48, 82, 88, 112–114, 121, 139; patients 6, 23, 25, 63, 114; protections 75; structure 105; transference 1, 7, 11; zones 121
publications 109, 154; *The Interpretation of Dreams* 119; 'Le divan bien tempéré' 30; *Les mots et les choses* 14; *The Psychology of Behaviour* 81; *Symbiosis and Ambiguity: A Psychoanalytic Study* 39–40, 43, 57, 72, 81–82, 137, 150

qualities 6, 18–19, 23, 73; benign 64; mental 135; psychical 135
quarantine 106, 113
Quinodoz, Jean-Michel 17

Rascovsky's theory of a fetal psyche 83
regression 8, 23, 29, 61, 83–84, 150; classifying 29; libidinal 89; psychopathological 29; therapeutic 29
relations 22, 26, 35–36, 49, 59, 98, 151–152; analytic 59, 99; asymmetrical 39; child's 44; condensed 66; ecological 151; invariant spatial 49; regulated 101; screen 48; social 151; symmetrical 120
relationships 2, 4, 6, 8–9, 11, 66–67, 72–73, 83–85, 91–92, 101–102, 121–122, 131, 133, 137–138, 151–152; analyst-patient 9, 11; bodily 83; distant 104; emotional 20, 85; extra-analytic 11; formal 18; frequent 140; fused 76; idealized 11; mother-child 23; narcissistic 10; professional 104; psychoanalytic 140, 153; social 4, 92, 98; stable 3, 18; symbiotic 3, 6, 11, 42–43, 65–66, 86, 114; two-body 59, 72
representation 19, 59, 112, 115, 121, 125; artificial 48; deficits 125; fueled by introjective identification processes 59; of internal mental structure 110
repression 1, 65
research: expanded psychological 84; prenatal 57; psychoanalytic 127–128
researchers 83, 99, 101, 142
resources 98, 101, 115; limited representational 121; optional 98; of the site 110

rhythm 26–27, 34, 65, 70–71, 74; annual 45; process of 134; shared 62; steady 18; sustained 27, 34; and tone 70–71
Rio de la Plata 25–26, 80–81, 84, 127
risks 3, 15, 20, 31–32, 34, 36, 66, 92, 124, 129
Riviere, Joan 16
robots 47, 49
Rochefort, C. 43
Rodrigué, Emilio 1, 2, 9, 150, 156
rules 14, 16, 18, 20, 23, 33, 98–99, 110, 120, 150, 152; basic 3, 99, 110; disposition of 16; fixed 104; framing 16; fundamental 33–34, 98; technical 27, 98
ruptures 2, 10, 17–18, 100, 113, 149
Russell, Gillian Isaacs 47–48

Sabbadini, Andrea 45, 48
Schilder, Paul 43
schizophrenia 10, 105
schools 41, 81, 83, 91–92, 127, 151
science 3, 128, 155
Second Life 47
security 7–8, 18
self 26, 29, 42, 44, 58–63, 65, 70, 75, 77, 80, 86, 109, 111–112, 133–134, 136–137; analysis 19; deception 50; destructive behavior 112; differentiation of 44, 134; discipline 142; esteem 92; granular 86; perception 138; subjective 63
seminars 2
sensations 57, 60–61, 70, 76, 132–134, 136–137; bodily 62, 71, 132; external 132, 134; new 134; objectless 60; pleasurable 122, 135; self-generated 137; unpleasurable 134, 136
senses 40, 58, 61, 63–66, 68, 70–71, 74, 135
sensuous impressions 133
separateness 62, 65–66, 68, 72, 77; facilitated 71; patient's 61; psychic 62
separation 18, 26–27, 30, 60, 62, 64, 68, 77, 125, 153, 155
separation anxieties 26, 30
sessions 1, 7–8, 10, 21–22, 24, 26–27, 29, 32–34, 36, 48, 66, 89–92, 122, 124–125, 153–154; analytical 26; canceled 32; group 34; in-office 113; in-person 153; missing 32, 124–125; psychoanalytic 40, 80, 85; scheduled 88; supervision 10; telephone 153
settings 14, 16–36, 40–46, 48–49, 51, 59, 61, 63, 73–77, 80–81, 83–87, 120–122,

138–139, 141, 148–152; analyst's 45; behaviour 86; classical 46, 48–49, 111; clinical 97–98; embodied 49; historical 83–84; internal notion of 33, 35; modified 39, 46; notion of 21, 33–34, 83; one-sided 83; patient's 76; psychoanalytic 17, 39–41, 43–45, 47, 49–51, 96, 138–139, 142; therapeutic 113; traditional 33
sex 104
sexual intercourse 7
silence 8, 65–66, 69, 92, 102, 106, 110, 122–125
skypanalysis 48
Skype 46, 48, 106
smell 60, 70, 135, 137
social distancing 113
social media communication 154
sociological' dimensions 43
space 18–19, 34–35, 42–43, 46, 51, 66, 68–72, 75–77, 115, 121, 137, 139, 141; common transference of 142; experience of 61, 75; hybrid 47; internal 63; physical 46, 48; predefined 14; real 47; three-dimensional 131, 137; virtual 47
space-time (concept) 110, 120–122
speech 16, 19, 32, 65, 71, 74, 99, 102, 106, 110; patient's 19; patterns 75; relationship between two participants 99
Steiner, John 142, 155
Strachey, James 16, 18, 27
Structural Theory 111–112
structure 6, 9, 11, 19, 75, 110–111, 115, 120, 130, 132, 141–142; α-elementary 134; basic 88; external 35, 110; internal 35, 110; primitive 132; psychic 89, 128; relational 42; repetitive temporal 45; stabilizing 85, 112; syncretic 83, 132
Stuart, Susan 44
study, post-pandemic 154
suicide 4, 121, 124–125
surgical operations 47
symbiosis 2–3, 42–43, 57, 59–61, 63, 65, 67–73, 75–77, 80, 82, 112–113, 121, 128, 130, 132; early 42; functions 68; original 11; pathological 77; primitive unresolved 76; published 137; silent 17, 112–114
Symbiosis and Ambiguity: A Psychoanalytic Study 39–40, 43, 57, 72, 81–82, 137, 150

symbiotic 9, 28, 153; attachment 70, 138; body relations 62; bond 87; connection 59; core 113; dependence 87; fusion 66, 115; interdependence 82; link 62, 67–68; relations 51; relationships 3, 6, 11, 42–43, 65–66, 86, 114

symmetry 119, 125; principle impregnates the transfer with functions that may be of a constructive or destructive nature 121; principle of 119, 121

symptoms 4, 8, 30, 57, 64, 84, 86, 114, 125, 150

syncretism 1, 10, 80, 83, 86, 131

systematic analysis 9–10

Tabakin, J. 46

techniques 1, 12, 23, 25, 32, 75, 97, 148–149, 152–154; analyst's 1; articulate 27; clinical 119; interpretative 26; mechanization of the 98; strict 35

technology 46–48, 50–51, 154

telecommunications 39, 46, 48–49, 51

telephones 46–47, 51, 122, 153; conversations 51, 89; give a reasonable experience of auditory presence 50

theoretical loyalty 16

theory 3, 26, 30, 69, 110, 112, 116, 128–130, 136, 150, 152; analyst's 26, 114; analytic 115; field 84, 127–130, 151; psychoanalytic 130, 148, 152

therapeutic relationships 1, 8, 11, 149

therapists 6, 10, 48, 61, 87, 105

thinking 15, 18, 26–27, 65, 67, 89, 92–93, 119, 123, 125–126, 137, 148, 153–154; concrete 19; defect of 125; paleological 119; pluricausal 15–16; processes 148; psychoanalytical 15, 36

thought 7–8, 14, 17, 24, 27, 29, 32, 109, 111, 122, 125, 133–134, 136–137; defects 125; disorders 136; experiments 39, 41, 46, 48–50; final 115

Topographic Theory 112

transference 1–6, 9, 19–20, 28–29, 40, 76–77, 85, 90, 93, 111, 115; analysis 31; autism 139; conditions 22; neurosis 10, 29, 32; neurotic 1; pending 1; positive 18; projective 19; relationships 88; resistance 129

transformations 33, 57, 115, 133–135

translation 24, 39, 84, 86–87, 92, 139; first 24; preferred 45; problems 16

trauma 58–60, 154, 156; derailing the normal course of development 76; early 76; original 62; surviving childhood 58

treatments 7, 11, 23–25, 27–28, 32–35, 85, 87–88, 103, 105, 110, 114–115, 120; analytic 26, 33; techniques 130

Tubert-Oklander, J. 43

unconscious 25, 99, 110, 125; collaboration 125; conflicts 45, 89; delusions 68; phantasies 74, 129–130, 140, 150–152, 155; repressed 119; sensory use 61; transmission and interaction 34; unrepressed 119

'The Unconscious' 109, 114, 119

unconscious meanings 152

understanding 58, 68, 71, 75, 127–129, 131–135, 137, 139, 141–142, 151, 155; analyst's 152; contemporary 72; psychoanalytic 45, 152; symbiosis and undifferentiation 58; theoretical 26

undifferentiation (concept) 58, 60, 66, 69, 82, 130–131, 135–138; Bleger describes symbiosis and ambiguity as being a function of 57; implies a specific structure and organisation with Bleger 42; moments of 58; primitive 12, 70, 80, 83, 132; states of 57–58, 131–132

variation 1–2, 8, 12, 17–18, 26, 31, 39, 97–101, 110; external 33; potential 33; quantitative 9; standardized 154; technical 31

verbal attacks 4

video 47–48, 50, 154

vignettes 32, 66, 72, 92, 156

virtual environment technology 50

virtual sex 156

visual arts 16

voices 50, 65, 70, 137; gentle 134; mother's 123; muffled 123; steady 124

Winnicott, D.W. 1, 9, 17–18, 23–24, 29–30, 66, 113, 115, 149

Zac, Joël 26

Zahiu, Anda 50

For Product Safety Concerns and Information please contact our EU
representative GPSR@taylorandfrancis.com
Taylor & Francis Verlag GmbH, Kaufingerstraße 24, 80331 München, Germany

www.ingramcontent.com/pod-product-compliance
Lightning Source LLC
Chambersburg PA
CBHW070342270326
41926CB00017B/3947

* 9 7 8 1 0 3 2 1 7 2 0 6 4 *